Looking towards the market square through the toll-house gates.

BUILDING HISTORY

Weald & Downland Open Air Museum

1970-2010 – the first forty years

Edited by
Diana Zeuner

with
Richard Harris, Kim Leslie and Carol Brinson

Contributions from
Fred Aldsworth, Julian Bell, Keith Bickmore, Roger Champion, Robert Demaus, Dr John Godfrey, Ivan Hicks, Bob Holman, Edward Hopkinson, Elizabeth Newbery, Richard Pailthorpe, Bob Powell, Sue Shave, Dr Danae Tankard, Mike Wall and memories and anecdotes from museum supporters from the last 40 years

Pendean farmhouse rises from its new site at the museum in 1976.

Published in 2010
Copyright © Weald & Downland Open Air Museum, the editor and contributors

ISBN 978-0-90525-930-7

Mixed Sources
Product group from well-managed forests, and other controlled sources
www.fsc.org Cert no. TT-COC-002610
© 1996 Forest Stewardship Council

A CIP catalogue record for this book is available from the British Library.

Published by Weald & Downland Open Air Museum, Singleton, Chichester, West Sussex PO18 0EU. www.wealddown.co.uk

Designed by Dorchester Typesetting Ltd, Bridport Road, Dorchester, Dorset DT1 1UA.

Printed by Pensord, Tram Road, Pontllanfraith, Blackwood, South Wales NP12 2YA. www.pensord.co.uk

Front cover: *Top row: left to right*, Pendean farmhouse; the house from Walderton; Bayleaf farmhouse. *Centre row: left to right*, geese in Bayleaf farmyard; the medieval hall from North Cray; the solar in Bayleaf farmhouse. *Bottom row: left to right*, looking through the doorway of Bayleaf farmhouse; hay-making with the museum's working Shire horse; the market hall from Titchfield.

Back cover: The market square with the South Downs beyond.

Acknowledgements
The editor is indebted to all the many people who have made contributions to this commemorative publication, especially those listed on the title page and to others who have offered assistance with research and have passed on their memories and anecdotes. In particular I would like to acknowledge the help given generously by Roy Armstrong's daughter, Jean MacWhirter, and her husband, Ian. I would also like to acknowledge especially the assistance and support given to me by Kim Leslie. The help with photographic research from Carol Brinson, early memories from Roger Champion, information about the 1980s and early 1990s from Richard Pailthorpe, the contributions from Richard Harris, publishing wisdom from John Rotheroe (founder of Shire Publications), additional proof-reading by Jenni Leslie and design expertise by Melvin Parvin and his colleagues at Dorchester Typesetting Ltd were also much appreciated. Photographs are from the Weald & Downland Open Air Museum archives incorporating the Roy Armstrong photographic archive and: Julie Aalen, Carol Brinson, James Clevett, Jan Elliott, Marjorie Hallam, Richard Harris, Bob Holman, Tony Hirst, Kim Leslie, Virginia Lyon, Ian and Jean MacWhirter, Denis and Sylvia May, Elizabeth Newbery, Portsmouth & Sunderland Newspapers, Ian Serraillier, Richard Pailthorpe, Bob Powell, The Edward James Trust and Chris and Diana Zeuner. The front cover was designed by Paul Houlton. The index was compiled by Chris Dance.

Re-erecting the framework of the upper hall from Crawley in 1978.

Contents

Dedicated to
Roy Armstrong and Chris Zeuner
whose energy and passion created the
Weald & Downland Open Air Museum

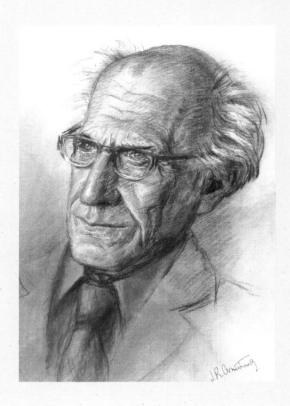 

“ *The founders of the museum were inspired by fire – the bonfires*
of important medieval timber-framed buildings that they
regularly witnessed in the 1960s – and timber framing has
remained a central interest of the museum ever since. ”

The museum's application for designation as an
outstanding collection, 1998

From the Duke of Richmond, Museum Vice President

From the Chairman of the Museum Trustees, Paul Rigg

It is well known that the Weald & Downland Open Air Museum was the brainchild of Roy Armstrong. His drive was to save timber-framed buildings that were threatened with demolition by road schemes, new town developments and housing, and even new reservoirs. Indeed it has been said that the founders of the museum were inspired by fire – the bonfires of important medieval timber-framed buildings that they regularly witnessed in the 1960s.

The happy coming together of Roy's ideas and the search for a location to store and reconstruct his 'saved' buildings with those of Edward James, owner of the West Dean Estate, who was looking to set up an educational foundation, resulted in the establishment of the museum in its magnificent setting in the Lavant valley. It makes a worthy neighbour for my own family estate at Goodwood.

It is both as a neighbour and keen champion of local tourism that I have watched and encouraged the museum's development from its early days. I was delighted to be invited to become a vice president in the mid-1970s. The museum has gone from strength to strength over its 40-year life, for nearly 30 years under the directorship of Chris Zeuner, and it has rightly established the highest reputation for the quality of its contribution to our regional heritage, to national and international research, and to learning in the field of vernacular architecture and related skills.

To record that contribution in a book is a great idea. I congratulate all the staff and volunteers who have worked so hard over the past four decades and wish the museum every success for the next 40 years!

I had long admired the museum as a fascinating place to visit in a beautiful setting. However, since becoming a trustee in 2007 and learning about the detail of its beginnings and the extraordinary journey to the present day I have become almost overwhelmed with wonder! Wonder at its very foundation – it has been referred to as 'the impossible museum' – and admiration for all those through to the present day who have given so much of their time to make the dream come true.

It is the story of that remarkable journey over four decades that is the material for this special book. In fact there are lots of stories which make up the history and capture the ethos and distinctive nature of the place and its activities. Moreover there is its achievement in becoming a museum of international renown. The museum is one of only seven 'independent' museums with no core public funding to have its collections designated by the Government. Designation implies pre-eminence, the highest level of scope and character, demonstrable quality and cultural significance.

The trustees are well aware that we are the custodians of a regional, indeed national, treasure, one that requires stewardship of the highest order. Our challenge is to live up to the standards set by our forbears and to continue to foster ideas and qualities that will inspire future generations. The editor of this book, Diana Zeuner, provides some thoughts for the future in the concluding chapter.

On behalf of the trustees, I should like to express thanks to all those who have contributed, and especially to our editorial team. This is a very special book about a very special place.

1

Roy Armstrong – the Museum's Founder

Historian – Teacher – Visionary 1902–1993

Kim Leslie

Roy Armstrong — the Museum's Founder

Forty years on and we're celebrating Roy Armstrong's dream — the opening of the museum in September 1970. Flash back another 40 years, to 1930, and Roy was then starting the other big project in his life, building his own home and taming its huge 11-acre garden from the surrounding heathland. Two pioneer projects on two quite different scales, both full of insight into Roy's remarkable energy and determination.

To discover Roy in the 1930s, building and landscaping his own version of paradise under the South Downs and finding his voice in the world of adult education, is to explain much about his position and the influences that inspired his lifetime's work. But what of the background that led to this fulfilment?

Jack Roy Armstrong was the third son of William Wallace Armstrong, a senior civil servant with the Local Government Board. The family lived in a substantial double-fronted house at West Norwood, south London, a neat Victorian suburb, once a magnet for wealthy bankers, lawyers and professionals working in the city or, in the Armstrong case, in Whitehall; they also had a seaside home at Broadstairs in Kent — Serene House — where Roy was born in 1902. His two brothers both fought in the First World War: Harry was killed and Wallace lost a leg, but went on to distinguish himself as a noted anthropologist and later an economist as professor of economic theory at the University of Southampton.

Educated at Dulwich College, Roy went up to Oxford in 1921, where he studied music for a year (he was a gifted pianist) and took his degree in history as an open history exhibitioner of Jesus College, graduating in 1925. With three student friends he started the Fish & Chip Society "to combat hypocrisy and promote intellectual advancement". His sport was athletics. According to his tutor, Roy read widely, particularly into the literary and artistic aspects of history, spending the long vacations in France, Germany and Italy. He loved exploring England, looking at buildings and landscape, either on foot or on bicycle, sometimes with the collapsible canoe he made himself so it could be carried by train. He canoed on all the major English and Welsh rivers, and just after coming down from Oxford in 1925 was paddling and camping down the Arun in West Sussex. Exploration and discovery were deeply engrained in Roy's life from an early age. (Perhaps his most ambitious trips were much later on in his open-topped car with his companion, Lyn — later to become his second wife — when they motored to Russia in the 1950s, where he was arrested as a spy for photographing an historic bridge, and then beyond the Arctic Circle in Norway.)

After Oxford, Roy took up school-mastering with three appointments lasting just a year each between 1925 and 1928 — in Devon, Lancashire and in Norfolk — but he was unhappy with this type of teaching, wanting to take up either tutoring or coaching. In 1927 he met a schoolmistress, Sheila Ward, and they married in Guildford the following year. Their home was a bungalow Roy built out of the frame of an old chicken shed at Albury near Guildford, Roy's first project with a timber-framed building.

From his comfortable family background, public school and Oxford, he had seen privilege and power at first hand, but played out against the inter-war shadow of the suffering and despair of low wages, unemployment and depression. Roy's social conscience and belief in the need for education and informed discussion in facing the complexities of such a confused and divided world led him to the Workers' Educational Association (WEA) for which he became the West Sussex organiser in 1932. But it was as an 'honorary' organiser, the work unpaid; his sole income came from tutoring WEA classes as well as giving private coaching. In Roy's early days in adult education he was particularly concerned with social issues, planning and extending educational opportunities into rural communities. One matter of great concern was town and country planning and the

Roy and Sheila Armstrong, c1932.

despoliation of the countryside by jerry-building and ribbon development. In July 1932 he gave an open-air lecture to the Steyning WEA at Chanctonbury Ring on 'The Future and Preservation of the Countryside', suggesting that Sussex should be scheduled as a National Park "free from the horrors of industrialism"; in the following year, in Storrington, Roy lectured on a report from Brighton and Hove Town Planning Committee.

A year or two before taking up with the WEA, he had been drawn towards making his home on Heath Common, on the outskirts of Storrington, then a focus of intellectuals and idealists, the legacy of a failed venture known as 'The Sanctuary' where Vera Pragnell had bought a tract of land, divided it up and given the plots away to anybody that wanted them. She called it "freeing the land" – "references were, of course, not required" she insisted. Roy and Sheila stayed here with one of the Sanctuary's residents in 1928 and clearly fell in love with the area, returning to buy 11 acres of nearby land. Here they built two homes in the 1930s, 'Longridge' and 'Highover'.

Artists, poets and others were drifting into the area, like the Scottish poet and communist, Hugh MacDiarmid, and just up the road was the self-styled 'King of Poland', pagan, poet and *enfant terrible*. Roy's friend, Reginald Reynolds, takes up the story in his memoirs, *My Life and Crimes* (Jarrolds, 1956):

Heath Common, Storrington, where I lectured once a week, was a lively place in those days. After the breakdown of an idealistic venture known as 'The Sanctuary'… the Common had become a sort of Bloomsbury colony in the heart of Sussex.

Far into the night, after the classes were over, some of us would sit by the fire, weaving fantasies, for we were all good at talking about what we would like to do. The only practical man among us was Roy Armstrong, who had ambitious schemes for a new type of education which presupposed a new type of community. As a community had to live somewhere he had begun by building – a brave enterprise for a man with no experience, and one in which he had shown himself a natural builder, architect and landscape gardener….

Roy, who in some indefinable way 'presided' over the clique, preached and practised a tolerance which was all-embracing.

Fundamental to Roy's all-embracing tolerance was fellowship and sharing. As he said in his own words:

We kept a rather open house and a number of friends who stayed with us were or had been members of extreme left-wing groups, some being German refugees … other friends were members of the Peace Pledge Union or eccentrics who had attracted some measure of attention….

Two others were Trotskyists who quite seriously asked if they could hide a secret printing press in his house – this was a venture too far, even for Roy – he refused.

Also welcomed was Jomo Kenyatta, the future first president of Kenya who had originally come to England as spokesman for his people, the Kikuyu, trying to redress their grievances against British colonial rule in Kenya. Unable to return home because of the Second World War, Roy offered him a home – he rented part of Highover – and gave him his own area of scrubland to clear where he grew his own maize and vegetables. A silver birch became his 'sacred tree' through which he communicated with the spirits of his people back in Africa (Jomo's tree survives to this day). For work, Jomo took a job as a labourer at Linfield's nursery at Thakeham where he spent much of his time boiling beetroot. More to his heart was lecturing to adult classes, organised by Roy – for example at Watersfield on 'Africa, Customs and Problems' – and whilst living with Roy he wrote *My people of Kikuyu and the life of Chief Wangombe*, published in 1944. It's not difficult to imagine them both talking late into the night about their dreams for an ideal world, of

Roy with Jomo Kenyatta, on his visit to his former war-time home at Highover after the Lancaster House Conference in London, 1963. The following year Jomo was inaugurated as the first president of Kenya.

Roy's other passion – Highover and Sandgate   *Kim Leslie*

Highover on Heath Common near Storrington, c1936 – the house built by Roy.

"…my own small garden, a few acres of reclaimed heathland, eats into my time far more than I ought to allow it." This was Roy writing in January 1966, just three months after launching his idea for the museum, frenetic months when he was not only considering his future plans, but also coping with the heavy demands of his WEA and university work. Whilst the museum came to take over much of Roy's life after he retired in 1967, his capacity for tending his "small garden" – his huge 11-acre garden – continued unabated. He may have been better known for his work at Singleton, but in the museum's shadow was always this other passion, his much-loved garden and home at Highover, near Storrington. Tamed and drained from the roughness of Heath Common since he first arrived in 1930, the perennial tasks were controlling the ever-encroaching bracken and invasive rhododendrons that love this sandstone ridge under the downs. Here Roy made an oasis of calm hidden away amongst the wooded sandy heathland, his home for over 60 years.

The 11 acres were purchased at £30 an acre in several plots between 1930 and 1934. As soon as Roy and Sheila secured the first plot they started to build their home, a timber-framed bungalow called 'Longridge'. Roy drew up his 'Ten-Year Plan' for future work on his new estate. Then a year after the bungalow was finished in 1932, they commandeered friends, took on some hired labour and started on 'Highover', a much larger and more ambitious brick-built property, a crescent-shaped sun-trap house with six bedrooms, and a 'common room'. This was to be a guest house for their friends, for lectures and meetings, to be managed by Lyn Birtles, an artistically-inclined young lady whom Roy and Sheila first met when visiting the Sanctuary. But by the time it was finished in 1936 the idea was abandoned, and the family – there were now two children, Jean and David, plus their friend Lyn – moved in.

Roy took great delight in shaping its surrounding acres, firstly draining the boggy heathland by digging out a pond, a massive task he undertook by hand. Then he built 12 little stone-arched bridges across the two tiny streams. The area between the two he called 'Mesopotamia' (between the Tigris and Euphrates). He delighted in its wildlife – particularly the butterflies, an interest since his student days – and the ever-changing seasons, keeping a remarkable series of weather records from 1937 until 1993, the year he died. What he created at Highover was a perfect setting for the children and their friends. One of Jean's happy memories of their idyllic childhood was boating along the pond in home-made punts and rafts made by Roy.

Whilst the underlying sandstone has given the essential character to this landscape, it has also been the cause of threats to its attractiveness through the relentless spread of industrial sandpits. Coupled with another threat, from housing development on the breaking up of the big local estate – the Sandgate Estate – Roy took a leading part in safeguarding its future by helping establish the Sandgate Preservation (now Conservation) Society in 1974.

Roy was an active member from its earliest days. Until the age of 90 he remained a regular helper on society 'field days', cutting, chopping and digging to open up and control this wild landscape. He started the society's newsletter as its first editor, to which he contributed numerous articles. And in an act of typical generosity, Roy donated three acres of his garden to help the creation of what is known today as Sandgate Park. When he was made the society's first president in 1982, the chairman said that Roy had been "a major force" in its formation and that his work to protect the area "has been outstanding". Today this peaceful place is one more tangible reminder of the legacy Roy left behind.

Moon Bridge under construction in 1954, one of a dozen bridges built by Roy across streams in his garden at Highover.

freedom and democracy, about Kenyan independence and breaking the yoke of colonial rule.

Unfortunately the habits and political views of some of those staying with Roy caused a considerable amount of gossip and concern. The West Sussex director of education even felt obliged to warn the WEA district secretary about these activities. Roger Fieldhouse, writing in *The Search for Enlightenment: The Working Class and Adult Education in the Twentieth Century* (Lawrence and Wishart, 1990), highlights Roy's case in his study of WEA tutors under siege for their liberal views, "an illustration", says Fieldhouse, of the "McCarthyite proscription of tutors and ideas" then threatening progressive left-wing thinkers throughout the country. It was just one of the hazards in working for the WEA to promote 'workers' education' at this time, particularly in such a staid political climate as rural West Sussex.

Roy was also actively involved in membership of the Left Book Club, founded in 1936 by the publisher Victor Gollancz to alert the country to the dangers facing the world through poverty, fascism and international hostilities. Its list of radical books, issued monthly at half-a-crown each, gives a good idea of what intellectual socialists like Roy were reading at the time: George Orwell's *The Road to Wigan Pier* (perhaps its most iconic title), Leonard Woolf's *Barbarians at the Gate,* G D H Cole's *The People's Front,* and Harold Laski's *Faith, Reason and Civilisation.* Members were encouraged to join local groups to discuss these books. Roy took a leading part in the Chichester group of the Left Book Club alongside another prominent member, Ernest Wishart of Binsted, near Arundel, an interesting combination of wealthy gentleman farmer and high-profile publisher of working class histories and Communist Party classics. In July 1938 we find Roy leading the local group on a downland walk and picnic to the top of Stoke Clump near Chichester where he led an open-air discussion on the club's new book, *A People's History of England* by the Marxist historian A L Morton. WEA and Labour Party members were invited to join club members for the occasion.

Roy's adult education work for the WEA widened in 1936 when he was appointed extra-mural resident tutor in West Sussex by Hartley University College (known as Southampton University from 1952), work that expanded even more with the outbreak of war and the university's response to the need from the military to provide classes on political awareness and cultural and leisure topics for the huge population of soldiers in the county. But, without warning, his permit to lecture to the troops was withdrawn through the intervention of MI5. The permit was eventually renewed, but Roy was never told the precise reasons. (Years later he said he thought it was because of allegations that he was a communist and security risk. Roy stoutly denied the claim, saying he always regarded himself as a "rather woolly liberal".)

But even with this increased burden, Roy optimistically used the war years to set out what has been described as a remarkable series of development proposals for adult education in West Sussex, including detailed plans for a major centre in the county. The opening of the Worthing Adult Education Centre in 1948 was one of Roy's landmark achievements and came to make a major contribution to adult education in West Sussex. As well as providing a focus for local town organisations, it became a county-wide centre for such bodies as the National Council for Women and the West Sussex Council for Educational Advance.

After the war had ended Roy started to make a name for himself nationally with articles in journals and magazines aimed at tutors in adult education; one theme was about the use of visual aids in adult education in which he was a pioneer, a theme that underlay all his teaching — to make knowledge and ideas accessible to as wide an audience as possible. For the WEA journal *The Highway,* in 1948, Roy highlighted the work of Dr Otto Neurath and his demonstration of the value of visual presentation in the 1920s, ideas we take so much for granted today but which then were appreciated by few teachers. The conference Roy organised on 'Visual Aids in Adult Education' at Lodge Hill, Pulborough, in 1950 was the first of its kind in the country and where it was reported that of 71 tutors questioned, 58 felt deterred from using them. By the 1960s Roy was making his own slides that became such a noted feature of all his classes, at a time even then when many tutors were still using chalk and talk. His vast collection of slides, mostly black and white, is now in the archives at the museum.

And it was after the war that Roy's work started to shift towards teaching local studies. This is really the prelude to Roy Armstrong, the local historian, who years later founded the Weald & Downland Open Air Museum.

His first publication to capture his widest audience was about locality and community history, a document revealing a lot about Roy's ideas and some of the principles that drove his work throughout his life. Co-authored with

How Roy Armstrong touched lives   *Kim Leslie*

All those who worked closely with Roy have their own personal stories and memories about how he touched their lives.

I first met him in the old police cells under Arundel Town Hall when new museum displays were being discussed in early 1967. Roy needed an exhibition about the old Arundel Theatre in Maltravers Street. Would I help? Would I put its history together and do a display?

He gave me my first opportunity to contribute to his work: research that took me to the Theatre Archive at the Victoria & Albert Museum and to West Sussex Record Office, a link that was later to change the direction of my life. And as an aside, at one of our Arundel meetings, he mentioned his other project, his attempt to start an open air museum, if only the land could be found. Would I like to come along to a meeting of its promotion committee? I went along to the meeting at the chairman's house at Ifield and was promptly appointed its first honorary treasurer in April 1967, forging a link that led to all sorts of activities within the new organisation over the founding years.

The point about all this is that Roy always wanted to involve

Deep in discussion: two 'like-minds' — Roy with museum director, Chris Zeuner, who developed a close bond. Behind them are the timbers of Cowfold barn awaiting re-erection on site following repair.

> ❝ *Roy Armstrong was speaking at a residential course at Lodge Hill near Pulborough. I was 18 and busy with A levels. He was electrifying and in the space of an hour I was totally captivated by the idea of this pioneering museum. I spoke to him after his lecture, offered my services as a volunteer, and thus began the start of a life totally devoted to the museum! The first time I saw Chris Zeuner was at a talk for volunteers and supporters at West Dean College. What he had to say was extremely interesting, but he wouldn't stand still — in fact I was to discover that he rarely stood still, either physically or metaphorically. The first time I spoke to them both at once was in Bayleaf where the three of us were in discussion. With me then were the two people — Roy and Chris — who were to have the most influence on my life. Today, their portraits face each other across the meeting room in Crawley upper hall, both now, incredibly, and sadly, passed away, but whose influence on the museum, building conservation and national heritage, and me personally, was formative and inspirational.* ❞
>
> **Diana Zeuner**

others in his projects, giving them opportunities to participate, discuss and contribute. At the time I taught history in Worthing. Meeting Roy now opened the way to tutor for the WEA (Workers' Educational Association) throughout West Sussex and to work side by side with him in shared teaching projects and courses. I well remember his kindness in making slides from maps and books for use in my own classes, his interest in using visual aids always so important for the work.

On the strength of all these activities I was appointed the first education officer of West Sussex Record Office — with the brief to promote the study of local history throughout the county. So it became possible to link record office duties with the museum in a great variety of ways, including making the first tentative steps towards the provision of a museum education service. These were exciting times that owed so much to Roy Armstrong whose great gift was enthusing others in all his ventures. I was fortunate to be one of those brought together by this inspirational friend and founder of the museum, to join an organisation that has been both life-enhancing and exhilarating.

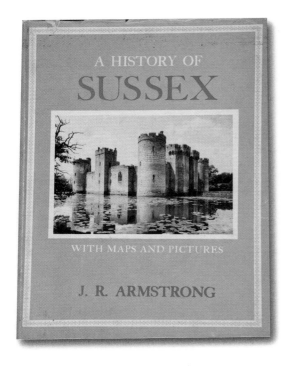

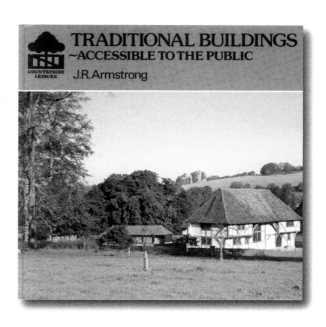

another WEA tutor, this was a 77-page booklet published jointly by the WEA and the Workers' Educational Trade Union Committee in 1955. Its lengthy sub-title is indicative: *Local Studies: a pamphlet addressed by its authors J. R. Armstrong and P. G. H. Hopkins to all those interested in local studies whether tutors or students in adult classes, or school teachers or ordinary citizens who wish to know more of the world immediately around them.* It was this world, the local world – what was "immediately around" – that became Roy's focus in his future work.

In it he says that the key to a better understanding of the wider world is to be found through "an intimate knowledge of one's own community", going on to suggest that the most revealing clues about a community are through studying its "less spectacular local buildings" and to urge the need to record them because of the dangers they faced through post-war redevelopment. Here he gave some of his early thoughts on vernacular architecture that eventually led to a new direction in his life by co-founding the Wealden Buildings Study Group and founding the museum. But at this stage in his thinking his advice on museums is restricted to the more traditional museum: that there should be a "local" museum for "every town or village of any size". He put his own advice to good use when he acted as historical adviser in setting up Arundel Museum in 1963.

Roy's work in tutoring adult classes throughout the county led to many local study projects and opportunities for his own research into local history. Out of this came *A History of Sussex* in 1961, his comprehensive account of the county's development from geological times to the 20th century. The third edition in 1974 widened its scope considerably with eight additional chapters, including material about buildings and the open air museum. In its scope and approach the book is without parallel and still in print some 50 years after it was first written, an unusual record in books about Sussex and testimony to Roy's authoritative but popular approach in making history so accessible. The latest edition, the fourth, updated and re-designed by Roy's two museum friends, Diana Zeuner and Richard Pailthorpe, ensures that Roy's work continues to stimulate interest in the county's past.

It was in Roy's much enlarged third edition that he introduced a new chapter 'Conserving the Past', giving the opportunity to put the recently established museum within the wider context of conservation and preservation movements. He stressed the need for their effective action against the "tremendous pressures in the south-east which are changing the environment more rapidly than in any previous epoch …".

And no more rapidly in Sussex than in Crawley New Town, relentlessly pushing out its tentacles in designated 'neighbourhood units' far in excess of its original plan. Whilst Roy clearly saw good social purpose in these new-town creations with

Above left *The first edition of Roy Armstrong's A History of Sussex.*

Above *Traditional Buildings – Accessible to the Public, written by Roy as part of EP Publishing's Countryside Leisure series, in 1979. Roy believed in making information and knowledge available to the widest possible audience, hence this popular book focusing on buildings which the public could visit. About a fifth of the illustrations were drawn from the museum, and most of the drawings were by Richard Harris, later the museum's research director.*

their decent homes and opportunities for London's overspill population, he nevertheless despaired at the needless destruction of what remained of medieval Crawley, smashing the town's links with its past. What was happening here was the first trigger that set in motion Roy's ambition to create a safe haven for threatened buildings that eventually led to the creation of the museum.

For all his endeavours the rewards of recognition followed. In 1972 he was awarded the MBE in the Queen's Birthday Honours and then in 1992 an honorary doctorate from the University of Sussex was conferred at the museum, the first time such a ceremony had been held outside the university campus.

His oration before the vice chancellor touched on his life's work in his involvement with what he called "*informed* organisations" such as the WEA, the Vernacular Architecture Group (of which he was a founder member in 1952) as well as small local societies.

It is my belief that the future of any form of democratic government will largely depend on the development of such voluntary, underline organisations [Roy's underlining in his notes]. The key word is 'informed', differences of interest and view-point can only be resolved by a willingness to reach a consensus through underline discussion and compromise. The alternative is likely to lead to confrontation and destruction....

For example, a conservation society with which I have been closely associated [the Sandgate Conservation Society at Storrington] has recently been divided on the question of rhododendrons. Some regard this shrub as an alien introduced in the 18th century to be totally eradicated ... others disagree, considering the evergreen leaf and large colourful flower attractive. At length everyone seemed to be *appeased by the acceptance of the phrase 'rhododendron control' — but this does not specify just how <u>much</u> control and exactly <u>where</u>; there will be many differing views about details and one trusts that discussion will be both informed and conducted with understanding and tolerance. This may seem a very trivial example but typifies wider and more important issues and much larger groups and organisations.*

Just as local studies can lead to a better understanding of the wider world, so smaller social entities, as in Roy's "trivial" example, echo their larger counterparts. Informed organisations, discussion and consensus rather than confrontation and destruction — these were essential elements behind Roy's teachings and the operating principles by which he worked to achieve his goals, be it in the museum or the many groups with which he was involved. In accepting his doctorate for his lifetime's work, Roy declared that he was "someone fortunate enough to be provided with a

For "untiring work and enterprise" — the Chichester Observer *paid tribute to Roy Armstrong's vision and inspiration by commissioning his portrait in 1978. From left to right: Geoffrey Godber, museum chairman; Juliet Pannett, the artist; Graham Brooks, editor of the* Observer*; Roy Armstrong and his wife, Lyn.*

platform and the means of bringing individuals together who share similar aims". His ability to do this with such success was Roy's supreme achievement.

Roy Armstrong's memorial – Poplar Cottage   *Diana Zeuner*

Poplar Cottage re-erected at the museum.

In 1998 the museum re-erected the 16th-century smoke-bay house, Poplar Cottage, as a memorial to Roy Armstrong in view of his close associations with the building.

Built of oak and elm between 1550 and 1630, it was situated at the edge of the scarp slope of the Downs at Washington Common, on what is now the Wiston Estate, close to Roy's Storrington home. Originally the home of a landless labourer, it was built where sheep pasture, arable land and common pasture meet — an important feature of the West Sussex landscape. The cottage was donated to the museum by the Goring family and dismantled in 1982. It retained a special link with Roy, who led a detailed research project into the buildings of the Wiston Estate, and discovered the cottage's importance as a smoke-bay house.

Partly funded by a Heritage Lottery Fund grant, the house was restored by Roger Champion under Richard Harris's direction, and provided the museum with the missing link in the story of house development on the site. Being heated by a fire lit within a smoke bay it represented the transitional type between the medieval open hall and houses with brick chimneys.

Poplar Cottage enabled the museum to contrast its construction and social status with that of Bayleaf farmhouse, a much more substantial dwelling. It has been furnished as the home of a landless labourer and provided with a cottage garden of the period.

The timber frame rising on its new site.

2

'The Impossible Museum'

Catherington treadwheel; thatching in progress in early 1970.

– from idea to reality: 1965–1970 *Kim Leslie*

At the start the challenge was enormous. Threatened buildings – the *raison d'être* of the museum – were freely available. They were quite literally free, otherwise they'd be destroyed, in one place for a new reservoir, at another for a road-widening scheme, at another for sand quarrying. Any cost for the actual buildings wasn't an issue. Their days were numbered because of their location; they were simply in the wrong place, in the way of development. The sticking point was that there was nowhere to take them. What we needed was land – at least 30 or 40 acres – hopefully for free again (maybe a rather naïve hope in this part of the world), but even if there was a site there'd be heavy lifting, transport and labour costs for the rescue operations. Then the dismantled timbers would have to be put together again. More labour costs. Such meagre funds as we had – less than £12 when I took over as honorary treasurer – would barely pay for all the postage stamps needed for any appeal for money let alone cover any ambitious wish list. It seemed an impossible task.

Of course Roy Armstrong, founder of the museum, ever the optimist, believed funds would come from somewhere; it seemed reasonable to think that there might be a sympathetic response from charities, from public bodies and possibly individual well-wishers anxious to see a safe haven for condemned buildings. The problem was more one of urgency. Important buildings would be lost unless there was speedy action.

And yet, amazingly, just three years after our funds had stood at under £12, the museum was opening its gates to the public for the first time in September 1970.

The site had been found, a limited company set up, charitable status granted, buildings transported and re-erected, the timbers of more safely in store at another nearby site, a labour force had been mobilised, the first director appointed, and funds were at last coming in. Considering the hurdles we faced, and even outright opposition to the project from some quarters, a miracle had been achieved.

So how did it all begin? What actually

happened in the founding years before the museum opened to the public in 1970?

In any formal sense the museum dates from October 1965. This was when the suggestion was first discussed at a conference of the Study Group on Timber-framed Buildings of the Weald at Balneath Manor, Chailey in East Sussex, held against an alarming background: that so many historic buildings, even those listed for protection, were being condemned to make way for new development. It was a sad and distressing story. In Surrey over 350 historic buildings had been destroyed between 1951 and 1965. The demolition rate in Kent was probably as high as *three a month*. Roy Armstrong underlined this catalogue of destruction by what had been happening in Sussex in the construction of Crawley New Town.

Writing about Crawley in June 1965 he said that within the last six months he had seen "three buildings worth preserving … two with unique features – literally consigned to the flames, the buildings being pulled apart with cables and caterpillar tractors … the main timbers, although in excellent condition, burnt on gigantic bonfires". To save others similarly threatened from the developer's claw, Roy suggested creating an "Open Air Museum of the Weald" (there was no 'Downland' in the title then) on a site somewhere central to the Weald: "possibly the Ashdown Forest district would be ideal". There was reference to a specific house: "Bayleaf … could well become available for removal to a museum. It is threatened with submergence in a reservoir within the next two years."

Within a year, in September 1966, Roy was convening the first meeting of the Committee for the Promotion of an Open Air Museum for the Weald and Downland. This cumbersomely-named committee took on all the initial groundwork that set the museum in motion: finding a site, rescuing the first buildings, all the initial publicity and fund-raising and setting up a business company acceptable to the Charity Commissioners.

Destruction of medieval Crawley for the New Town development

Bonfires of ancient timbers, the original catalyst for the museum – the destruction of medieval buildings for Crawley New Town after the Second World War.

Awaiting re-erection – timbers of Winkhurst stored in the disused railway cutting at Singleton, 1968.

The museum might never have found its home at the far end of West Sussex had one of a number of other sites been successful. Although the original suggestion for a Wealden site somewhere around Ashdown Forest in central Sussex was never pursued, the wider title – since 1966 incorporating 'Downland' – reflected the widening search for a location that might well have been on the chalk downland somewhere around Brighton or Worthing. Investigations looked at possibilities in Stanmer Park, on Beacon Hill, Rottingdean and Sweet Hill, Patcham, as well as in the grounds of the demolished mansion of Muntham Court at Findon. Other possibilities investigated were near Maidstone (linked to a projected centre illustrating 'The English Way of Life' promoted by Richard Hearne, aka TV comic 'Mr Pastry') and on manorial wasteland at Ifield, near Crawley. Roy thought the National Trust might be able to help,

maybe at Wakehurst, Nymans, Sheffield Park or Batemans. None of these possibilities turned out to be either practical or suitable. There was still nowhere to go, still the urgency to act before more demolition gangs moved in to repeat the distressing Crawley saga elsewhere. Considering what was about to happen, it was fortunate that all these sites were non-starters.

The key to the dilemma was provided by one of the members of the promotion committee, Victor Sheppard, who had just come down to Sussex from the Museum of English Rural Life at Reading. Now senior keeper of folk life and ethnography at Brighton Museum, he discussed the project with its director, Dr Clifford Musgrave. Importantly, Musgrave was advisor to the trustees of the Edward James Foundation, a recently formed educational trust based on the West Dean Estate near Chichester. Fortuitously the trustees were ready for an approach by an organisation with an underlying educational purpose.

By the summer of 1967 a possible solution to all the searching had been found; Victor Sheppard's timely intervention was the first big step towards all our subsequent success. By October the trustees agreed on a location adjacent to West Dean village. The landscape setting seemed ideal, with the little river Lavant running through the proposed site (when it flows, that is, as it's a seasonal winterbourne). Edward James himself, whose family had owned West Dean since 1891, was delighted at the prospect. Larger than life, a millionaire patron of the arts, a poet and writer, the eccentric backer of so much creativity, his support was vital. The planners were encouraging and no objections were lodged within the statutory three-week period; we thought we were home and dry. But any euphoria was short-lived. When the proposals were presented to the villagers at a public meeting at West Dean there was uproar. The village erupted, alarmed at the prospect of traffic squeezing through its narrow lanes and loss of their seclusion. The tenant farmer would lose valuable grazing land. For the community it was clearly a bad decision. We listened – and retreated.

Edward James of West Dean, patron of the arts and supporter of the museum project. He is pictured with his macaws at his Mexican estate, Xilitla.

> " *...the grassy slopes of a Sussex estate near Chichester...may become one of the most famous showplaces in the south...* "
>
> **The Daily Telegraph, 1969**

Early site exhibits – 1. The charcoal burners' camp   *Diana Zeuner*

The charcoal burners' camp was one of the first non-building exhibits which came into the category of 'reconstructions' and was built for the opening year of 1970. The museum undertook a number of these in its early years, to add to its exhibits and help visitors understand structures, such as the Saxon weavers' hut, which had long disappeared from the landscape, or to interpret rural crafts.

Charcoal burning was an important Wealden industry and the museum was fortunate in its relationship with Arthur Langridge, the son-in-law of the last charcoal burner in Sussex, and his wife, who had experienced living and working with the craft in its most traditional form. Lyn Armstrong (Roy's second wife, then Lyn Sharf) took an early interest in assisting them, nurturing successive camps through various phases and teaching charcoal burning to others, such as Alan Waters, who at one time carried out charcoal burning at the museum

Mr and Mrs Arthur Langridge who built the first charcoal burners' camp at the museum.

on an almost full-time basis, latterly using more modern charcoal burning kilns. Lyn contributed to the then small volume of published material on the craft by writing *Woodcolliers and Charcoal Burning* in 1979.

A traditional earth burn is an atmospheric sight, and an early example was noted by volunteer Matti Denton, whose diaries of her involvement at the museum are now in its collection. In the first Museum Magazine, No 1, November 1972, she described what she saw:

> *On Monday the 11th September we saw Mr & Mrs Langridge back at the museum once more. They came to build another charcoal kiln on the same site as last year's burn. This time the kiln was about twice as big as the previous one.*
>
> *On the following morning by 9 a.m. the kiln was lit. The weather was ideal, not too windy, not too hot. A number of local newspaper reporters came to see the burn and write up their notes on this romantic and ancient craft.*
>
> *White steam belches from the kiln as the wood dries and soon the sand and earth covering is beginning to show signs of scorching. Mr Langridge and his helpers went around with sand and water to repair any overheating breaks in the outer crust. Already the burn was being declared a success. The helpers and enthusiasts had supper by the*

Lyn Armstrong and Alan Waters, the museum's charcoal burner, lighting the kiln in 1980.

> *charcoal burners' huts on a warm, lovely, evening and a most enjoyable evening it was. Evening became night and the long vigil went on. Strangely enough the time passes quickly – with intermittent conversation on many subjects. The dawn came and all looked in pleasure and amazement at the now almost completed burn. The shape of the kiln had changed during the night after hours of damping and patting down, but not changed too much. All was now blackened and spent-looking. Then began the careful task of opening up the kiln, starting at the apex, bringing down the earth with the wiper, wetting the charcoal as it was uncovered, then down again with the wiper and so on until all 20 hundredweight [1.016 tonnes] of lovely metallic charcoal was revealed. A most rewarding 24 hours.*

Above *Geoffrey Godber, right, whose support for the museum at county council level was crucial. He is pictured here in 1981, when he was museum chairman, escorting the Duke of Gloucester around the site on the occasion of the opening of the hall from Boarhunt. Victoria Leslie sits nonchalantly on a log.*

Below *Open pasture in the Lavant valley – the museum site in 1968 before the first buildings were erected.*

An alternative site must be found. With the full support of the Edward James' trustees another was identified at the Singleton end of the West Dean Estate. This time no estate residents complained about the choice. But it was now the planners' turn to object. They were concerned at access from the two main roads bordering the site as well as the need to preserve the strategic gap between Singleton and West Dean. There was talk of 'ribbon development' between the two villages, of encouraging the spread of Singleton down the valley. One prominent member of the planning committee feared a Disney-type theme park might emerge. Even the possibility that we might be linked to Billy Butlin was cited. Emotion and unfounded rumour-mongering could have killed the project – the planners might well have rejected the second site and we would need to start all over again. The frustration was that this site had so much to offer: a generous space of open pasture and woodland set on a rolling slope

of downland with parkland views down the valley – quite as fine a site as any other open air museum in Europe. It was perfect, too good to lose. And we were already stacking up timbers from rescued buildings on the estate through the immense co-operation of the resident estate agent, Edward Jermy. Would they have to be moved all over again?

The museum's honorary architect and planner, John Warren, patiently drew up more plans for the local planning department, redrafting, negotiating, endlessly explaining. More bureaucratic than visionary, its officers and members could well have buried the project under a mass of technicalities and procedures. This is where Geoffrey Godber came into the picture. A resident of Singleton – he had only just moved into the village – he was crucial to our purpose. Importantly he was clerk of West Sussex County Council, the chief officer of the local authority, an influential figure who saw the museum as an imaginative opportunity not to be missed. He didn't suffer fools – or opposition – gladly. By December 1968 outline planning permission had been granted by West Sussex County Council. Godber had been working behind the scenes. He personally called John Warren by telephone with the news that the area planning officer would be glad to finalise details.

Events had been developing fast. We now had the land, 35 acres, offered on a lease of 42 years at a remarkably generous price, at a peppercorn rent of just £1 a year and, vitally, with planning permission. Buildings were being rescued and piling up ready for reconstruction. But, and it was a big but, there was little money in hand and no proper administrative organisation to handle the next stages.

Disturbingly, the doubters had been surfacing. From one quarter we'd been told we shouldn't be saving buildings at all without substantial resources

> *A complete village with houses, cottages, farm buildings, inns and shops may be 'created' in the south of England…. The strange thing about the little community is that it would be a museum. An open air museum of buildings through the ages is now becoming more than just a dream for a well-known university lecturer from Storrington.*

Worthing Gazette, March 1967 (the first news article to cover the museum)

behind us; without these we couldn't guarantee the way ahead. Whatever the urgency, even if it meant sacrificing valuable buildings, we should wait. Raise the money first, save buildings next.

Then there was the museum establishment, highly suspicious of this new type of venture. Some prominent museum professionals voiced concern at this upstart project, insisting that the first essential was to make a detailed and comprehensive survey of the architectural heritage of the south-east *before* any collecting began, whatever the losses. Make a survey first, save buildings next.

Roy was ideal in countering any opposition. Criticism was never a deterrent. He ignored it. His other strength was his ability to bring together professionals, experts and influential people to advise and guide. An indefatigable letter writer, he sought opinions from a wide field, seeking comments, suggestions and contacts for the way ahead. His correspondence shows him writing to Frank Atkinson, himself busy setting up the Beamish Open Air Museum in County Durham; to Nigel Nicholson at Sissinghurst; to the archaeologist Sir Mortimer Wheeler who'd been advocating the idea of European-style open air folk museums since the 1930s; to Ingemar Liman of Skansen in Sweden, prototype of all open air museums in Europe. Roy developed a vast web of correspondents.

To serve on his committees, Roy recruited people like John Warren of Horsham, an architect and planner, who did so much to lay down the original framework for the museum, and Norman West, an accountant from Bognor who offered himself as company secretary, ensuring that all our dealings were in line with company law. Then

there was Robin McDowall, senior investigator for the Royal Commission on Historical Monuments, and Stuart Rigold, prolific scholar, a leading authority on medieval buildings, and chief inspector of ancient monuments, who brought vast knowledge to committee decisions. Betty Murray, principal of Bishop Otter College, Chichester, administrator, academic, archaeologist and historian, always added old-fashioned wisdom and sensitivity to discussions.

There was James Farmer, first chairman of the museum, a local landowner from Ifield (who had been at school with Roy), a senior alderman of Surrey County Council and chairman of its records, historic buildings and antiquities committee, who knew so many influential people, including the Duke of Norfolk whom he enlisted as the museum's first president. Major General Arthur Hawes of Harting brought his vast military background into the museum circle as its vice chairman. He had been in charge of relief work after the 1935 Quetta earthquake in India and was the brains behind the planning and movement of the British Expeditionary Force to France in the Second World War. To this retired officer the problems the museum faced were simple. He produced a series of 'Appreciations' – military-style appraisals of the situation: "In spite of all the difficulties, the project is, in fact, relatively a simple one if approached in a realistic and methodical way". General Hawes brought order and confidence when the way ahead seemed fraught with problems. Personalities such as these made for a formidable team.

They gave respectability and professionalism to the venture, buttressed by John Lowe who

Above *Major General Arthur Hawes, left, the museum's first vice-chairman, who brought "order and confidence" to the early development of the museum. Here he is speaking at the retirement presentation to the museum's first senior warden, Doug Bryant, and his wife, Marjorie, in 1983, who seem momentarily distracted by something in the air. Behind them is Jim Hampshire, site manager, and Richard Pailthorpe, assistant director.*

Above left *Three key figures in the early days of the museum. From left to right: Roger Champion, who was to become master carpenter; John Lowe, the first museum director, and Kate Barson, museum trustee, 1970.*

Early site exhibits – 2. Hangleton cottage and the reconstructions
Richard Harris and Diana Zeuner

Archaeologists and volunteers building the conjectural flint walls of the 13th-century Hangleton cottage, based on the excavations at the structure's original site.

The year 1970 was an intense time for members of the museum's archaeological committee who were discussing the proposed reconstruction of a Saxon weavers' hut and two buildings based on excavations at Hangleton, Hove. Its members were Roy Armstrong, founder; John Lowe, museum director; Betty Murray, principal of Bishop Otter College, and two archaeologists, Eric Holden of the Sussex Archaeological Society, and John Hurst, an inspector of ancient monuments. Nearly 20 years earlier (1952-4) they had excavated the deserted medieval downland village.

Three projects were considered: the reconstruction of a Saxon weavers' hut, a replica 13th-century longhouse, and a two-roomed cottage, based on the Hangleton evidence. The weavers' hut, based on excavations at Old Erringham Farm near Shoreham, and at Bishopstone, near Seaford, was constructed in time for the museum's first opening, complete with a replica loom. Regular weaving demonstrations took place.

The longhouse proposal was aborted, partly on cost grounds and partly because of a concern that the museum should not focus on archaeological reconstructions (for which many elements were conjectural) at the expense of its efforts to rescue 'real' buildings.

Work on the smaller house proceeded, however, with the blessing of the museum's sites and buildings committee, supervised by the archaeologists. Despite some concern about the necessity to conjecture the building above ground level, the completed project was well received by visitors and provided them with a contrast between a medieval peasant's dwelling and the house of a yeoman farmer, such as Bayleaf.

The museum's third experiment in reconstruction was the creation of the footprint of a large Saxon hall based on evidence from a Saxon village deserted in the ninth century on the Downs above Chalton in east Hampshire. The evidence was reproduced to the exact scale on the ground, with short timbers marking the position of post-holes (popularly known at the museum as the 'dragon's teeth') and gravel marking the trenches revealed by the excavations. No attempt was made to reconstruct the superstructure.

The archaeological committee also discussed other projects, including medieval iron smelting, a replica glass furnace and the medieval pottery experiment. Its work was part of a Europe-wide movement in experimental archaeology, which encompassed Avoncroft Museum of Buildings' Iron Age huts, the Iron Age project at Butser Hill run by Peter Reynolds, and the reconstructed Saxon village at West Stow, Suffolk, as well as others in Denmark, Austria and Poland. However, in 1983, the weavers' hut and 'dragon's teeth' were removed: there were ongoing maintenance problems with the hut and it was felt that the reconstructions were not at that time being underpinned by active archaeological involvement.

The Hangleton cottage remains an important exhibit, not least because it was the first time such a reconstruction had been attempted. The original excavations continue to be widely cited in publications on dwellings of this early period.

The Saxon weavers' hut, with the footprint of a Saxon hall laid out with timber posts in the foreground.

generously agreed to work as the museum's part-time director for the first year without salary from May 1969. John came with considerable and prestigious museum experience behind him; from senior posts at the Victoria & Albert Museum and then as director of the City Museum and Art Gallery at Birmingham. Before this he had been a story editor at Pinewood Film Studios, edited Collins Crime Club books and Faber's furniture series and had published works on Thomas Chippendale and ceramics. He went on to become a leading authority on Japanese life and culture and produced the first major biography of Edward James, as well as being appointed the first principal of West Dean College. A man of wide learning and many parts, John injected style and efficiency into the day-to-day running of the infant museum. John's first major task was organising an appeal for £100,000.

> " The early months saw Susan, Alan and I attending history lectures in East Wittering Primary School. Our tutors were Mr J R Armstrong and Mr Kim Leslie. Never were three people more enthralled with their new evening lectures on cold winter nights. So much so, that we got caught in the current interest of the lecturers — namely the Weald & Downland Open Air Museum. ... I was told there were many jobs I could do such as laying and clearing pathways through the woods and burning unwanted wood and rubbish. This thrilled me no end but no one at this point seemed to want to say exactly where the museum site was. I realised later that the secrecy was important because until Mr Armstrong was assured of one's sincerity he did not want people let loose among such valuable properties. ...On Sunday 17 May 1970 we were taken on a tour of the few buildings erected on the museum estate. It was a lovely day, the weather good and everyone so nice explaining what Weald & Downland was all about. We were also taken to the old railway cutting to see other buildings in store. We laughed and chatted and pledged to do all we could to help this venture get off the ground. "
>
> **Matti Denton's diary, 1970**

With Geoffrey Godber agreeing to take on the museum's legal work at County Hall — and promising all sorts of office help from West Sussex County Council — the jigsaw of pieces was rapidly coming together. There may not have been much money at the start, but there were friends and supporters in the right places, offering an enormous range of time and talents.

As did the site volunteers. Progress on the museum site depended on a growing band of helpers, also giving their skills and labour for nothing, recruited and co-ordinated by Pam West (company secretary Norman's wife), whose Bognor home rapidly submerged under museum affairs. Her volunteers regularly met together in all the free time they could muster for opening up the site for public access: cutting footpaths,

Above *Lintott's walking-stick workshop during its working life — its tools and equipment and remaining products were the first rural life artefacts to be collected by the museum in 1968.*

Below *Volunteers stripping the roof of the Upper Beeding toll house in 1968.*

Above *Roy Armstrong on the site of Pendean farmhouse during dismantling in 1968 with Marjorie Hallam, one of the earliest supporters of the museum, who became the second honorary librarian and was made a vice president. The lady in the foreground is Pam West, later to be appointed volunteer co-ordinator.*

Above right *Boys from St Andrew's School, Worthing, unload the timbers of the Littlehampton granary, with volunteer Pam West, 1969.*

coppicing woodland, planting trees, making picnic areas. A regular weekend contingent came from the Chichester Wine Circle – home-made wine and summer sunshine made for some jolly occasions! Then there were rescue missions away from the site, again co-ordinated by Pam West, collecting old farming implements and craft tools such as the entire contents of Lintott's walking-stick workshop near Chiddingfold, made possible by Chris Zeuner (later to become the museum's first full-time director) who offered his Land Rover and trailer. Anthony Simmons put his van at the museum's disposal. I lent my caravan for early site meetings.

The Upper Beeding toll house from near Steyning (nearly demolished after a road traffic accident) was the first of several buildings to be dismantled by volunteers (the heavy transport provided at no cost by West Dean Estate). Pupils from St Andrew's Church of England School for Boys at Worthing helped dismantle the 18th-century granary at Littlehampton. The following month, in July 1969, they were at a week-long work camp – repeated the following year – unloading lorries, making wattle panels for Winkhurst, helping Roger Champion put up the framework around the Catherington treadwheel and working with our charcoal burners, Mr and Mrs Langridge, to build a traditional charcoal burners' camp in the woods. St Andrew's was the first school on the site. Theirs were magical experiences, making real history, fondly remembered by former pupils who still relish their significant contribution all those years ago. Hidebound by health and safety regulations, none of this would now be possible in today's timid environment.

Whatever the tasks, we all knew we were involved in pioneer work, all sharing in Roy

Armstrong's dream. For quite a lot of volunteers, time away from the excitement of the museum site was time lost. Caught up in this very special atmosphere, the museum changed the direction of several peoples' lives. There was an excitement in the air, still nostalgically remembered today by those touched by Roy's infectious enthusiasm.

Although the site was on a peppercorn rent and so much time and so many talents were freely

> " *My introduction to Roy and Lyn (it was always 'Roy and Lyn', as you might say 'apples and pears' or 'chalk and cheese') was in autumn 1968 on the original site of Pendean. Other 'founder members' were there, such as Marjorie Hallam and Pam and Norman West together with a group of archaeologists digging for gold within the house footprint. All that remained of Pendean at this time was the low sandstone wall upon which the oak sole plate had rested undisturbed for the previous 350+ autumns. Even now, with the sand extracting company's mechanical shovels taking greedy mouthfuls of sand from Pendean's feet, and the turmoil of the site itself with its rejected broken bricks, stone, mortar, plaster, sundry bits of wood, fencing, corrugated iron and the general detritus of an abandoned farm, it was still a very peaceful place upon which generations of farming families had left their mark. "*
>
> **Roger Champion, master carpenter**

given by well-wishers and volunteers, there was still clearly a need for funds – it couldn't all be done on a shoe-string. Money was needed for paying essential staff and covering the expenses of running an office, printing appeal literature, publishing the first guidebook, buying building materials and hiring equipment. And there were not only historic buildings to think about, there was the need to lay out the essential site infrastructure with a car park, lavatories, telephone and electricity, water and drainage.

Money came from a patchwork of sources. The original promotion committee started with the modest sum of just under £12, handed over to me by Roy Armstrong when I became the committee's honorary treasurer. These few pounds represented gifts from local organisations addressed by Roy on his early campaign to promote the museum, headed by three pounds three shillings (£3.15), a modest sum, but a landmark donation, from a church group in Tarring. Roy continued to hand over many similar gifts and lecture fees, even the money given to him on his retirement.

Some substantial gifts followed to support specific projects, such as from John Lowe and Kate Barson (a member of the museum's Council of Management) who gave £250 and £100 respectively for Winkhurst. The first grant from a public body came from West Sussex County Council – £400 towards the dismantling of Pendean, near Midhurst. Littlehampton Round Table did a sponsored walk towards the rebuilding costs of the Littlehampton granary and raised £464. The Friends of the Museum – with some 400 members by 1970 paying a minimum annual subscription of £1 – made its first donation to the new museum company by handing over £872 for stage one of the car park and the main entrance. An offshoot, the Manhood Friends (geographically covering the Manhood Peninsula south of Chichester), set up by Diane Wilson of Sidlesham, organised a jumble sale, a sponsored walk, a barbecue and carol singing, raising just over £200 for the Catherington treadwheel. A matching grant from the Victoria & Albert Museum then doubled this sum, so all costs for the wheel were met. (Another similar Friends' offshoot was started at Hurstpierpoint by Frances Taylor. We wanted more of these local offshoots, but they never developed.)

To help with the administrative side of the museum – and strictly not to be used for any buildings – West Sussex County Council made an interest-free loan of £1,000 (soon converted into a gift) and the Society of Sussex Downsmen met

all the legal costs for the formation of the museum as a limited company – £160.

Responding to specific needs in these various ways, individuals and organisations rallied around and gave their support. Projects would be started without all the money in hand, but it always eventually came from somewhere, as if by a miracle. Roy's persistence and dogged determination to succeed permeated the whole organisation, much in the way of Dickens' impecuniously optimistic Mr Micawber, for whom something always turned up in the end.

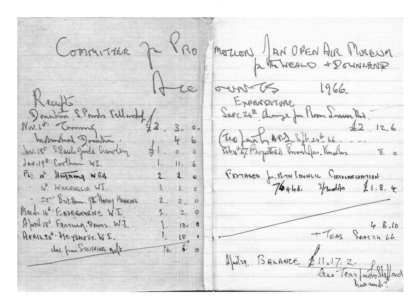

Above The first museum accounts: Roy Armstrong details the origin of £11.17.2 (£11.86) handed to the promotion committee's first honorary treasurer to open the museum's first bank account in April 1967.

Below Early fund raising, 1970.

MANHOOD FRIENDS OF THE OPEN AIR MUSEUM

J U M B L E   S A L E
In Aid of the

D O N K E Y   W H E E L

Now Being Erected

You are invited to a Jumble Sale to be held at the Church Hall, East Wittering on Saturday, 29th August at 2.30 p.m. Produce, Toys etc.

If you have any jumble you would like to give, would you please deliver this to the Church Hall on the Morning of 29th August (open 10am) OR Previously to either Mrs A.Wade, 79 Fletchers Estate, Sidlesham or Mrs Bennett, Onaway, Longlands Road, E.Wittering

12th August 1970.

Early site exhibits – 3. The Medieval Pottery Research Project   *Diana Zeuner*

From the outset the museum aimed to represent the traditional crafts and trades of the Weald and Downland region. In 1971 a project began to research how the pottery of the Middle Ages – familiar from museum displays – was actually produced. Small medieval potteries were present wherever suitable clay beds were at hand and near an abundant supply of wood. But little was known about the conditions in which they were made, how kilns were constructed and fired, the length of their working life and the number of pots that could be fired at once. The objective was the reconstruction of a medieval kiln and the making and firing of pots to shed light on these archaeological questions.

There was no evidence for the superstructure so this was conjectured. It was fired twice, consuming two lorry-loads of 'bavins' (brushwood bundles), and was watched overnight. Parts of the kiln reached 1100°C, but the firing was uneven. A second firing in September proved more productive. A great deal was learned during the first season, and students acquired considerable skill in 'dry throwing' pots on primitive wheels.

In 1973 the project continued with a newly-designed top-bearing spoke wheel and a kiln based on an example excavated at Heyshott, near Midhurst. This time 55 people were involved. The first firing achieved relatively poor results, but the second provided much-improved pots. The project eventually ended in 1975, coinciding with a national petrol shortage and the appointment of Denis May, now a doctor of sociology, as principal lecturer in educational studies at Portsmouth Polytechnic.

A workshop was established at Easter the following year in Lurgashall cattle shed near Bayleaf farmhouse to represent a 12th-14th century Wealden pottery based on one known to have existed at Binsted, West Sussex where tiles and Sussex jugs were made and fired. It was led by artist and potter, Denis May, from Portsmouth Teacher Training College, and his wife, Sylvia, with Fred and Mary Seyd playing key roles. Four subgroups were set up to research wheel construction, kiln building, clay artefacts and clay sources. Forty volunteers came from craft colleges around the region to take part in the project, many camping on site.

Clay was sourced from the region, including the clay pits at Fareham (now covered by the M27) and Pitsham, near Midhurst. A direct drive wheel of the sort thought to have been used was designed by Peter Fletcher of Farnham College of Art with a second modified version produced later by Fred Seyd. Pots were made by the project's members, based on existing examples in museums and other research.

With the help of Worthing archaeologist Con Ainsworth, who had excavated the Binsted kiln, a replica was built at the museum. Made of local clay and broken tiles, it had two arched firing tunnels under the floor of the kiln chamber.

Pottery fired in the Binsted kiln.

A major milestone was reached in spring 1969 when Gunolt Greiner arrived on site with his tent and mobile workshop. The task: to re-erect Winkhurst, the museum's first landmark building. Living and working on site was much in line with the style of itinerant medieval craftsmen – a good omen: indeed Gunolt's skills had already earned him a reputation as one of the last carpenters in the country with knowledge of medieval crafts-manship. Born at Jugenheim in Germany, he was a woodcarver by trade. A peace-loving man, he had been ordered to join the Wehrmacht by Hitler's Nazis, but refusing to serve, and with a price on his head, he fled his native country and eventually landed up as a refugee at an agricultural work camp at Avoncroft College, Bromsgrove during the war. Gunolt was to return in the mid-1960s to put up the first building for the new Avoncroft Museum of Buildings, from where he went on to restore Birmingham's last working watermill, Sarehole Mill, under John Lowe's directorship at Birmingham Museum. And it was through John that Gunolt came to work on Winkhurst. (It is a curious coincidence, indicative of how small the historic buildings field was at that time, that Richard Harris, later to become the museum's research director, provided some of the working drawings for the mill while working as an assistant to architect Freddie Charles.)

Roger Champion acted as Gunolt's assistant, his first job cutting the wooden pegs for pinning the frame together. With his incredible skills and instinctive talent for handling timber, Roger soon became the key worker on the site as the museum's master carpenter after Gunolt's depar-ture. Many of the museum's exhibits as we know them today were put together by Roger.

On Saturday 5 September 1970 the museum opened its gates to the public for the very first time. The first of six weekends to see what was

Above *Gunolt Greiner (right) and Roger Champion working on the frame of Winkhurst, 1969.*

Below *The frame grows.*

Right *The toll house as originally reconstructed at the museum, just inside the front entrance (it was later moved and its interpretation changed). The sign advertises the museum's first season of open weekends in 1970, when adult entry was four shillings (20p, equivalent to a little over £2 today).*

> *From this time (1968) and for the next six months or so I spent the majority of my time on the museum site. I found it difficult to keep away; besides I had no other occupation, paid or otherwise. After 40-odd years one's memory fades, but my time was spent happily removing old fencing, cutting trees and undergrowth on proposed woodland paths and general fetching and carrying, not to mention playing with Silas, my six-month-old Boxer pup.*
>
> **Roger Champion**

advertised as 'work in progress', these were experimental trial runs anticipating the first full season beginning the next year. We seriously wondered whether anyone would turn up, but were not to be disappointed. Visitors poured in. The new car park behind its screen of trees was soon full to capacity and cars were forced to overflow onto the open field below the treadwheel. Shiny metal and windscreens glinting in the sunshine at the very centre of the museum were a seriously out-of-place distraction to the magnificent setting. The need for more screened car parking was one early lesson learnt.

Between Saturday 5 September and Sunday 11 October a total of 7,198 visitors came through the gates, adults at four shillings (20p) each and children under 14 at one shilling (5p). This immediately opened up yet another source of income for the very first time: entrance money. Over these first six weekends we took £1,802, then a huge sum and a massive injection to our funds.

At the time we first went public there were just seven exhibits for visitors to see: Winkhurst, Littlehampton granary, Catherington treadwheel, the charcoal burners' camp, the saw pit, the Saxon weavers' hut, and the Upper Beeding toll house serving as the museum's first shop selling guide books and local history publications. What we lacked was a place to buy a cup of tea and refreshments – there was fierce opposition to the very thought of this type of commerce on the site. It would be out of place, quite unnecessary and only create litter. How thinking has changed since 1970!

Below *Saturday 5 September 1970 – waiting for the first visitors. From left to right: Norman West, museum company secretary; James Farmer, museum chairman; John Lowe, museum director; Douglas Robertson-Ritchie, volunteer steward.*

The museum's first publicity poster, 1970.

Friendly Friends *Carol Brinson*

The first mention of the 'Friends' appears as early as 1968 when at Expo Sussex, Ardingly, the museum's Promotion Committee staged its first major public exhibition, launched its first appeal brochure, seeking £35,000, and extended a first invitation to subscribe to the 'Friends of the Museum'.

The Duke of Richmond, left, visiting the Friends' stand during one of the museum's special events, with, left to right, Richard Pailthorpe (assistant director), Virginia Lyon (Friends' chairman) and Bruce Pailthorpe (Friends' vice chairman).

This set the tone for the Friends as primarily a fund-raising body, separate from the management of the museum, and unlike many other museum friends' groups, not a vehicle for volunteer membership – it's not necessary to be a member of the Friends to be a volunteer, and vice versa.

So, the Friends exists to provide financial support for the museum. However, there has always been an accompanying social role, building a friendly group of supporters and providing additional sustenance for the museum in public relations and goodwill.

It was not long after the 1968 launch that word spread. By 1970 it was reported that there were 400 members and there were two 'local' Friends groups assisting the main body. The Manhood Friends set up by Diane Wilson of Sidlesham is reported to have raised £213.4.8 which was matched by the Victoria & Albert Museum in 1971, and another was established at Hurstpierpoint, founded by Frances Taylor. Kim Leslie, then honorary treasurer, remembers "… the thrill on opening a letter with a cheque from one of the earliest and perhaps best-known names to support us – the late Sir John Betjeman".

The Friends held its inaugural meeting as a registered charity on 29 August 1970. Its chairman was Major General L A Hawes; honorary secretary, John Lowe; honorary treasurer, Kim Leslie and committee members were Roy Armstrong, Kate Barson, Jack Kessler, Douglas Robertson-Ritchie, Frances Taylor, Pam West and Diane Wilson.

John Lowe wrote in the autumn 1977 museum magazine:

Much has happened since then [1970]. A year later we had seven hundred members and had raised £6,444. Over the next year or two the membership rose to over a thousand and the Friends were able to give money to many important projects at the museum. The summer parties became an institution … and the Friends became an integrated and vital part of the museum's organisation making a major contribution to its remarkably rapid success. Material support is always valuable, but so is moral support, and the continuing interest and enthusiasm of the Friends has been a great encouragement to the staff.

John Lowe was succeeded as honorary secretary by Bernard Johnson, and Major General Hawes continued as chairman for another two years. Since then the Friends has flourished and grown under hardworking and influential chairmen: Sir James Waddell, Virginia Lyon, Tim Heymann, Frances Messenger and Jean Piggott, as well as its honorary secretaries: myself, Jean Piggott and Sarah Casdagli (now the Friends' chairman). The finances were at first in the sound hands of Kim Leslie (who was also the museum's honorary treasurer), followed by two years when West Dean College accountant, John Hill, received a

Ethel Buvyer, seated at the table on the right, recruits a new member on the Friends' stand at the Rare Breeds Show.

Friendly Friends

small remuneration for the work. Following criticism of this payment from the membership, Mrs Elsie Kessler returned the role to an honorary footing. Since then the treasurership has continued to be voluntary, despite the growing complexity of legal requirements, in the care of Bernard Rush, Mike Doran, Maurice Pollock (who was, like Kim, also the museum's honorary treasurer) and Richard Wilde.

> *The Chairman of the Friends in 1973 was Major General Hawes. No-one new to minute-taking could have been more fortunate in their first chairman. General Hawes would allow an item to be discussed until he thought the topic had been aired enough, then provide an instant summary, which was all that was needed for the minutes. He was also a frequent volunteer on the site, and was often to be seen picking up litter with the help of a pointed stick. Following the death of his wife he used to say that coming to the museum was to be recommended to anyone living alone: after a day surrounded by noisy children he relished the peace of home!*
>
> **Carol Brinson**

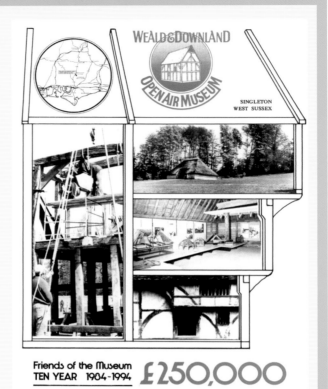

The Friends' £250,000 Development Fund Appeal was launched with this brochure in 1984.

Fund-raising methods over the years have been varied and lively. In 1981 a major auction of donated items was described in the museum magazine as "the Friends' most ambitious fund-raising project to date": it raised nearly £9,000, for the re-erection of North Cray hall house. Held at the Assembly Rooms in Chichester, Henry Adams and John Haywood of Wyatt & Son gave their professional services as auctioneers and advisors. The following year there was a grand draw, with donated prizes, which made £4,000 for the Wittering School project. Much of the administration for these two events was undertaken by the museum's senior assistant (later assistant director), Richard Pailthorpe, demonstrating how closely the museum and the Friends interacted. This was also the case, in reverse, when I was paid an honorarium by the Friends to work one day a week in the museum office on its Development Fund Appeal in the mid-1980s.

Other events included a series of lunches with speakers in Slindon, a 'Cavalcade of Costume', produce stalls at museum events, barn dances, food tastings, recitals and art exhibitions (including one in 1989 on the theme, *Traditional Buildings*, with contributions from eminent artists such as Sir Hugh Casson, and sponsored by architects Roth

Partnership). The events were not always a resounding success: committee member and long-standing volunteer Walter Greenway records in the 1982 museum magazine that the attendance was "disappointing with the result that the profit was small" at a concert at Petworth House, but "it was possible to give the impression that it was fuller

> *One of the museum's most remarkable qualities is the loyalty and devotion it has inspired in many of its earliest Friends. Daphne Chandler's ... earliest memories are of manning the ticket office and selling our first black and white postcards in the toll cottage in 1970. She remained one of our principal ticket office stewards right to the end, even when she gave up driving and came all the way from Bognor by bus.*
>
> **Virginia Lyon, 1996**

than it was, so there were no reproving empty rows of seats. Those of us who attended were all agreed that the Friends who ignored the opportunity to attend had made a great mistake."

> *Doris and Ted Nash joined the Friends in 1970… A few years later while stewarding at the museum Doris met the proud possessor of [Friends'] membership card No. 1, Mrs Morton of Findon. In 1974 when she retired [Doris] mentioned to Doug Bryant, the warden, that she would be able to help if volunteers were required. He replied, "Can you come tomorrow?" In some trepidation Doris turned up the next day and was sent to Winkhurst with a pile of guide books to sell. Each day was a challenge as she stewarded all the buildings then on the site. The shop had moved to the granary, where tall men lived in fear of their heads meeting low beams.*

Virginia Lyon, 1996

The Friends, being friendly, have always also organised events for its members which are not necessarily intended to make a profit but provide social and educational benefits. The spring tours have been a fixture in the calendar for over 30 years. Organisers have included Bernard Johnson, Walter Greenway, myself, Virginia Lyon, Keith and Beryl Bickmore, and Mike and Jean Piggott. A great deal of work but enormously rewarding, the tours – usually based on cities in the UK – were always over-subscribed. To try and alleviate this one year, two coaches were hired instead of the usual one. It was something of a nightmare keeping track of everyone, so we called the two groups 'Bayleaf' and 'Pendean'.

Day tours and talks are also organised for members, and Walter Greenway ran quizzes: I treasure the Peter Iden painting of Chichester Cathedral which was my prize one year. More recently the Friends held another grand draw, in 2002; family barn dances; events with an appeal for children, such as the Shaun Winter Marionettes, and two 'Proms by the Lake' (2007 and 2008) when the audience brought their own supper, "a bit like a mini Glyndebourne for the common man!" says former Friends' chairman Jean Piggott.

The Friends of the Museum had grown from small beginnings to one of the largest museum friends' organisations in the country. In 2010 it had 5,500 memberships, representing more than 12,000 individuals.

Welcome to the Museum

Join the Friends of the Museum today for around £12 – your first year's membership will be reduced by the admission fee

ENJOY …
- Unlimited free entry
- Free entry to special events
- Regular magazine
- Friends social events

WEALD & DOWNLAND OPEN AIR MUSEUM

Singleton, Chichester, W Sussex PO18 0EU
Telephone 01243 811348 www.wealddown.co.uk

The Friends' 'Welcome leaflet' introduced in 1997, which had a substantial effect on recruitment. By 2010 the Friends had a total of some 5,500 memberships representing over 12,000 people, one of the largest museum friends' groups in the country.

Its financial contribution to the museum's work is significant – by 2010 it had grant-aided the museum to the tune of some £1.7 million. Funding in 2009 alone amounted to £182,040, including a core grant split into four quarters, of £120,000, and support for individual projects amounting to £62,040. In 2009 the money was spent on such items as the thatching of Gonville Cottage, the Vehicle and Implement Gallery, repairs to tiled roofs, toilet renovation and picnic tables, the Mills Archive project, paving stone for the market square and intercom radios for site staff.

3

Sublime Setting

Diana Zeuner

The landscape in which the museum has developed has played a significant role in its fortunes. Nestled in the stunning Lavant valley between the villages of Singleton and West Dean, visitors cannot fail to be overwhelmed by the natural beauty of this eastern end of the West Dean Estate. Entering the museum through the ticket office in Longport farmhouse near the top of the hill draws expressions of delight.

From the earliest days the museum's guardians have been careful to treat this noble environmental advantage with respect. Hours of discussion, in the early days by the sites and buildings committee, preceded any decision about the siting of building exhibits and visitor facilities. The retention of important sight lines and views, the conservation of high quality grassland and woodland and preservation of the landscape from the effects of

Aerial view showing the museum's setting in the historic South Downs landscape, photographed by museum trustee David Russell in 2004 while piloting a plane above the site. The village of West Dean is to the right. The museum is in the foreground, in the eastern-most part of West Dean Park, with the Lavant valley sweeping away south towards Chichester.

high levels of activity have characterised the development of the museum. As museum director, Chris Zeuner took a particular interest in the site, initiating an extensive tree-planting and coppicing programme in the early years, thus enhancing the interpretation of the traditional buildings and helping to preserve rural skills at the same time as husbanding the landscape for the future.

West Dean Park is a grade II★ listed historic landscape. The first steps towards the creation of a park to the south of West Dean had been taken in the 1760s when the highway was diverted to run north of the house. By about 1810 it had become a rather old-fashioned 'pocket park', but a significant change shown in a map of that year is the northern realignment of the road between Singleton and West Dean, which had meandered through the water meadows, thus removing it from the museum's future site. Over the next 20 or 30 years the park was greatly expanded and an arboretum was created when Caroline Harcourt inherited the estate in 1835.

After William James purchased the estate in 1891, shooting became a major activity, resulting in new and enlarged game covers in the upper park, but he also extended the roadside tree screen a short distance up to Town Lane, fronting the area now occupied by the museum, and planted new circular clumps of trees to enhance the view eastwards from the house.

William James died in 1912 but his son Edward did not take possession of the estate until he was 25, in 1932. He took a great interest in the gardens and arboretum, and in 1964 created the Edward James Foundation to ensure the estate's continuation. It was the greatest good fortune that when the committee seeking a site for the museum made contact with the foundation, Edward James himself supported the project. The woodland at the museum continues to be managed by the foundation, which, in the traditional way, retains the timber rights.

In his 1978 survey, West Dean's gardens manager, arboriculturalist Ivan Hicks, said the trees at the museum acted as "a frame to the picture – a visual backcloth to detail and [they] create a sense of tradition to the whole scene. They also represent one of the essential amenities and as such their educational role is paramount." In the museum's successful 1998 application for the Government's designation of its collections as being of national importance, the significance of this historic landscape setting was singled out: "It is in effect part of our collections".

By 1975 large areas of over-mature beech trees in the woodlands to the south of the museum site

Above *Aerial view of the site in about 1975. Bayleaf farmhouse and the two cattle sheds to the west can be seen at the bottom of the photograph, with the Littlehampton granary further up the track and Gonville Cottage to the left. To the right Winkhurst is in its original position by the wooded hill, much of which had to be felled in 1979-81. At the top of the photograph the car parks can be seen top right, with Hambrook barn, the Upper Beeding toll house and Titchfield market hall, in glorious isolation but with its nearby clump still standing. In the centre top, the upper mill pond has been dug, but not yet filled with water. The lower mill pond is still to be excavated. The Southwater forge is the final building visible, to the left.*

Below *View of the site, again in 1975, from the current path to Hangleton cottage, with Bayleaf farmhouse and the Littlehampton granary to the left and Pendean farmhouse being re-erected on the right. Winkhurst is on the right further along the woodland edge and Hambrook barn can be seen in the distance.*

SU 872127 *Diana Zeuner*

Above *Gonville Cottage, at Ordnance Survey grid reference SU 872127. The only original structure on the museum's site, it was the home of museum director, Chris Zeuner, and his family for many years and later that of stockmen and of the site manager. When it became vacant in 2008 it was the opportunity to take it in hand for the museum: built in 1847 it is a good example of a common type of house of the period, with central entrance and staircase between two living rooms with a rear outshot. Research has shown that in 1851 it was occupied by a shepherd and archaeologists discovered the remains in the garden of a structure thought to be a sheep-fold. Re-thatching provided information about the roofing material used: three layers of wood shavings were found – the waste from hoop-making for barrels – and six coats of wheat straw, making eight coats in 160 years. In the photograph below is the archaeological trench through the thatch layers.*

"What is this? It's the Ordnance Survey (OS) grid reference for Gonville Cottage."

George Newell, the museum's honorary surveyor, writing in 1974, was introducing newsletter readers to his survey of the museum site, which proved so invaluable in establishing the basis for the historic building sites and infrastructure for the museum.

He reasoned that eventually the OS would plot the references for the newly re-erected buildings. But at that time he was working with the 1912 edition of the 1/2500 scale local survey sheet. He notes how "sadly depleted" were the cedar in the meadow between Gonville Cottage and the Southwater forge, and also the chestnut near Titchfield market hall.

To reduce guesswork and for future good planning George Newell embarked on a survey of the whole site. With Pam West on the end of his measuring tape, he set about the task during the late summer of 1973. He wrote:

> Much of the site slopes steeply, and this fact, together with the many trees and other landscape features, increased the physical difficulties (personal and technical) and made a trigonometrical survey necessary. This method (on which the Ordnance Survey is based) depends upon overlaying the area with a network of triangles. On the micro-scale of my survey the blue topped pegs scattered about, in what might appear to be unlikely places, are my triangulation points. A lot of effort has been needed to establish them and so, please, do not disturb them.

The sides of George's triangles were aligned to follow natural boundaries and other important features and the fieldwork was completed by measuring short offsets from the survey lines. "The extent of the survey is about 750 yards east to west and 220 yards north to south," he said.

To take account of contour lines and altitude, bench marks are used all over Britain and George was pleased that he was able to arrange for the museum to have its own officially-recorded bench mark, the milestone near the Upper Beeding toll house. This has appeared on all relevant Ordnance Survey maps since: all the site levels are related to it and hence to the national network. It stands 204.42 feet above Newlyn, Cornwall.

George's triangulation pegs were to be found all over the site, including in the woodlands, and became an integral part of the museum's story; no doubt one of them is there still, tucked under a bush somewhere.

were the cause of some concern. Over 120 years old, they had been nurtured for pheasant cover and shooting, but gales were now bringing them down regularly. Trees on the hillside fared particularly badly, and combined with beech-bark disease and lime-induced chlorosis, were in serious decline. A particularly heavy gale in 1977 blew out the centre of the wood, and West Dean Estate's forestry department decided to clearfell in compartments from 1979 to 1981, allowing natural broadleaf regeneration to take over. For a while the work resulted in a changed landscape. "It is very important to be aware that the artificial landscape we are so used to is not permanent," said Chris Zeuner, "and to realise that the planting we undertake will not be mature for us to enjoy. It will be just as essential for future generations to take steps to change and therefore secure the woodland for the future."

The parkland clumps were also showing their age, and many of the site's elms were forlorn as a result of earlier Dutch elm disease. In 1976 the museum suffered the loss of the elm clump north of Titchfield market hall, and many of the mature trees were greatly affected by the extreme drought that summer. The clump was replanted to mark the Queen's Silver Jubilee in 1977.

To assist with the museum's revised master plan in 1978, Ivan Hicks was commissioned to undertake a survey of the museum's landscape and make recommendations for future management. He said new planting should be sensitive to the current landscape, taking into account existing planting, the exhibit buildings and farming activities, and ensuring vistas and sight lines were preserved and enhanced.

He suggested removing dead and dying trees and planting informal clumps of new trees in some areas with an under-storey of smaller trees and shrubs to soften the edges of the groupings. Among these were plantings of alder and white

willow around the lower lake, a group of trees on the bank of the upper lake to soften the view around the watermill, and a clump of Scots pine, silver birch and gorse separating the café area from the upper millpond. Other planting took place around Gonville Cottage and to continue the tree line south from Gonville drive, uphill to the woodland; while a linear grouping of juniper, yew, whitebeam and blackthorn was planted between Pendean farmhouse and Hangleton cottage, softening the edge of the traditional woodland planting.

New planting around Bayleaf following the felling of a mature clump south-west of the building was later extended as part of the Bayleaf Medieval Farmstead project and included the

> " My memories of the museum include tree planting weekends with Chris and Diana [Zeuner] and Roger and Heather [Champion], plus volunteers, all over the site. These trees are now really showing their mark, especially the white willows down by the mill. And desperately trying to retain the cathedral-like beech trees on the slopes above Hangleton cottage for as long as possible, although, ironically, the natural regeneration that occurred after their inevitable felling looks more in keeping with the museum than a planned plantation. And spending weekends with Roy and Lyn at their home discussing oak trees. Edward James told me that he was proud that he had helped such a worthwhile and important project to establish itself. "
>
> **Ivan Hicks**

Visitors at the **Trees and Woodlands in the Landscape** *exhibition, 1982, which linked the museum's South Downs landscape with the natural materials it produced.*

The museum's shaws were allowed to establish and were cropped in winter 2001.

The museum's landscape is not only a haven for plants, but animals as well, from the wildfowl attracted to the mill ponds to a wide variety of birds suited to the woodland and pasture, not least a family of barn owls which reared four chicks annually for several years after the millennium.

In 1982 the museum opened a major new exhibition, *Trees and Woodlands in the Landscape*, in the Coldwaltham cattle shed re-erected in the woods. It was written by Ruth Tittensor, who had a particular interest in the history of landscape, and included a series of paintings of the changing historical landscape of the upper Lavant valley based on archaeological, historical and ecological research undertaken by the Chilgrove Valley Landscape Project. The exhibition also made the links between natural materials harvested from the woodlands and the museum's exhibit buildings and rural crafts. Ruth described landscape as "the busy factory-floor of industries such as farming, forestry and country sports, as well as being of immense historical, cultural and conservation value". At the museum she was allowed the freedom to explore new ideas about landscape history and nature conservation, alongside her ecological and historical surveys of local landscapes, including those of the West Dean Estate. The following year Ruth produced a woodland trail to expand the theme.

The exhibition was dismantled in 2008 as part of a new focus on live interpretation and the shed itself removed to the newly reconstructed woodyard close to the charcoal burners' camp.

establishment of two small fields surrounded by woven fences of hazel, an orchard planted with older varieties of fruit and a traditional 'shaw' on either side of the approach road from the south-west. Common features in the Weald, shaws consisted of belts of trees and shrubs harvested in rotation for their timber and producing wild foods such as bullace, black and redcurrants, plums, pears and gooseberries. Researched by ecologists Ruth and Andrew Tittensor, they consisted of different species planted for different purposes – hazel for fencing, pea sticks and nuts; blackthorn for tinit (dead hedge material); ash for handles, pole lathes and firewood; hawthorn and crab-apple, field maple, gean (wild cherry); goat willow and oak.

Three of the six historical landscape paintings by Pat Donovan, used in the 1982 exhibition, Trees and Woodlands in the Landscape. *They showed how the landscape seen from the museum was likely to have looked at different historical periods, viewed north from the woodland edge between Catherington treadwheel and Pendean farmhouse. Pictured from top left are the paintings depicting the same landscape in 1000 AD (the time of the Saxon weavers' hut), 1600 (by which time Bayleaf had been built on its original site), and 1880 (showing two features familiar today – Gonville Cottage in the foreground, and Singleton railway station in the centre).*

The hazel coppice   *Diana Zeuner*

Some 18 acres of neglected hazel coppice in the woodlands on the southern boundary of the site were managed by the museum from the early 1970s, providing much-needed hazel for fencing, spar-making and wattle panels for the building exhibits. Older wood was useful for fires in the houses. The coppice included 70-year-old hornbeam standards which were pollarded in the traditional way, and some newly planted hornbeams.

Blocks of hazel were cut on a seven-year rotation, demonstrating to visitors a typical managed woodland landscape of the 17th-19th centuries. Deer damage to the growing hazel shoots from the coppiced stools was a constant problem and a tall deer fence was established at one time on the southern side of the coppice to try to prevent their entry.

As the museum's needs for hazel for wattle panels and fencing grew, it was able in 1982 to acquire the lease to over 20 acres of coppice on the Goodwood Estate. This also enabled the activities of the museum's new subsidiary company to expand, with the sale of thatching spars, bean poles, pea sticks and faggots.

Above *The hazel coppice in the wood to the south of the museum site, showing stacked cut hazel and mature hornbeam pollards alongside the woodland path to the charcoal burners' camp, photographed in about 1975 and* **below right** *in 2009.* **Below left** *Albert Peacock working in an off-site coppice in East Dean Park leased from the Goodwood Estate in 1983.*

The coppice had other benefits too. A group of Sussex Downs Conservation Board volunteers studying the coppice woodland for flowers and butterflies expected to see primroses and violets as it was early April but they discovered another 47 species besides. Later visits that year brought the flower species up to 65 and butterflies to 11. There were four species of orchid, butterflies including brimstone and orange tip, a common lizard, and an unusual false oxslip (a cross between a primrose and a cowslip). The list demonstrated the value of coppice for a wide range of different plants, mainly thanks to the flush of light provided at different stages of the rotation.

Behind the museum's woodyard an area of traditional wood pasture was created, combining grazing and woodland management. Tamworth pigs churn the ground and eat new growth, so to provide timber, trees are pollarded in the traditional way – described by Jon Roberts, the museum's woodsman responsible for the upkeep of the woodland and the supply of firewood to buildings, as 'high-rise' coppicing.

Jon Roberts' experience with utilising the museum's woodland resource has challenged some of his preconceptions. "A medieval farming household would be hard-pressed to find the man-hours necessary to sustain [even] the museum's level of consumption," he says. "Sustainability may be fashionable today, but on a medieval farmstead it was essential."

In 2009 the museum drew up a woodland management plan covering all the regular tasks involved in caring for the wooded areas and extracting their products.

Ivan Hicks, West Dean's gardens manager, planting the Lord Bonham Carter memorial garden south of Longport farmhouse, with the Goodwood granary in the background.

In 1986 the trustees of the Edward James Foundation agreed to extend the boundary of the museum by 20 acres, incorporating the field at the centre of the museum, Greenways, and the three fields to the west of Gonville drive. This enabled the museum to run a range of activities independent of the needs of West Dean's home farm. That year's museum magazine recorded the museum's appreciation for the continuing help and assistance the project had received from the foundation, especially from Tim Heymann, the agent, and staff in the woods and farms departments. Chris Zeuner wrote: "Now that the museum has grown into one of the foremost attractions in the south of England it is able to make a valuable contribution to the fulfilment of the [educational] aims of the Edward James Foundation".

The care of the museum site was always a priority for Chris Zeuner, who understood well the potential wear and tear to the pasture, woodlands and tracks and the need to constantly nurture them. He dealt strictly with anyone who drove their car onto the grass, left baler twine hanging on a fence, or put up an unsanctioned notice. Grazing land had to be harrowed and rolled, litter had to be collected promptly, special-event detritus had to be cleared away before the museum was open for the following day. It was a discipline which contributed greatly to the reputation the museum developed for a neat and tidy site. Jim Hampshire, Andy Hodby and Nick Conway have been among the most vital members of staff with site responsibilities whose duties included upholding these tenets.

1987 was the year of the Great Storm when a hurricane tore through south-eastern England on the night of 15 October, bringing down power lines, damaging buildings and felling large numbers of trees in its path (a total of some 15 million trees were lost). The museum did not escape, losing several mature specimens. The following morning an eerie silence had descended, traffic having been halted by fallen trees across roads. Museum staff armed with chainsaws went to work, both on site and in local villages, clearing debris in an effort to return life to normal.

In 1995, as the re-erection and conversion of Longport farmhouse as the new visitor entrance facility, shop and offices drew to a close, a new contribution to the museum's landscape grew to the south of the building. Ivan Hicks designed a modern garden, with funds donated by museum trustee Lady Elizabeth Benson and her husband, David (a former chairman of the Edward James Foundation), and their friends in memory of Lord Bonham Carter of Yarnbury, a frequent visitor to the museum. The garden was inspired by the type of garden popular in the 1930s which Roy Armstrong had created at his home in Storrington.

A report in 2004 by Tim Heymann, museum trustee, ex-chairman of the Friends and former agent of the West Dean Estate, and Rod Stern, a forester and botanist, confirmed that the activities of the previous 30 years had resulted in a site well-wooded and maintained with no need for major radical works. Ian Odin, the Edward James Foundation forestry manager, continues to undertake an annual survey of the health of individual trees, and some new planting will be needed to replace existing and maturing specimens. The maintained woodland, downland grazing, arable fields, field strips and recreated period gardens give the museum "a landscape resource of huge interest," says Richard Harris, museum director since 2001.

Two years later, a Landscape Conservation Management Plan was commissioned jointly by the Edward James Foundation and the museum, with English Heritage funding, to guide future management and development of the grade II★ listed West Dean Park, including the museum. The report, by Nicholas Pearson Associates, underlined "exemplary standards" of husbandry but highlighted the pressure on the historic landscape from vehicular traffic from those visiting the museum and the nearby West Dean Gardens. The development of a new visitor centre and car park on the northern boundary at the bottom of Gonville drive, favoured by the museum's trustees, was endorsed by the report, a development which is intended to alter and transform visitors' arrival and experience at the museum.

The South Downs National Park   *John Godfrey*

The market square today, with the South Downs landscape soaring above it.

The South Downs has long been recognised as one of the exceptional landscapes of England, celebrated by poets, writers and artists for its homely, pastoral charms and comfortable, almost feminine, contours.

Not surprisingly, the South Downs was included in the list of areas deserving special protection produced during the Second World War, in anticipation of what became the National Parks and Access to the Countryside Act 1949. Indeed, as we have seen, Roy Armstrong was already calling for this in the early 1930s. However, the extent of cultivation of the downland to increase food production during the war led the then National Parks Commission to conclude that the area did not provide sufficient opportunities for recreation which, along with conservation, is one of the two statutory purposes of National Parks.

Subsequently, the Downs in Sussex and East Hampshire were designated Areas of Outstanding Natural Beauty (AONBs), providing similar protection to National Parks, but without the obligation to promote recreation. Over time, however, evolving statutory guidance and changing public expectations led to a blurring of the distinction between the two designations and an energetic campaign began to persuade the government of the day to designate a South Downs National Park. In 1999, the deputy prime minister announced his intention to proceed with such a designation and the necessary statutory procedures got under way.

While welcomed by conservationists, some local authorities and farmers and landowners had reservations about the merits of the proposal. Their concerns, and issues relating to the boundary of the proposed National Park, were explored at a lengthy public inquiry. Eventually, in 2009, the decision to confirm the designation was announced in Parliament, and a public proclamation took place at the museum. The National Park came into effect on 1 April 2010.

As a major visitor attraction and educational resource within the new National Park, the Weald & Downland Open Air Museum is well-placed to act as a gateway to the park and to play its part in bringing together all those who love the South Downs to secure the future of these very special landscapes.

The decision to go ahead with the South Downs National Park was announced at the museum in 2009, by Hilary Benn MP, secretary of state for the environment (centre), pictured here with Richard Harris, museum director, left, and Charles Anson, chairman of the South Downs Joint Committee.

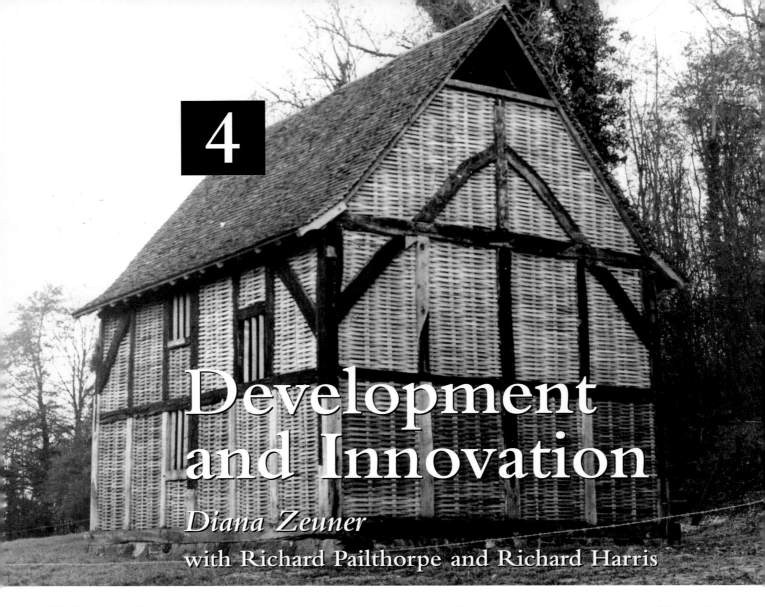

4

Development and Innovation

Diana Zeuner

with Richard Pailthorpe and Richard Harris

Winkhurst, here with its completed wattle awaiting daub, was the iconic image for the museum's early publicity, appearing as part of its logo.

The 1970s

Since the first 7,000 visitors came through the turnstile in autumn 1970 the museum has captured the public's imagination. Its opening coincided with a national growth of interest not only in heritage matters, but also tourism generally and a rise in leisure time and car ownership. It was one of a series of independent heritage projects launched in the late 1960s, including Ironbridge Gorge Museums Trust, Avoncroft Museum of Buildings and the National Motor Museum, Beaulieu.

The museum quickly established itself as a major attraction, not only in the Chichester area, but in the wider region of the Weald and Downland – Sussex, Surrey, and parts of Kent and Hampshire – and numbers of visitors increased rapidly through the early 1970s to over 150,000 in 1975.

In 1973 – when the museum welcomed 111,042 visitors – John Lowe, the first director, wrote:

Every day of the opening, seven to ten volunteer stewards manned the museum, keeping an eye on the buildings, answering questions and making the public feel at home, something much appreciated by all our visitors who continually comment on the friendly atmosphere of the museum.

One of the most staggering statistics in these very early days was the number of children

Time-Line

1961 *A History of Sussex* by Roy Armstrong first published

1965 (24 October) Roy Armstrong introduces the idea of an open air museum for the

Weald. The first reference is made to a building in danger – Bayleaf farmhouse. At the initial meeting at Balneath Manor, Chailey, the following are present: J R Armstrong, Mrs S Bright, Miss J Duce, K Gravett, Mrs M Hallam, Miss J Harding,

Mr & Mrs H Lacey, J Ludlow, R Mason, R Wood

1966 (September) Inaugural meeting of the Committee for the Promotion of an Open Air Museum for the Weald and Downland

Bayleaf farmhouse soon became a focal point for activity; this is one of the first visits by a group of morris dancers in the early 1970s.

" *I remember the journeys through country roads somewhere in the Weald and Downland region to look at yet another building potentially requiring saving and removal to the museum site, Roy's red car weaving dramatically along the road as another interesting structure came into view; traffic lights were often jumped. Once at the building, much discussion took place about its history and structure; out with the penknife to check condition; up into the roof to examine the timbers. More discussion. Back at the museum, more and more discussion. We always seemed to sit on the hill by Hambrook barn at lunchtimes – with its wonderful view across the site and over to the downs. Roy and Lyn were vegetarians. So Lyn had a huge Tupperware container full of peanuts. "Protein, Roy", she would interrupt, as she handed it to him, and he would absent-mindedly take a small handful, as the discussion continued.... "*

Diana Zeuner

welcomed in school groups. Only two years after opening, John Lowe reported that some 35,000 children had visited with their teachers, and this was long before the current preoccupation with the importance of education in museums.

In 1974 the season was extended and the problems of overcrowding were such that on Sundays and Bank Holidays the admission charge was increased from 30p to 40p for adults in an attempt to encourage people to visit on weekdays and Saturdays.

One of the defining elements of these early years of the museum's development was the rapid pace of rescuing and dismantling buildings and their re-erection on site. This demonstration

Chris Zeuner, the museum's first full-time director. His practical skills – here he is pictured driving the museum's tractor in 1971 – and his ability to run the project on a daily basis were considered equally important.

held at the University of Sussex. Present are: J R Armstrong, Lt Col B A Capell, Alderman J A Farmer, F W Gregory, Mrs M Hallam, W C Holder, C A Jewell, R McDowall, R Milner-Gulland, S E Rigold, Miss M Rymill, A V Sheppard

1967 Edward James Foundation reacts favourably to the idea of providing a site for the museum; the final site is decided upon the following year, and outline planning permission granted – the museum is 'launched'

Kim Leslie appointed first honorary treasurer: balance in bank account – £11.17.2

1968 Arrival of the first building on site: the timbers of Winkhurst, one of the Bough

The rapid pace of dismantling and re-erecting threatened buildings characterised the first years of the museum's life. **Clockwise from top left** *Volunteer Mike Coviello and museum director Chris Zeuner load tiles removed from Fountains Farm (Berrylands) barn onto a low loader for transport to the museum stores. The Goodwood granary arrives, in one piece, on the back of a lorry after its journey uphill from the Goodwood Estate. The roof timbers of Titchfield market hall are craned into position in 1974.*

The museum's mission

The purpose of the Weald & Downland Open Air Museum is to stimulate public interest in and to promote and encourage the preservation of buildings of architectural or historical interest and to stimulate public interest in ancient crafts, trades and manufactures.

(First object as stated in Memorandum and Articles of Association, 1969)

Key aims

- To run an open air museum that inspires and delights its users
- To provide lifelong learning based on the museum's collections and other resources
- To ensure high standards of collections care
- To pursue research and scholarship

Beech Reservoir houses
Sites and buildings committee established to agree the acquisition and siting of exhibit buildings; it continues until 1990
Master carpenter Roger Champion's

involvement begins, helping to dismantle Pendean farmhouse
Chris Zeuner becomes a volunteer, using his own transport to help rescue buildings and artefacts, later being employed as

keeper and finally museum director
Toll house from Upper Beeding and medieval shop from Horsham dismantled. Tudor wall paintings rescued from Fittleworth, Wealden-house roof truss

of energetic and continuous growth was a major factor in drawing in large numbers of visitors, many of whom awaited with keen interest the arrival of the next building on site. In those first five years, 26 buildings were rescued and dismantled, and 15 buildings re-erected, together with other exhibits such as the charcoal burners' camp. The frenetic pace continued, certainly until the mid-1980s.

> " *For a whole year I had the somewhat surreal experience of dusting a Henry Moore. When the museum won the National Heritage Museum of the Year Award in 1975, the trophy was Moore's sculpture, Moon Head, a thoroughly pleasing piece of modern art. Unfortunately in those early days there was nowhere secure enough within the museum itself to keep it: even the small office in Goodwood granary was deemed too vulnerable. So Chris and I kept it on our sideboard at Gonville Cottage. I was very sad to see it go.* "
>
> **Diana Zeuner**

In 1975, just five years after opening, the museum received the National Heritage Museum of the Year Award, the most prestigious accolade in the museums and heritage sector. It was given primarily for the introductory exhibition in Hambrook barn, but the judges also praised "the initiative and enterprise shown by the open air museum in Sussex [which] gave them the edge over the other candidates". In many ways this single joyful event helped set the scene for the museum's success over the next two decades.

Although the museum was succeeding in attracting visitors it needed greater resources to meet the ever-increasing challenge of site development and maintenance, and for ten years from 1977 advantage was taken of job creation schemes run by the Manpower Services Commission. For the first six years successive teams carried out site and project work and from 1984 these included the creation of indexes of books and slides in the library using the first Apple computer system.

Above *Just five years after opening to the public, Chris Zeuner receives the National Heritage Museum of the Year Award, £2,000 and the Henry Moore porcelain sculpture* Moon Head, *from the American Ambassador, Elliot Richardson. On the right is James Bishop, editor of the* Illustrated London News *which sponsored the trophy. The judges' citation included: "…in the end…the initiative and enterprise shown by the open air museum in Sussex gave them the edge over the other candidates. The museum has recently set up a new exhibit in an 18th-century barn saved from demolition and re-erected on the museum site which serves as a fine introduction to all the exhibits on display. The museum as a whole is a free-and-easy place, without rigid direction of the public, so that a visit is both rewarding and relaxing."*
Below *The introductory exhibition in Hambrook barn, for which the museum won the award.*

saved from Billingshurst and Lintott's walking-stick workshop collected from Chiddingfold
Timbers of Bayleaf farmhouse arrive on site

1969 (1 April) Weald & Downland Open Air Museum Ltd incorporated as a company, followed by charitable status being granted by the Charity Commission. Subscribers to the Memorandum and Articles of Association are: J R Armstrong, Alderman J

A Farmer, Mrs M Hallam, Maj Gen L A Hawes, K Leslie, J Warren, N West. In addition to these, other members of the first Council of Management are: Miss C E Barson, Dr K M E Murray, J E Whittome

Right *The barns complex in the nearby village of Charlton, which enabled the museum to bring together facilities for collections storage and care and building conservation in the early 1980s.* **Below** *Master carpenter Roger Champion making replica medieval furniture in the new workshop at the complex.*

By 1978 it was apparent that there would need to be a revision of the master plan, partly because of the changing landscape and partly because of visitor circulation and site-servicing needs. Museum director Chris Zeuner said:

It is clear that the museum has grown faster than was expected. Many of the facilities were provided on the basis that the museum would cater for around 50,000 visitors per annum. In addition, the buildings erected so far dictate the type of development that can be undertaken elsewhere on the site.

The plan, informed by Ivan Hicks' landscape report, led to a series of new pathways and vehicle tracks, improved lavatory facilities, changed entrance arrangements, and fresh areas of tree planting.

Roy Armstrong wrote that in the future, 1978 may be regarded as a turning point in the museum's development, as it also saw the completion of major buildings enabling the realisation of some of the original aims. The Lavant building and the upper hall from Crawley furthered development of the museum's research and educational work.

Edward James Foundation grants lease of the site (35 acres) for 42 years at annual peppercorn rent of £1

John Lowe takes up part-time appointment as the first museum director

Re-erection of the first building, Winkhurst, by Gunolt Greiner with Roger Champion assisting

Granary from Littlehampton, treadwheel house from Catherington and granary from Yapton dismantled

Charcoal burners' camp constructed

First guidebook written by Roy Armstrong

St Andrew's School, Worthing becomes the first school to help with site work

Making and selling craft products   *Richard Pailthorpe and Diana Zeuner*

In the late 1970s the museum established a trading company, Singleton Museum Services Ltd, enabling it to undertake appropriate commercial activities to generate income for its work and assist restoration projects off-site.

Albert Peacock making thatching spars from hazel, for use at the museum and for re-sale. He was able to make 1,000 in a day. In the year 1995 alone, he had made 150,000 spars by the autumn.

The arrival on the staff of Sussex countryman Albert Peacock led to the museum making and selling thatching spars and laths. Other conservation building materials and craft products followed, with the museum taking on the management of hazel coppice at Goodwood and other local estates. Bringing a working coppice back into rotation was in itself a worthwhile conservation exercise. Hazel was also brought in from the Sussex Wildlife Trust's coppice on the West Dean Estate for use on the museum site and re-sale.

Thatcher Chris Tomkins using the museum's own-grown thatching straw to provide a new roof for the hall from Boarhunt.

Maris Widgeon, a traditional variety of wheat, was grown for thatching straw in fields adjacent to the museum site in agreement with the West Dean Estate, and used by the museum for its own buildings and also further afield. The straw and hazel spars were sold to thatchers, including Chris Tomkins who still works on the museum's thatched buildings. Chestnut laths made by

Albert Peacock and George Marshman from Petworth were sold to a number of prestigious conservation projects including the Historic Dockyard, Chatham (some 8½ miles of the product), King's College, Cambridge and the Globe Theatre in London.

Other outside contracts included the restoration of wagons and agricultural equipment for the Greater London Council, sub-contracted to the West Sussex Rural Engineering Company which rented a workshop in the Charlton Barns complex, and the *in-situ* restoration of an important but deteriorating historic brick-kiln on Ebernoe Common, near Petworth for West Sussex County Council.

The charcoal burners' camp was a favourite exhibit with visitors. Alan Waters, assisted by Lyn Armstrong and volunteer Ted Nash, continued the tradition of demonstrating earth burns. With the increasing popularity of home barbecues, the museum decided to go one step further and produce charcoal commercially using metal kilns. Cordwood was readily available from West Dean Estate and the museum's leased coppices. Several tons of charcoal were produced each year and sold on local garage forecourts and through the Chichester ironmonger, G. Pine. The 'fines' or smaller grades of charcoal were sold to gunmakers, James Purdey & Sons, for 'blueing' the barrels of their distinctive guns. The company

Charcoal burning on a commercial scale; Alan Waters is tending to the modern metal kiln.

sponsored a new interpretation board about charcoal burning. In 1995 the museum's charcoal went on sale at one of the largest superstores in the region, B&Q in Bognor Regis, through the museum's links with the Bioregional Charcoal Company; the first delivery was made by horse-drawn wagon, providing an excellent publicity opportunity.

These trading activities gave the museum a new dimension, the income helping subsidise its building restoration work, providing quality on-site craft demonstrations, assisting local craftsmen and raising the museum's profile in the conservation sector. Today, with these products increasingly available commercially, the museum has turned its attention to pioneering other aspects of conservation.

The museum was also considering an opportunity to lease redundant farm buildings in the nearby village of Charlton from the Goodwood Estate Company. This would enable it to establish a permanent workshop, bring all its artefact collections together in one place, let some units commercially to appropriate craftsmen and set up a materials bank.

The arrangements were completed by 1980, primarily by Richard Pailthorpe, who had been appointed senior assistant (later made assistant director) in 1979. The Charlton Barns project represented a great step forward in improving the museum's infrastructure and helping to generate income. In many ways it was ahead of its time as it enabled the retention of a traditional complex of buildings as a working unit, and for conservation purposes, rather than their conversion into residential housing.

The museum's establishment had followed on closely from the opening of Fishbourne Roman Palace in the late 1960s, and together with Goodwood, the Festival Theatre and the Cathedral, Chichester had become a major tourist destination. However, tourism was not a popular development with some local politicians and it was due to the visionary effort of the present Duke of Richmond, then the Earl of March, that tourism gained proper recognition as an important sector of the local economy.

The Duke founded the Chichester Visitors' Group (CVG) as a consortium of the main visitor attractions together with local authority representation. The museum supported this initiative from the start, with Richard Pailthorpe succeeding the Duke as chairman. The CVG produced an annual tourist leaflet promoting Chichester, and was instrumental in persuading Chichester District Council to open Chichester Tourist Information

| **1970** | (5 September) Museum established "through voluntary determination and effort, inspired by Armstrong's leadership" and opens to the public for the first time; there are seven exhibits | Launch of £100,000 fundraising appeal

Saxon weavers' hut is built, the first archaeological reconstruction

Re-erection of Littlehampton granary, treadwheel house from Catherington and | toll house from Upper Beeding. The hall from Boarhunt, the medieval house from Sole Street, the cattle shed from Lurgashall and the roundhouse from Bersted are dismantled. The cattle shed from Rusper is dismantled and re-erected |

Centre and West Sussex County Council to appoint a tourism officer. Through CVG the museum was closely involved at the heart of local tourism, including travel trade fairs organised by the Southern and South East England Tourist Boards, the creation of the 'Goodwood leaflet exchange' and in 1994 promoting 'Chichester, City of Culture'.

At national level, the museum was a founding member of the Association of Independent Museums (AIM), a self-help organisation formed to promote independent museums and to lobby government and national institutions on its members' behalf. Independent museums were a vital new force representing grass-roots community determination to preserve aspects of history, notably industrial heritage, which were neglected by the established museum sector. Museum director Chris Zeuner became its honorary treasurer and later its chairman, with his wife, Diana, becoming the association's magazine editor. This close involvement with a countrywide body enabled the museum to establish a high profile in national museum matters.

By the end of its first decade the museum was receiving an average of 160,000 visitors per year and this was achieved on many fewer open days than today and with no special events. However, these were about to be introduced.

The 1980s

In its first ten years the museum had staged demonstrations of crafts and rural life, but in the 1980s it became a pioneer in the development of special events and promotional activities on a bigger scale. A country fair in 1980 was soon followed by the autumn ploughing and threshing event (1981) and a Heavy Horse Day (1983). These quickly established themselves as major occasions in the museum calendar, and continue to be popular today. Further events followed, including the Rare Breeds Show (attracting attendances of over 5,000), and others focusing on themes such as timber and its uses, and sheep dog trials. In 1984 a successful Festival of Building was staged in association with the Chartered Institute of Building and this led to the holding of building conservation events. The museum's first Food Fair was held in 1989 in association with Taste of the

Richard Pailthorpe   *Diana Zeuner*

Senior Assistant, then Assistant Director, 1979-1995

Completion of the lease arrangements for Charlton Barns was the first task for Richard Pailthorpe, the museum's senior assistant, later assistant director, a post he held for 15 years. Richard came to the museum in 1979 from the Goodwood Estate where he was assistant land agent.

A member of the Royal Institution of Chartered Surveyors, with a BSc in estate management, his role evolved as the museum grew, involving him in tasks ranging from wardening and volunteer rotas, organising special events and the sale of craft products, to marketing and tourism, strategic planning, and fundraising. From 1990 to 1995 he was chairman of the Chichester Visitors' Group (CVG). Richard's interests include local history, rural life and photography. Among other titles, he is the author of *The Downland Shepherds* (with Gordon Beningfield); *Goodwood Country* (with Ian Serraillier); *Chichester: A Contemporary View* (with Iain McGowan) and fourth edition editor (with Diana Zeuner) of Roy Armstrong's *A History of Sussex*. After leaving the museum he became manager of Syon Park, the London home of the Dukes of Northumberland, and in 2007 general manager of Parham Park, West Sussex. He is vice chairman of the South East Regional Committee of the Historic Houses Association. Richard says his time at the museum taught him "the invaluable lesson of multi-tasking".

Friends of the Open Air Museum launched at West Dean village hall
Balance in bank – £5,705

1971 Re-erection of Bayleaf farmhouse begins

Chris Zeuner becomes the honorary curator of crafts and craft equipment and establishes first collections' cataloguing system
Smithy from Southwater, West Sussex,

dismantled and re-erected. Cattle shed from Lurgashall re-erected. Aisled barn from Hambrook, market hall from Titchfield, cattle shed from Kirdford and roundhouse from Binsted dismantled

The magazine *Diana Zeuner*

The annual visit of the History Re-enactment Workshop, based at Pendean farmhouse, enabled the museum to show domestic life at the beginning of the 17th century.

The museum is unusual in that it has published a magazine for its supporters and stakeholders for most of its life. Its origins were in newsletters produced for the volunteers and Friends which merged at an early stage to become a fully-fledged magazine including news, features and academic articles, reflecting all the museum's activities, mailed out currently to over 10,000 Friends, volunteers and supporters. It won a British Association of Friends of Museums award in 1999.

Diana Zeuner has been its editor for over 30 years, producing it alongside two other magazines she publishes. The first article she wrote for it was in 1973, *August Charcoal Burn*. Authors of articles in the first issue included Chris Zeuner on the collection of craft artefacts, Kim Leslie on buildings and equipment demonstrating horse power and John Warren on the re-erection of Titchfield market hall. Other aspects covered included the thatching of Hambrook barn, the re-erection of the Kirdford sheds, the daubing of Bayleaf farmhouse and the Medieval Pottery Research Project.

In the early 2000s, Walter Greenway transferred the magazines' contents onto a database usable by museum staff. Today the magazine is published twice a year in full colour with 40 pages, supported by the Friends of the Museum and advertising.

South East. All these events served a dual purpose, bringing in greater numbers and a broader range of visitors, and also providing the opportunity to explore new themes and interests.

The museum was regularly invited to attend shows and national events such as the South of England Show at Ardingly, the Museums & Heritage Show and the Country Living Magazine Fair at the London Design Centre. A former

military caravan was converted for promotional purposes and manned at events by teams of volunteers. This mobile promotional outreach vehicle travelled to numerous venues throughout the region, from ploughing matches and heavy horse parades to county shows, steam rallies, seafronts, shopping centres and even Hyde Park, London.

Good media coverage was invaluable. In 1982, BBC 2's *Chronicle* television programme featured the re-erection of the house from Walderton; fortuitously it was broadcast just before the museum opened for the season. At that time there was no planned overflow parking, and the resulting bumper Easter led to the site itself becoming a virtual car park. The programme was undoubtedly the major factor contributing to 1982 as the museum's record attendance year, with 176,374 visitors.

But it was the variety of promotional methods that led to the museum's success in attracting visitors, says Richard Pailthorpe. Whilst leaflet distribution and advertisements in tourist guides contributed, surveys showed that 'word of mouth', 'following a school visit' and 'good PR' were the principal reasons for visits. The museum was quick to take advantage of national or regional promotions, such as British Food & Farming Year in 1989. This approach led to an unusually high number of repeat visits, which has also resulted in continuing growth in the number of Friends. Many of the museum's activities attracted valuable

Medieval cottage from Hangleton reconstructed Medieval Pottery Research Project begins, lasting until 1975	**1972** First master plan of exhibit building sites drawn up by the museum's honorary architect John Warren Bayleaf farmhouse completed Roy Armstrong appointed MBE	Chris Zeuner appointed keeper (curator) Windpump from Pevensey dismantled and re-erected. Upper hall from Crawley and granary from Chilcomb dismantled

The shop *Diana Zeuner*

Visitors seek mementos of their visit at the museum shop in the building from Lavant in the early 1990s, and below, assistant warden Frank Knights welcomes visitors to the new entrance facility at Longport farmhouse.

From its earliest days the museum ran a shop, not just to generate income, important though this was, but to provide visitors with the opportunity of buying a memento of their visit. The educational potential of selling items related to the museum's theme was also considered important. Staffed entirely by volunteers for many years, by 1979 it was making a profit of over £10,000 per year.

Among the first items for sale were postcards of drawings of the museum's buildings made by the museum's honorary architect, John Warren, and 'cut-out' models of the buildings from card, designed by Marie Hett. These became one of the best-selling lines over many years.

The first shop was extremely small, operating from the Upper Beeding toll house, soon moving to the Littlehampton granary, and then to the building from Lavant, where, under Keith Bickmore's management, the extra space and increasing number of lines helped raise its profit. One innovative line was a board game featuring the museum

buildings, devised by Richard Pailthorpe. The shop moved to Longport farmhouse in 1995, where it shared space with the museum's new entrance facility and the post office.

Chris Zeuner was especially keen on building its reputation as a bookshop, and today it is regarded as one of the best specialist bookshops holding titles on vernacular architecture, rural crafts and countryside matters. For many years Shire Publications, which published books on a wide range of historical subjects – including those on timber-framed buildings by Richard Harris, the museum's research director and later director, on heavy horses by Diana Zeuner, and on Scottish agricultural implements by former curator, Bob Powell – regarded it as one of its best outlets.

In 1989, coinciding with the Bayleaf Medieval Farmstead project, a series of carefully replicated items, including pewter platters, treen, and horn spoons and mugs, were specially commissioned for sale in the shop. In 2003 Richard Harris introduced Swedish-made Gränsfors Bruks axes, already being sold to course participants. Sought by woodsmen and timber-framers from the UK and overseas, these have now become one of the top selling items. Another popular line is the range of herbs and traditional plants supplied by Don and Helen Baldwin from their Black Dog Nursery at North Mundham.

Today the shop is run by Paul Maxted, with part-time assistants and volunteers, and comes under the operations department headed by Henry Warner. In 2009 the shop contributed £54,000 to the museum's income.

Postcards were sold of drawings of the museum's buildings made by the museum's honorary architect, John Warren; this shows Bayleaf farmhouse before the over-mature beech trees were felled.

People's interest in rare breed farm livestock was burgeoning in the 1980s, with the foundation of the Rare Breeds Survival Trust and the growth in smallholdings focusing on breeding animal lines threatened with extinction. At one of the museum's early Rare Breeds Shows the championship went to John Dunlop's Sussex bull Tarrant Havelock shown by Chris Blyth, here receiving the trophy from Sylvia Stone of show sponsors, the West Sussex Gazette.

sponsorship from local businesses, keen to support this thriving cultural business in their midst.

The museum's rapid growth made it necessary to make a radical change in its governance. The Council of Management had met four to six times a year since its inaugural meeting in 1969 but in November 1985 chairman David Biart and honorary treasurer and secretary Jimmy Woollings, presided over changes to a two-tier system, with trustees meeting three times a year and an executive board meeting monthly, enabling quicker and more responsive decision-making. The structure has stood the test of time and is still in use today. The museum director continues to be responsible for daily operation and development, reporting to the board.

Surveys backed Chris Zeuner's view that visitors wanted to experience more about domestic life from the past and see how the buildings may have been furnished or equipped. Great strides were already being taken in the agricultural interpretation of the site and buildings, through the introduction of livestock, the growing of wheat for thatching straw and a wide range of farm tasks undertaken with the use of the working horses and implements from the collection. During the early 1980s the museum turned to additional methods of interpretation. The first building to receive this treatment was the Upper

The café *Diana Zeuner*

The museum had no on-site catering until 1981. Visitors to the museum brought picnics or made use of the local pubs. Cafés at museums were unusual. But this was all to change with Lord Montagu of Beaulieu's infamous phrase, that visitors wanted "a pee and a cup of tea", and the

Victoria & Albert Museum's high profile promotion: 'Ace caff with museum attached'. The museum's concept was to keep the catering as simple as possible and locate it near the picnic area with its views over the lake. It was easily accessible for deliveries, did not interfere with the exhibit buildings, and was based in a restored wagon shed from Pallingham Quay, north of Pulborough. Adapted by local building company, John Booker & Co, it was initially run in-house by staff and volunteers, led by Richard Pailthorpe, before being taken over on contract by the Ellis Family Partnership. Its quality was recognised by an Egon Ronay award in 1995, and flour ground in the museum's watermill and vegetables and herbs from the period gardens were used in the production of food for sale. Demand and expectations grew and the aisled building from Sole Street was re-erected to provide undercover seating. Today the catering is provided by Rachel Dempster (née Ellis) and her husband Brian as Shenlowe Catering Ltd. Pictured is Guy Ellis serving customers at the museum's new café.

First children's guide produced, written by Kim Leslie
35,000 school children have visited the museum already

1973 Visitor attendance records broken, with 111,042 people visiting this year
Roy Armstrong writes *The Open Air Museum: Idea and Reality* for the *Transactions of the Ancient Monuments Society*

Main track across the site completed
Goodwood granary transported intact, re-erected and converted to the museum's first on-site office
Aisled barn from Hambrook and cattle

To mark the presentation of the Times/Shell Community Museum of the Year Award 1989 a staff photograph was organised in the Market Square. Grouped around the museum's president, Geoffrey Godber, and the award trophy are, left to right: seated – Roger Champion (master carpenter) and Zak, Carol Hawkins, Clare Nicoll (Chris Zeuner's secretary), Heather Champion, Richard Pailthorpe (assistant director); standing, back row – Jimmy Redrobe (assistant warden), Mike Tighe (miller), Keith Bickmore (senior warden), Dave Gabbitas (site labourer), Alan Waters (charcoal burner), John Chattaway (horseman); front row – Lynn Shaw (museum secretary), Thelma Jack (Bayleaf interpreter), Neil Wilkins (assistant miller), Jon Roberts (honorary librarian), Albert Peacock (site labourer), Percy North (book-keeper), Elizabeth Newbery (education officer), Les Whitecall (site labourer), Andrew Hodby (site manager), Richard Harris (research director) and, in the front, Chris Zeuner (museum director).

Beeding toll house where mannequins were introduced and a cottage garden established, sown with old varieties of seeds from the Henry Doubleday Collection. A rescued privy from the nearby village of Charlton and a derelict pig sty from Coultershaw Bridge, near Petworth, were added.

The challenge of new interpretive methods was also met by the introduction of an annual visit from the History Re-enactment Workshop during the summer holidays. Carefully chosen for its rigour in historical accuracy, the group was based at Pendean farmhouse, its members using period clothing and replica artefacts to portray domestic life at the beginning of the 17th century. Their

parallel use of 'modern' interpreters in red T-shirts proved a highly successful way of breaking down any barriers such living history interpretation might produce for visitors.

In 1986 the museum embarked on its most ambitious interpretation project – to 'furnish' Bayleaf farmhouse and its curtilage, giving visitors an unprecedented insight into the social and working life of a Wealden farm in c1540. The project would involve fresh research into the world of a yeoman farmer of the period and high quality replicas of his domestic and agricultural equipment. It would take in the interior of the farmhouse, the garden, and the barn and farmyard,

shed from Kirdford re-erected. Sheds from Coldwaltham and Selsey are dismantled

First donation from The Peter Minet Trust (£2,500) for the Lurgashall watermill project

1974 (1 April) Chris Zeuner appointed full-time museum director. John Lowe retires, but remains as consultant

Heather Jackson appointed museum education officer (eventually taking on

curatorial duties, until 1990)

Market hall from Titchfield and cattle sheds from Coldwaltham and Selsey are re-erected. Stable from Watersfield and Tindall's Cottage from Ticehurst dismantled

The nerve centre. The smooth running of the whole organisation is in the hands of the office. Successive director's secretaries and office managers – Julia Hett, Marion Maxwell, Cathy Hicks, Val Price, Clare Nicoll, Pat Melhuish, Janet Sandys-Renton and Julie Aalen – along with their assistants and volunteer helpers, have been vital to the museum's success over four decades. Tackling the administration of the latest ideas and projects with a combination of energy, enthusiasm and quiet dedication, most of them have also volunteered, staying on late after a busy day to help with evening activities. In the photograph, at work in the office in the portacabin and looking forward to more space in Longport farmhouse, are Chris Zeuner's secretary, Pat Melhuish, right, and Jean Piggott.

and be accompanied by a History of Farming Exhibition, in association with the NFU (National Farmers' Union), bringing the story of agriculture up to date. After the launch in May 1989 by Sir Derek Barber, chairman of the Countryside Commission, it was described as "the most extensive project yet undertaken by the museum". It was certainly the biggest single challenge since bringing Lurgashall watermill back into operation, attracting substantial public interest, and proving a valuable aid to increasing visitor numbers.

The following year the museum turned its attention to policy appraisal and Chris Zeuner made recommendations for development over the next 15 years. His report included combining entrance arrangements and shop close to the car park; the upgrading of storage facilities for the museum's collections and the continuation and expansion of its acquisition of historic building exhibits and rural life and buildings artefacts; upgrading the existing car parks to provide a 20% increase in capacity and improving catering arrangements. The plan to move the library to the Lavant building and the office to the upper hall from Crawley was to be superseded by the acquisition of Longport farmhouse which would solve entrance, shop and office facility needs in the 1990s. 1987 was also the year in which the museum celebrated the 20th anniversary of its foundation with a party in the market square. The

following year winter openings on Wednesdays and Sundays began. And two years later the museum was to experience the best season in its history, when it was visited by nearly 186,000 people.

The 1980s had seen a period of sustained growth; by the end of the decade the museum had attracted well over three million visitors and its work was being recognised in other ways. In 1989 the museum won the Times/Shell Community Museum of the Year Award, another recognition of its ability to bring together the goodwill and commitment of people in the local community. The £10,000 grant which came with the trophy enabled the development of the 'hands-on' exhibition exploring traditional building materials and techniques, *Getting to Grips*. In 1990 Chris Zeuner was awarded the OBE for his development of the museum and his work with museums nationally, and two years later Roy Armstrong received an honorary degree of Doctor of Letters from the University of Sussex.

The 1990s

But as the 1990s dawned, change was in the air for all heritage attractions and visitor numbers started to drop. A downturn in the economy and increased competition from other attractions and Sunday shopping all contributed. It became necessary to explore new markets through advertising

Sunday winter openings begin

1975 Hambrook barn opens with introductory exhibition designed to help visitors; it forms the subject of the museum's entry to that year's Museum of the Year Award

Museum wins the National Heritage Museum of the Year Award

Dismantling Lurgashall watermill begins

Re-erection of the upper hall from Crawley

Timbers of medieval house from North Cray, Kent arrive on site (it had been dismantled in 1965)

Richard Harris researches timbers of the hall from Boarhunt, and is subsequently

on TV and radio, discounted vouchers for the summer holidays, and new extensions to the season, opening between Christmas and New Year, and for the February half term. Mothering Sunday became a popular annual event, with free admission for mothers and the gift of a bunch of daffodils. School visits had reached a peak at the end of the 1980s with 35,000 child and student visits a year. But the increasing costs of travel and the necessity of meeting National Curriculum requirements meant fewer school trips as the new decade progressed and the museum needed to plan for more structured educational visits.

The early 1990s saw the start of an important new initiative at the museum. The Joint Centre for Heritage Conservation and Management was launched in 1991, with the museum entering into a partnership with the newly-established Bournemouth University. This was the stimulus for the development of adult teaching and training at the museum, starting with workshops in October that year and the validation by the university of the MSc in Timber Building Conservation in 1994. From these small beginnings the museum's programme has grown to the point where in 2009 over 3,500 student days of adult training were delivered.

In 1992 the museum was registered under the Museums & Galleries Commission's new Registration Scheme, designed to ensure high standards in all fields of museum work. Registration was the stimulus for the creation of the museum's first formal forward plan (referred to

> ❝ *One of the characteristics of our museum that attracts so many people, and so many to come again and again, is the fact that it continues to develop. Development does not only mean major new exhibits, but the thought given and the steps taken to enhance the quality of the visitor's experience, to improve facilities and to widen the museum's role in the fields of education and conservation.* ❞
>
> **Nigel Stephens, chairman of trustees, 1992**

The re-erection of Longport farmhouse in 1994.

then as the corporate plan), which incorporated a site master plan and a landscaping plan.

Towards the end of that year a great opportunity presented itself for improvement of the museum's facilities. A large farmhouse within the site of the Channel Tunnel terminus in Kent had to be removed, and the museum, in partnership with the Canterbury Archaeological Trust, made a successful competitive bid to carry out its dismantling. Its removal and transport to the museum over such a distance was a substantial undertaking, but its reconstruction was completed in time for it to become the museum's ticket office (replacing the kiosk in the car park) and shop for the 1996 season, with administrative offices on the first floor. Chris Zeuner wrote:

> *When completed the effect of the project on the museum will be considerable. We will be able to welcome visitors in a way which meets the expectations of today, and the problems of providing office accommodation and an improved shop will have been solved. The revenue potential of the museum's sales activities will be greatly enhanced.*

As part of the fund-raising effort for the removal of the building to the museum, Chris Zeuner took up the opportunity offered to charities of a sponsored walk through the 31-mile tunnel prior to the public opening, raising £14,000 for the project.

appointed assistant to the research director, Roy Armstrong

Lord Egremont of Petworth becomes president of the museum, succeeding the late Duke of Norfolk

Geoffrey Godber becomes the museum's second chairman with the retirement of Alderman James Farmer. Mr Godber lived in Singleton and was chief executive, formerly clerk, of West Sussex County Council

First museum loans service to schools launched

Wagon shed from Selsey severely damaged in gale during re-erection

Sponsors and supporters   *Diana Zeuner*

For any independent museum responsible for its own income and development, donations, sponsorship, legacies, loans and gifts are a vital part of daily life. The museum has been especially successful with its fund-raising for capital projects, generating very large sums of money, usually for the restoration and re-erection of historic building exhibits. Achievement in this field is always down to painstaking hard work; Chris Zeuner's irrepressible enthusiasm was critical in persuading many trusts, companies and individuals to make donations.

A crucial element in fund-raising activities was the need to alleviate cash flow problems. This was especially true in the early years when the museum was closed in winter and income from visitors ground to a halt. Revenue funding is always harder to secure, although the museum has had some success in this field.

The first bank balance of just under £12 came from donations by local organisations addressed by Roy Armstrong during his early promotional campaign. The first

The museum was proactive in obtaining sponsorship for its capital projects, as with this promotional brochure from the early 1980s.

group to donate funds was a church group from Tarring, the first individuals, John Lowe and Kate Barson, and the first grant from a public body was £400 from West Sussex County Council. The county council made an interest-free loan of £1,000 (converted into a gift) and the Society of Sussex Downsmen met the legal costs of the formation of a limited company.

Among the earliest and most enduring supporters were Peter and Wilhemina Minet, who gave money through their trusts, the Peter Minet, and Idlewild. The first donation was £2,500 from the Peter Minet Trust for the Lurgashall watermill project, and a later legacy was to enable a sea-change in the museum's financial security.

By 1977 the museum was publicising its sponsorship and

donations in order to recognise the givers and encourage further support. That year Simon Sainsbury's Monument Trust provided the museum's largest ever donation in its development thus far – £7,000 for the re-erection of the Lavant building. The trust also agreed to support three craftsmen for three years.

In 1977 other important donations included gifts from the King George V Jubilee Trust for education, the Victoria & Albert Museum for Watersfield stable, The Pilgrim Trust for the upper hall from Crawley, Gosport & Fareham Conservative Association for Court Barn, the Kleinwort Trust for the upper hall from Crawley, the Worshipful Company of Carpenters for general expenditure, the Idlewild Trust for the hall from Boarhunt and for general expenditure, and the Peter Minet Trust for electrical services.

In 1982 the museum promoted an interest-free loan scheme designed to ease cash flow. Those lending £200 and upwards would be issued with a gold pass for free admission to the museum: one substantial loan under the scheme was for £10,000. 1984 grants included £20,000 from the Museums & Galleries Commission towards the Horsham shop/Reigate town house project, and in 1985 the Victoria & Albert Museum offered £9,500 from the PRISM Fund towards the re-erection of the 17th-century house from Reigate.

Other devices to raise money included a grand draw for the re-erection of West Wittering school; the sale of prints of artist Gordon Beningfield's work for the

A publicity photograph to mark the sponsorship of the restoration of wall paintings in the town house from Reigate. Assistant director Richard Pailthorpe, left, and curator Bob Powell, right, are with Mike Mason, manager of the Chichester branch of Marks & Spencer and chairman of the Chichester Chamber of Commerce.

Horsham shop/Reigate town house project; an auction of items contributed in support of the same project carried out by Sotheby's, and the *Be a Brick* campaign for Longport farmhouse.

In 1987 the then Earl of March (now the Duke of Richmond) and the Goodwood Estate made a generous offer of a complimentary hospitality box at its June evening race meeting, together with discounted tickets for Friends of the Museum. A race was named after the museum. In an arrangement which continued until Chris Zeuner's death, the museum was able to host its sponsors and donors at the event each year, providing a convivial atmosphere in which to thank them for their support – and perhaps inspire further giving.

The museum continued to encourage supporters to take out a deed of covenant enabling the charity to claim a tax refund from the Inland Revenue. People were urged to provide legacies in their wills. In 1987 the museum received a £5,000 bequest from the estate of Arthur Plewis, together with his wheelwrighting tools and equipment which were already in the museum's collection. Ten years later the museum received £40,000 from the estate of one of its closest supporters, Virginia Lyon, former trustee and chairman of the Friends.

An astonishing £100,000 was raised by 1987 for the Museum Development Fund (launched three years' earlier to raise money for historic building projects, particularly the Bayleaf Medieval Farmstead and Horsham shop/Reigate town house projects). This was on top of £93,000 raised the previous year. These figures were large sums in the late 1980s. Among supporters of the Bayleaf project were: the John Lewis Partnership, the English Tourist Board, the Countryside Commission, Goodwood Estate Co Ltd and James Longley & Co Ltd. The National Farmers Union supported the accompanying *History of Farming* exhibition. An important contributor to the Reigate town house project was the UK Government/Wolfson Foundation Museum Improvement Fund.

Other key supporters of principal projects included: Seaward Properties (matched by ABSA's [Association of Business Sponsorship of the Arts] Incentive Scheme) and the Redland Brick Company (for Petersfield brick-drying shed); the PRISM Fund, Eurotunnel Group, the Basil Shippam Trust and the Garfield Weston Trust (for Longport farmhouse); the Leopold Muller Estate (for

Whittaker's Cottages); the European Union Raphael Programme (for Whittaker's Cottages eradication of pests), and the Radcliffe Trust (for education programmes).

In 1997 the unexpected legacy of £250,000 from the estate of Mrs Wilhemina Minet enabled the museum to establish an Endowment Fund to help ensure its future sustainability. With the 'windfall' of the VAT cultural reclaim in 2006, and other legacy income and non-restricted funds, the museum's endowment in 2010 stood at a total of £1,150,539.

More effort than ever before went into the fundraising campaign for the Downland Gridshell in the late 1990s, with the backing of a specialist sub-committee and advice from professional fund-raiser, Sarah Mansell. The spring 2000 museum magazine lists 46 supporters on its back page, most of these donating to this one project. Among them were the Heritage Lottery Fund, the Garfield Weston Foundation, the Wolfson Foundation, the Jerwood Foundation, the Mitford Foulerton Trust, the Esmée Fairbairn Foundation, Chichester District Council, UK Waste and Kleinwort Benson.

Virginia Lyon (left) presenting a trophy at the Rare Breeds Show. A long-standing supporter of the museum, at one time chairman of the Friends and a trustee, she left a £40,000 legacy to the museum in her will; it was used to assist with the funding of the Poplar Cottage re-erection project.

Throughout the museum's history the Friends has, not unexpectedly, been its greatest supporter. By the end of 2009 the amount raised by the body stood at an astonishing total of £1.7 million. The grants for 2009 alone amounted to £182,040.

The museum's rapid development and innovative projects drew national media interest. Here The Guardian *arts correspondent, Maeve Kennedy visits the Longport farmhouse site. With her are Chris Zeuner, right, and Richard Harris.*

The re-erection of the timber-frame – a highlight of every year in which a 'new' building joins the exhibits at the museum – was of special interest in the case of Longport farmhouse, in view of the number of new techniques developed by the museum to ensure the faithful restoration of the building's structure, materials and textures. The working horses and an historic timber carriage were used to transport the restored timbers from the workshop in Charlton to the museum – the 60 feet-long load causing great interest for Singleton villagers. More than 150 guests from all over the south-east attended the inauguration by Sir Alastair Morton, chairman of Eurotunnel, which had financed the dismantling and much of the reconstruction.

The museum's involvement with countryside activities and its partnership with the Goodwood Country Park expanded in 1994 with a special event on the Spring Bank Holiday weekend. *A Downland Celebration* was run in conjunction with the Sussex Downs Conservation Board (precursor to what was to become the South Downs National Park), which had an office at the museum. Richard Pailthorpe led the production of new interpretation panels covering the story of the Trundle Hill (also known as St Roche's Hill), its wildlife and ecology, and St Roche's Day on 16 August was celebrated with a service on the site of St Roche's Chapel on the hill, organised by the museum, which still continues annually.

1993 ended sadly with the death of the museum's founder and constant mentor, Roy Armstrong. Chris Zeuner wrote:

Roy exerted an unassuming yet strong influence on the development of the museum, believing steadfastly in sharing its direction with as many people as possible, in the usefulness of discussion and in the creation of opportunities for everyone involved. For those of us working daily on Roy's imaginative project he was a quiet and constant source of inspiration – he will be very sorely missed.

The final link was broken in June 1995 with the death of Roy's wife, Lyn. In her obituary in the museum magazine, Diana Zeuner wrote:

A tireless worker alongside Roy, Lyn's devotion to the museum and its aims was every bit as constant as that of Roy. It was Lyn, who during endless hours of conversation and discussion over 25 years, tempered with reality the most excessive ideas Roy was able to muster for his museum dream.

An era had ended. Roy's 'Impossible Museum' had not only been realised, but had contributed greatly to our understanding of our built and rural heritage, and become an iconic and popular institution. Many of the developments and innovations of the 1970s, 1980s and early 1990s laid the foundations for the museum's continued success today.

While the museum's progress and activity continued unabated, 1994 proved to be an extremely difficult year. The recession affected recreational activity, with museums and heritage projects across the nation suffering a downturn. Chris Zeuner pinpointed a truth common to all independent museums:

It is a strange anomaly that we are able to raise capital grants for development and support for special projects at a time when the main need is to achieve sufficient income to maintain running costs.

Yet a nationwide British Tourist Authority survey of attractions showed that the museum remained extremely popular; it was number 14 in the top 30 independent museums for visitors (there are over 1,000 independent museums across the country).

1976 Pendean farmhouse and stable from Watersfield re-erected

Dismantling of building from Lavant, wagon shed from Wiston and saw-pit shed from Sheffield Park

Plewis collection of wheelwrighting equipment arrives at museum

1977 Association of Independent Museums founded, with Chris Zeuner of the Weald & Downland Open Air

Museum a founder member

Richard Harris appointed research officer

Re-erection of Lurgashall watermill completed

First children's activity days introduced

Special events   *Diana Zeuner*

Special events have enabled the museum to expand the interpretation of its exhibits, at the same time attracting new visitors, enhancing the experience of Friends and supporters, and generating income.

Demonstrations of crafts and small-scale activity days had been held since the early days but special events as we know them today began in the early 1980s, with the introduction of heavy horses and steam threshing in June and October. They proved extremely popular and were followed by the Rare Breeds Show and weekends devoted to timber, sheep dog trials, building conservation and food fairs. Sponsorship from a variety of local businesses and income from trade stands help pay for costs. Large numbers of volunteers are drafted in to help staff on these very labour-intensive occasions.

Events held at the museum over the years have included: Country Fair, Fine Food Fair (originally called the Traditional Food Fair), Sustainable Building Event, Heavy Horse Spectacular, The Wood Show, Early Music Afternoon, Rare Breeds Show (originally called The Rare & Traditional Breeds Show), Children's Activities at half term and Wonderful Wednesdays in the summer holidays, Sheep Dog Trials, the History Re-enactment Workshop, Autumn Countryside Celebration, Tastes of a Tudor Christmas (later known as A Sussex Christmas), Romani Roots – a celebration of Gypsy culture, and the Steam Festival.

Left, from top *1981 – the first time horses ploughed at the museum (this is Bob Lomas), leading to the development of the special events programme. Heavy horses have been involved in two annual events ever since. Rob Dash ploughs the paddock in front of Bayleaf farmhouse; he later became the museum's part-time horseman. Rowena and John McDermott's horse-drawn steam fire engine is a regular visitor. The Rare Breeds Show. Show director John Bushrod checks the trophies, while volunteers Brian Weekes, centre, and John Ruffell, right, listen to commentary from the chairman of the Rare Breeds Survival Trust, Peter Titley. Dairy Shorthorn cattle, awaiting their turn in the ring, attract visitors' attention. Gloucestershire Old Spots breeder and regular show exhibitor, Dave Overton, receives his championship rosette from Chris Zeuner in 1997.*
Right, from top *Visitors discover traditional furniture at The Wood Show, where demonstrations included working with the pole lathe. Steam threshing in the 1980s. Visitors watch the museum's crop of wheat straw being threshed in the traditional way. A steam roller in use for a real job - relaying the Gonville Cottage track - during the Steam Festival. Wonderful Wednesdays – a young bricklayer is shown the technique by Alfie Pilcher during the summer holidays. The Sustainable Building Event, seen here in 2004, is the natural successor to earlier building conservation days.*

Development and Innovation

Above *The visit of HRH The Prince of Wales in 1996. Here he meets thatcher Chris Tomkins. Behind him are David Tomlinson, museum chairman and Chris Zeuner, museum director.*

Right *The newly re-erected Whittaker's Cottages were subjected to an unusual treatment in 1997, when it was enshrouded in silver foil and linked to a computer for the environmentally friendly eradication of pests. Pioneered by Thermo Lignum, it was the first time the treatment – mostly used on small objects – had been used for an entire building.*

By the end of 1996 the new visitor reception area and shop in Longport farmhouse were making a huge difference to the way in which visitors were received. At last the museum had appropriate office space on the upper floor and the new shop was bringing in increased income. That year's crowning event was the official visit of HRH The Prince of Wales, who showed particular interest in the rural crafts demonstrated at the museum.

Later in the year the museum continued to pursue its reputation for innovation when the newly re-erected framework of Whittaker's Cottages was subjected to a most unusual treatment. It was surrounded in silver foil and linked to a computer ready for the environmentally friendly eradication of pests pioneered by Thermo Lignum. This was the first time the treatment – mostly used on small objects – had been used for an entire building; it was funded by the EU under its European Cultural Heritage programme. When their rebuilding was complete the cottages were each treated differently, one furnished as it would have been in the 1880s and the other left unfinished to show the structure and with an accompanying exhibition and audio guide.

The museum's direction had taken another step forward two years earlier with the appointment of Sue Shave to the new post of interpretation officer, responsible for interpretation and education. She made considerable strides in a number of areas, ranging across the schools service, special events and activities, and interpretation development, alongside work for the West Sussex Countryside Studies Trust at Goodwood. Two years later the Heritage Education Trust awarded the museum a full Sandford Award, given annually for excellence in heritage education, one of several awards the museum has received for its education service over its lifetime.

| 1978 | Revised master plan drawn up to take account of high numbers of visitors and landscaping needs
Re-erection of the upper hall from Crawley
Re-erection of the building from Lavant, | achieved with the help of the museum's largest donation so far, £7,000 from The Monument Trust
Carpenters' shop from Windlesham, barn and cattle shed from Kirdford, and | woodsheds and pigsty from West Dean dismantled
Discovering Timber-Framed Buildings by Richard Harris published by Shire Publications |

The museum's audience – its visitors *Diana Zeuner*

During the life of the museum an enduring pleasure has been the positive comments received from visitors. The museum attracts a particularly high volume of repeat visitors – reflected partly in the huge Friends' membership – the envy of many similar attractions.

The museum has always sought to put visitors' experience at the heart of its work, and long before the government's emphasis in the late 2000s on 'social inclusion' and 'access for all', was attracting people from all walks of life to its varied programmes of activity. The admission fee was designed to ensure a visit was accessible by the vast majority of the population, and has remained reasonable, even while some competitors have been charging more. "The museum depends on visitors as its major source of revenue," Chris Zeuner pointed out in the designation application. "Our policy is to attract them through quality."

Over the years various surveys of visitors' responses have been carried out, helping the museum develop its activities according to their interests.

Visitors – lots of them. Cars overflow among the exhibits in 1982, before overflow parking was begun in adjacent fields.

The Light Sussex poultry queue for crumbs as visitors enjoy a picnic near Bayleaf farmhouse.

The 1983 survey showed that 62% of visitors were coming to the museum for the first time (with a repeat visitor figure of 38%). The ploughing event that year, one of the first, attracted 72% new visitors. A high percentage (52%) were visiting as a result of personal recommendation – 'word of mouth' proving once again to be the best form of marketing. A large percentage (97%) found the guidebook commendably easy to follow. The favourite building was Lurgashall watermill, followed by Bayleaf farmhouse and the house from Walderton; the same three buildings remained the most popular in subsequent surveys. A majority of people cited their reasons for visiting as their interest in architecture, building history or carpentry. Other motives included personal recommendation, a day out in the country, curiosity, and an interest in a particular building. Facilities did not receive quite such high praise, but the museum continues to make strenuous efforts to improve these.

The 1998 visitor survey evaluated a new marketing strategy in operation that year, which focused on a striking new approach to publicising the museum and its activities. A significant proportion of visitors had come as a result of leaflets and tourist maps, a form of marketing at its height in the late 1990s. Repeat visits remained high (44%) and 56% of visitors were coming for the first time. Most visitors read *The Daily Telegraph*, followed by *The Times*, *Daily Mail* and *The Guardian*. A majority (33%) were in the 35-54 age bracket, followed by age 55+ (30%), age 5-10 (12%) and 25-34 (11%). Geographically East Sussex was an area ripe for further marketing as fewest visitors came from there.

The re-erection of a timber frame always attracts much interest. Here visitors watch Cowfold barn rise behind Bayleaf farmhouse.

→

Engaging visitors with period cooking in Winkhurst Tudor kitchen.

Visitors' comments have included, overwhelmingly: "Had a very enjoyable visit". Others are: "Very well organised and maintained"; "Polite and helpful staff"; "Non-touristy feel, unhurried, quiet, not overcrowded or commercialised"; "Lovely to be able to touch things", "Seeing conservation in progress"; "Excellent presentation by volunteers: all questions we asked were answered"; "Feeling of country life in the past"; "Attention to detail, well laid out"; "Accurate and imaginative re-erection of buildings", and "Very good value for money". Some took the opportunity to make suggestions; "More working demonstrations" was one request.

In 2008 the Designation Challenge Fund supported an audience research and development project carried out by Stuart Davies Associates, which aimed to understand the subtlety of visitors' motivations and experiences through observation, questionnaires and focus groups. The main conclusion was that although people had enjoyed their visit, they had not found the site layout easy to understand, especially if they were visiting for the first time, and would like help with the best way to experience the museum. This information made an important contribution to the development of the Access Project intended to renew visitor facilities.

Volunteer Alan Wood explaining the process of creating the Gridshell to visitors. He was one of a number of volunteers who later gave daily guided tours of the completed building.

By 1997 the museum felt its development and stature warranted a by-line increasingly used in publicity material: "England's leading museum of traditional buildings and rural life". It had developed a national reputation for its development of repair techniques and high standards of research into traditional architecture. Richard Harris pointed out that this work had taken to new levels our understanding of the craft of the timberwright, which had received little attention compared, for example, to the craft of the stonemason.

The museum's next project, the boldest in its history, to construct a ground-breaking building conservation centre and open-access museum store, was to take this reputation to a new level.

Two applications for grants were made in 1997 to the newly-launched Heritage Lottery Fund, for the 16th-century smoke bay house, Poplar Cottage, which was to be re-erected as a memorial to Roy Armstrong, and for a £1.3 million building conservation centre and collections store to be housed in an "innovative greenwood timber structure sited uphill from Longport farmhouse". This highly ambitious project would also be the museum's most expensive. Both bids succeeded. The Downland Gridshell, as it was to become known, was a pioneer modern structure utilising timber and a range of new techniques, enabling the museum to move its collections and

First use at the museum of dendrochronology (tree-ring dating) to date timber in the solar of Bayleaf farmhouse (felling date 1505-10)

1979 Richard Harris appointed research director

Richard Pailthorpe appointed senior assistant, later to become assistant director

Traditional Buildings – Accessible to the Public by Roy Armstrong published

Woodcolliers and Charcoal Burning by Lyn Armstrong published

Re-erection of Court Barn from

its buildings workshop onto the site, where visitors would have much improved access. With this structure the museum was keen to show how sustainable natural materials could be used in modern buildings in the countryside.

In 1998 the museum received an unexpected and large legacy of £250,000 from the estate of Mrs Wilhemina Minet, who with her husband Peter had been a constant supporter since the museum's early days. It presented the museum with the opportunity to realise a long-cherished dream, the establishment of an Endowment Trust to help ensure its future sustainability. Part of the amount was invested by the trust and joined by further legacies over the next few years.

The previous year the Friends had taken steps to increase its membership recruitment, and thus the funds available for donation to the museum, with a 'Welcome leaflet' for every visitor, incorporating an invitation to join. Subscriptions doubled from 2,522 at the end of 1996 to over 5,000 at the start of 2010. Later, in 2003, Tim Heymann and Maurice Pollock, respectively chairman and treasurer of the Friends, led a change in policy in which a proportion of Friends' funds available each year would be donated to help develop the museum's core activities, rather than purely in support of capital projects. Approximately 60% of funds would be dedicated to core activities such as site and exhibits maintenance, publicity and training, with 25% allocated to capital projects, and 15% to additional opportunities arising during the year.

Independent museums are complex bodies, having to comply with company and charity law and maximise limited resources whilst protecting their collections, held in perpetuity. To secure this protection, legal opinion in 1998 led to the formation of a subsidiary charitable company, Weald & Downland Museum Operations Ltd, which became responsible for the day-to-day operation of the museum. The main charitable company, Weald & Downland Open Air Museum Ltd, retained responsibility for the collections, education and strategy. A separate subsidiary company established earlier, Singleton Museum Services Ltd, continued to run the museum's retail and catering trading activities. In 2003 further legal opinion enabled the museum to simplify its structure again by merging the assets of the museum operations

company back into the main museum company, whilst continuing to protect the collections.

1998 was also the year in which the museum was accorded 'Designated' status in a new government scheme to recognise outstanding historic collections. This was an extraordinary achievement for a medium-sized, regional institution dependent entirely on its own efforts for funding its development. At that time only 43 collections were designated (even in 2010 there were only 131), and unlike many museums in which only some elements were designated, in the case of the Weald & Downland Open Air Museum it was the whole collection – buildings and rural life – which received the distinction. Furthermore it is one of only seven independent museums without core government funding to have been so designated.

Above *Exhibit maintenance is constant. Here the Pevensey windpump is being replaced after repair by Robert Demaus.*

Below *Chris Zeuner with Edward Cullinan Architects' model of the proposed Downland Gridshell – the museum's new building conservation centre and collections store – with the market square in the background.*

Lee-on-Solent. The pugmill house from Redford and the brick-drying shed from Petersfield are dismantled

Establishment of Singleton Museums Services Ltd, a subsidiary company, to allow

the museum to undertake commercial activity separate to its charitable work

Kim Leslie retires as honorary treasurer

The first sheep and working horses arrive on the museum site

1980 Museum takes on redundant farm buildings at Charlton on a lease from the Goodwood Estate Company, bringing the majority of the museum's collections and the master carpenter's workshop together in one place

A successful new marketing campaign was launched in 1999: 'Come and Experience the Real Thing' was designed to appeal to people's interest in history as an escape from the challenges of modern life. To its right are leaflets from 1985 and 2003.

The Government earmarked £15 million funding for designated museums, and in the following years the museum successfully claimed grants for a number of schemes to enhance the collections' care and interpretation.

They included the appointment of a collections' manager (Mike Wall) to undertake a complete analysis and review of the museum's collections,

and the computerisation of the museum's entire collections' records, the ultimate aim being to enable visitors to look up information on a computer during their visit. It also enabled the re-interpretation of Pendean farmhouse, including alterations to the chimney and furnishing the interior, and the re-interpretation of Winkhurst, removing it to a new more appropriate site next

The certificate of the museum's designated status was formally presented to the museum at the Autumn Countryside Celebration in October 1998 by Loyd Grossman (right), the broadcaster and then Museums & Galleries commissioner, and now chairman of The Heritage Alliance. With him in the photograph are, left to right, museum director Chris Zeuner, museum chairman David Tomlinson and research director Richard Harris.

The house from Walderton, the barn from Cowfold and the dovecot from Milton Street are dismantled. Re-erection of the wagon shed from Wiston, the saw-pit shed from Sheffield Park, the pugmill house from Redford, the carpenters' shop from

Windlesham and the brick-drying shed from Petersfield

Worshipful Company of Plumbers' museum opened

Completion of the upper hall from Crawley enables the museum to establish the library, and provides meeting facilities

1981 Duke of Gloucester opens the re-erected hall from Boarhunt

to Bayleaf farmhouse. Winkhurst had been the first historic building exhibit to be re-erected at the museum in 1969, in its familiar position on the hill overlooking the museum, but subsequent research revealed that it was likely to have been a Tudor kitchen, a type of structure which would have existed alongside a farmhouse such as Bayleaf. Its new site would be more appropriate topographically and simple modern structures were added to represent the adjoining buildings which it was known to have had. It was now possible to interpret properly its original purpose and in the early 2000s it was furnished as an operational kitchen.

A new large object store at Singleton railway cutting was also made possible by designation funding as was the conservation and documentation of all off-site artefacts. It supported the writing of an Interpretation Strategy, the new Volunteer Support Project and under the 'Hidden Histories' category and in collaboration with the Museum of English Rural Life at Reading, a series of videos and manuals covering the operation of animal-powered agricultural equipment, to help bring to life these usually static exhibits. Thus most of the developments at the museum after the turn of the century were supported by the museum's designation status and accompanying funding.

In 1999 the museum's website went online for the first time – www.wealddown.co.uk – planned and run by museum trustee Jeff Houlton. In its first six months it attracted over 10,000 visits, which were responsible for 1.5% of visitors that season. By 2003 this had risen to just under 200,000 and in 2010 is approaching 800,000 visits per year. It represents a valuable additional string to the museum's marketing bow, and a channel for distributing news. In 2000 French, German and

A number of projects benefited from grants from the Designation Challenge Fund over a ten-year period. **Above** *Museum carpenter Roger Champion works on the back of an oak chair for the Pendean furnishing project.*
Below *The frame of Winkhurst Tudor kitchen, removed from its original hilltop location, grows on its new site close to Bayleaf farmhouse; two modern additions show the position of original structures which had disappeared by the time of its dismantling.*

> 66 *Considering the small labour force available at the time, it is astonishing to look back at the amount of work that was achieved in the first few years. I think it was mainly down to the phenomenal enthusiasm of everybody involved.* 99
>
> **Roger Champion**

Dutch language versions were added and the site was completely redesigned with virtual tours of the museum and expanded information on other local tourist attractions. A separate but linked site purely devoted to the museum's schools services was launched in 2006 and this provides a significant resource for teachers planning to bring school groups to the museum. In 2010 it was redesigned under the museum's Knowledge

Lurgashall watermill is officially opened and begins regular production of stoneground wholemeal flour, with Robert Demaus as miller

School from West Wittering, house extension from Reigate, horse whim from West Kingsdown and outhouse from Shipley dismantled
First computer arrives, enabling the

computerisation of the museum's building records
First horse ploughing demonstrations at the museum establish the precedent for 'special events'

The opening of the new Singleton Post Office within the Longport farmhouse entrance facility by Sue Farman, left, Singleton Parish Council chairman. With her are, left to right, postmistress Penny Barc, a Post Office representative and Chris Zeuner.

Transfer Partnership arrangement with the University of Reading.

In contrast to the start of the decade, the 1998 and 1999 visitor numbers were very buoyant. 1998's figures were 8% up on the previous year – an important indicator as many other museums and attractions experienced serious downturns at this time.

In the 30 years since it first opened to the public the museum had embedded well into its local community in the Lavant valley, proud to have such a successful cultural institution on their doorstep. When the local Singleton Post Office was closed, Chris Zeuner saw an opportunity to continue this vital service, and in 2000 a new post office was opened in Longport farmhouse within the museum's entrance facility and shop. Opened by Singleton Parish Council chairman Sue Farman, the postmistress was Singleton resident Penny Barc.

The 2000s

The decade began with the construction of the Downland Gridshell, a project for which the word innovation is an understatement. With the first earth being turned in May 2000 the museum was entering unknown territory. All previous building activity had been small scale and under its direct control, costing no more than around £100,000. But this project was eventually to cost £2 million, and involved a high level of risk – a new form of construction and the need to raise the final funding.

Cross-section of the Downland Gridshell drawn by Edward Cullinan Architects.

Cattle shed from Kirdford is lost following an arson attack
Café opens for first time

1982 Re-erection of the house from Walderton.

BBC *Chronicle* charts its dismantling and reconstruction
Renewal of introductory exhibition in Hambrook barn

Trees and Woodlands in the Landscape exhibition opens in the Coldwaltham cattle shed
Poplar Cottage from Washington and the joiners' shop from Witley dismantled

Then in September came an enormous shock. Chris Zeuner was diagnosed with cancer, and on 3 January 2001 he died. He had devoted 30 years of his life to the museum, which had lost its guiding light, and tragically he would not see the completion of the Gridshell project which he had piloted through all the development stages. Richard Harris was appointed museum director in June 2001 but in a re-structured role focusing on policy and strategy, while a new post of operations director, focusing on daily management, was filled by the museum's marketing officer, Gail Kittle. Richard replaced Chris supervising the Gridshell project, and led the remaining fundraising supported by trustees. £230,000 had been raised, but more than double that was still needed to match the Heritage Lottery Fund grant of £1.23 million.

February 2001 brought a further challenge: foot-and-mouth disease struck Britain, resulting in restrictions on livestock movements throughout the country. The museum had livestock on site and could not move the animals away without breaking the law. Visitors could bring infection and spread the disease so the museum was closed and stood to lose 2-3,000 visitors a week. Eventually, however, a licence was issued to move the livestock, and with the Government backtracking on its initial attempt to close down the countryside, public opinion was ready to support attempts to get things moving again. The museum reopened on 1 April, but the Fine Food Fair was postponed and the Rare Breeds Show cancelled. A craft show brought extra visitors and the season ended with a small increase on the previous year following a sustained marketing effort.

Owing to the work of an outstanding construction team the Downland Gridshell was successfully completed in two years, and in June 2002 it was officially opened by Sir Neil Cossons, chairman of English Heritage. "It was immediately clear that the museum had gained not only a workshop and open-access store, but also a large space for occasional gatherings, something it had never had before," says Richard Harris. Christened the Jerwood Gridshell Space to reflect major funding received from the Jerwood Foundation, it had already been used for a Museum Community Forum (which replaced the volunteer briefings) and the museum's first Sustainable Building Event.

After the opening it was the venue for a major international conference on the modern use of timber in building, *Time for Timber*, followed in August by *Frame 2002*, the conference of the Carpenters' Fellowship. Social events included a dinner for volunteers and in 2003, a fundraising ball.

Concerns by some that such a major project would prove a distraction from the museum's core mission and be to the museum's detriment were to prove groundless, Richard Harris says. The task of moving the museum's collections into the open-access store began in May 2002 and was completed by curator Julian Bell by the end of the year. This tight timetable was achievable because of the preparatory work by Mike Wall, supported by the Designation Challenge Fund (DCF). DCF projects begun at the turn of the decade continued with the furnishing and re-presentation of

Foot-and-mouth disease precautions in place at the museum entrance in February 2001.

David Biart, a prominent Chichester solicitor with Thomas Eggar & Son, becomes the museum's third chairman, succeeding Geoffrey Godber

Viscount Watkinson becomes museum president
Restoration of brick-kiln *in situ* on Ebernoe Common, near Petworth, for West Sussex County Council

Marjorie Hallam becomes honorary librarian
First working oxen introduced
First Volunteers' Briefing takes place

Development and Innovation

Pendean farmhouse, and the re-location of Winkhurst and its interpretation as a Tudor kitchen. A full-time interpreter was engaged for this new project, to present the daily tasks of a Tudor housewife, processing food and producing meals for the family and servants.

The following year the museum lost one of its most dedicated supporters with the death of Heather Champion at the age of 57. Heather had arrived as a volunteer in the embryonic years and as a member of staff played a distinguished role in the education service, the care and documentation of the collections, and the dismantling and re-erection of exhibits. Later that year her husband Roger retired; his carpentry skills had brought outstanding quality to timber work of all sorts at the museum, from the historic building exhibits to shelves for the shop. Roger continues to work part-time concentrating mainly on replica furnishings for the buildings. The museum's reputation for excellence in timber framing was carried on by carpenter Joe Thompson, who had in 2000 become the leader of the museum's *Timber-framing from scratch* courses. In 2002 he became

carpenter-in-residence, based in the workshop at the east end of the Downland Gridshell.

The early years of the decade saw the museum's financial position improve rapidly. In 2003 two additional sources of revenue became unexpectedly available. Firstly, it became possible for charities to treat visitors' entry fees as donations, and recover the tax through Gift Aid – worth 28p in the £. Even after a subsequent rule change made it more difficult, this brought a substantial new revenue stream: in 2009 for instance, 52% of visitors chose to pay in this way, representing a value of £80,200.

Secondly, following a six-year campaign, the museum heard that under EU law and in common with other cultural institutions, it would be able to reclaim VAT wrongly levied by HM Revenue & Customs on visitor admissions. A condition under the UK courts' ruling was that trustees, who receive no payment, must take active responsibility for the governance of the museum. After another court ruling on the time limit for back-payments, in 2006 the museum was repaid VAT back to 1990, plus interest, a total of £567,364.

1983 On Doug Bryant's retirement Keith Bickmore becomes senior warden and shop supervisor
Joiners' shop from Witley re-erected. Animal pound from Walton Heath

dismantled and re-erected
Junior Friends launched, led by Elizabeth Newbery

1984 Re-erection of the medieval house from

North Cray and the school from West Wittering
Festival of Building held to mark the 150th anniversary of the Chartered Institute of Building, and *Traditional Building Materials*

In 2000 the museum had established a separate Endowment Trust to build up and administer a long-term fund to support the museum's aims. Starting with £122,921 from Wilhelmina Minet's legacy, all unrestricted legacies received by the museum were immediately transferred to the Endowment Trust, whereas previously they had been committed to projects or used to offset annual deficits. Therefore, by 2010 the trust's investments stood at £583,175. The value of these two funds, totalling just over £1 million, represents long-term security beyond the wildest dreams of the museum over the previous three decades.

Exhibit development continued, in part fulfilling the forward plan of 2000-05. Two small buildings, the shed from Charlwood and the horse whim from West Kingsdown, were completed in 2000, and Winkhurst was moved and became effectively a new exhibit in 2002. In 2005/06 a timber crane dating from the turn of the 20th century and collected from Privett in Hampshire was fully restored to working order and became the centrepiece of a new exhibit depicting a rural timber yard, complete with a racksaw bench and sawpit. In 2006 a small church – a 'tin tabby' clad in corrugated iron – was dismantled at South Wonston in Hampshire. Its re-erection was scheduled for completion by March 2011 and is to be the subject of a BBC2 programme about vernacular architecture. A hay barn from Ockley which had been dismantled in 1985 was re-erected in 2008/09 and is used to house the three elements of a 'threshing train' – threshing machine, elevator and living van.

There was also a new emphasis on exploiting the collections by bringing objects into the public eye. For small objects the Downland Gridshell open-access store has proved extremely interesting for visitors, who enjoy the display of artefacts, familiar and unfamiliar as they wander through the store. For large objects a display gallery for vehicles and implements was created, using a grant from the DCMS (Department for Culture, Media & Sport)/Wolfson Museums & Galleries Improvement Fund, and a new shelter built for three large vehicles behind the Witley joiners' shop.

Agricultural developments have most recently centred on Bayleaf farmhouse, with farm manager

Chris Baldwin establishing field strips appropriate to the period, worked by the two pairs of oxen he has trained. A hop garden in front of the house relates to a nearby display of hop-making equipment from the collections.

In 2005 – the year the museum welcomed its five millionth visitor – a new interpretation department was established with the aims of supporting and enhancing live interpretation around the site. This reflected the success of Winkhurst Tudor kitchen and the challenge of bringing similar interpretation to the other domestic exhibits, but also the need to co-ordinate the development of interpretation around the site including craft demonstrations, the gardens and agricultural work. Close co-operation between the interpretation and schools' departments was also essential to ensure cross-fertilisation between schools workshops and interpretive demonstrations.

In 2003 a new forward plan focused on the concept of buildings at the centre of a 'web' connecting themes such as landscape, artefacts, historic and environmental conservation, and science and technology. It acknowledged the need to upgrade visitor facilities and especially improved 'orientation' to help visitors understand better both the physical shape of the museum and the diversity of what it offers. Encompassing both physical and intellectual access, this became known as the 'Access Project'.

One of the questions visitors ask is: "what was life like for the people who lived in the houses?" To enable more informed answers the museum

The new Vehicle and Implement Gallery enabled the museum to display some of its largest and most interesting objects and was funded by the DCMS (Department for Culture, Media & Sport)/Wolfson Museums & Galleries Improvement Fund.

The museum provides a unique and interesting venue for a wide range of events, conferences and meetings, helping raise income and providing a way of involving local, regional and national communities. Among organisations which have taken advantage of this resource are: the Society for the Protection of Ancient Buildings (1985), Historic Farm Buildings Group (1985), West Sussex County Council (1993), Folk Life Society (1994), ICOMOS (International Council on Monuments and Sites) International Wood Committee Symposium (1996), Rare Breeds Survival Trust (2008), the Museums Association, the Museum of English Rural Life, the Association of Independent Museums, the Architectural Association, University College London Museum Studies Department, the Victoria & Albert Museum, Historic Scotland, and the National Society of Master Thatchers.
Above Frame 2002, the annual conference of the Carpenters' Fellowship.

entered into a Knowledge Transfer Partnership (KTP) agreement with Reading University which provided two fully-supervised research associates, one in history and the other in IT. This work started in October 2005 and underpinned the access project by establishing a body of knowledge and the means to communicate it.

The physical need for new visitor facilities was much more difficult to solve and led to a long series of studies and reports. "One of the museum's most intractable problems is the wide range of visitor numbers, from a dozen on a cold winter's day to 5,000 at the biggest summer events," says Richard Harris. "For a single point of access, parking arrangements would have to be in the area of flat fields on the northern boundary of the site." This was established in a feasibility study by Edward Cullinan Architects in 2004, but was a contentious choice. An outline planning application was submitted and approved in 2006 and, with the support of English Heritage, the museum and the Edward James Foundation commissioned a Landscape Conservation Management Plan for West Dean Park in 2007.

With these studies supporting the new approach, the museum's trustees commissioned a feasibility study and sketch design for new facilities comprising retail, café, ticketing and orientation on a site near the proposed new parking. It was completed in November 2008, but the economic recession led to a re-appraisal, and in 2009–10 new proposals were developed for a series of smaller scale discrete

projects rather than one monolithic solution. One of these is for a new catering facility on the existing lakeside site, and another is to give improved interpretation in small pavilions around the site focusing on specific themes, such as early houses, farms and farmsteads, and woodland. This attracted a £175,000 grant from the DCMS (Department for Culture, Media & Sport)/Wolfson Museums & Galleries Improvement Fund.

While these proposals were being developed, the museum prepared the way by making a series of changes to its use of the site. The layout of events was altered to fit in with the new parking proposals, and the access road was improved. New paths were created to allow a circuit walk to be established, and research carried out to strengthen the museum's understanding of visitor needs. The KTP project established capacity for high quality social history research and distilled ideas about digital resources and communication with visitors. By the end of 2010 – a date that would also see the retirement of Richard Harris – these proposals would be brought together into a plan intended to underpin the museum's development for the years ahead.

The journey from 4 September 1970 has been a long but rich and productive one. As 2010 dawned preparations were under way to celebrate the 40th anniversary of the first public opening of the museum, and the opportunity was taken to compile the history of this remarkable project, to provide a lasting memory of a unique venture.

plumbers' workshop from Newick and dismantling of the hay barn from Ockley

Edward James, the museum's site benefactor, dies at the age of 77. He is buried at St Roche's Arboretum on West Dean Estate

Changes to museum's operational structure, introduced to reflect rapid growth, embrace three trust meetings annually and monthly executive board meetings

Museum hosts its first Rare Breeds Show

Museum takes part in an Association of Independent Museums (AIM) event, *Heritage at Work*, designed to promote independent museums, with a sheep fold,

5

Three Key Personalities

Diana Zeuner

One of the great strengths of the Weald & Downland Open Air Museum has been the clarity of purpose and determination of a small handful of people. Following Roy Armstrong's vision, they have ensured standards of the highest quality in building conservation and restoration, interpretation and education, and the management of a visitor attraction. Without dismissing the huge contribution made by a wider group of people, including trustees, volunteers and staff over the years, there are three who stand out, without whom the museum could quite possibly have languished as merely a regional heritage attraction without the influence and recognition it subsequently attained.

Chris Zeuner
Honorary Curator of Crafts and Craft Equipment 1971-1972, Keeper 1972-1974, Museum Director 1974-2001

The eminent 20th-century cultural commentator and broadcaster Kenneth Hudson was highly supportive of the new breed of independent charitable-trust museums being formed in the early 1970s which were to challenge the museum establishment. At an Association of Independent Museums seminar in Exeter he put his finger on the quality which he felt epitomised those who were running these innovative cultural businesses – "charisma". He was referring to some 10 individuals and Chris Zeuner of the Weald & Downland Open Air Museum was firmly in this group.

In his covering letter to potential supporters of

Chris was an ardent interpreter and would always take advantage of interested groups of visitors to explain and describe.

Southdown sheep and a shepherd's hut outside Guildhall, City of London

The museum grows its largest ever crop of wheat for thatching on site, 20 acres, yielding some 7,000 sheaves

1986 Stevenson collection of farming equipment arrives at museum

Re-erection of the house extension from Reigate. Cattle shed from Goodwood dismantled

The Edward James Foundation agrees to an extension of the museum's boundary by 20 acres

Bayleaf Medieval Farmstead interpretation project begins

Three Key Personalities

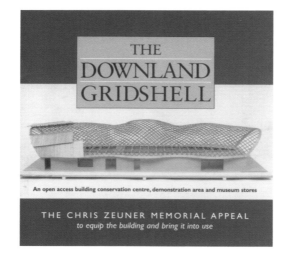

THE DOWNLAND GRIDSHELL

An open access building conservation centre, demonstration area and museum stores

THE CHRIS ZEUNER MEMORIAL APPEAL
to equip the building and bring it into use

the Chris Zeuner Memorial Appeal to raise the final funds for the Downland Gridshell, museum chairman David Tomlinson said the building reminded him very much of Chris: "brave, pioneering and simply a one-off". Cruelly, Chris was never to see his final and most ambitious project completed as he became suddenly and unexpectedly ill and died of cancer aged 55 on 3 January 2001.

But in the previous 27 years of his directorship of the museum he choreographed one of the most inspirational museum projects of the time – an exciting presentation of our built and rural history with no walls, few rules, ever innovative through building conservation developments and

Chris and Roy – walking together to the official opening of the hall from Boarhunt in 1981.

unashamedly commercial and business-like in its approach without ever compromising its academic integrity. Its huge success after only five years of opening, by which time it was attracting some 150,000 visitors annually, brought it the National Heritage Museum of the Year Award; there was a potential pool of some 2,000 other museums to choose from.

Chris was one of the earliest volunteers at the museum. A pupil at Seaford College, near Petworth, he was drawn back to Sussex from his London home at Kew after a short uninspiring period with the Metal Box Company, to learn to teach at Bishop Otter Teacher Training College, Chichester, under the motivating leadership of Betty Murray. He was working as a teacher with special needs pupils on Hayling Island when he first learned of plans for the museum. He was immediately drawn to it; his specialism was rural life and he already had a private collection of rural and agricultural items of his own. No doubt the fact that he possessed a Land Rover and trailer endeared him to Roy in those early days as the loan of suitable equipment at no cost was a pressing need. But the two men soon formed a close bond which was crucial to the successful development of the museum in its first years. At the dedication of a memorial to Chris in June 2002, museum trustee Tim Heymann said: "Chris's relationship with Roy was crucial in the development of the museum. They were like minds having a determination and passion for the subjects of vernacular architecture and rural life and its communication to the public."

In 1971 Chris was appointed honorary curator of crafts and craft equipment, managing the growing collection of rural craft artefacts. The following year he became the museum's first full-time employee as keeper (curator), with overall responsibility for all activity on the museum site, including the re-erection of buildings, administration, and the organisation of volunteers. Then in April 1974, at the age of 28, as a result of what John Lowe called "his devoted service to the museum" he was appointed as its first full-time director. By 1976 museum chairman Geoffrey Godber was describing him as "a human dynamo". He proceeded to develop the project with "passion and energy", reflected in the message on his memorial.

1987 Re-erection of the house extension from Reigate and the cattle shed from Goodwood. Whittaker's Cottages are dismantled.

The museum raises £100,000 in a year for

the Development Fund – an extremely large sum at this period

Nigel Stephens, senior partner of Whiteheads Estate Agents, becomes museum chairman

Marjorie Hallam retires as honorary librarian

Bob Holman appointed museum gardener

The 'Great Storm' hits the museum, with the loss of a number of trees. Staff help

Chris's interest in history had its origins in his father's work as a distinguished archaeologist at the University of London Institute of Archaeology. He was born in 1945, the younger son of Frederick and Ilse (Etta) Zeuner who, with the onset of Nazi activity (Etta was Jewish), had escaped Germany for England in 1933 with the assistance of the British scientific community. In 1946 the Institute offered Frederick the new post of Professor of Environmental Archaeology. In addition to publishing more than 200 papers during his working life he wrote three books, the most important of which are *Dating the Past* (1946) and *A History of Domesticated Animals* (1963), the latter still regarded as a seminal work on the subject. This interest resonates completely with his son's later focus on farming and livestock, further nurtured during summer-time archaeological digs in South Devon where the young Christopher stayed with his father on a local farm, helping the farmer with his daily livestock duties. In later life Chris was often to meet former students of his father on their visits to the museum; they would rarely miss the opportunity of seeking him out and sharing the memory of Professor Zeuner's inspirational teaching.

Sir Neil Cossons, former chairman of English Heritage and director of The Science Museum, contributing an obituary to *The Independent* in January 2001, said:

> *Chris Zeuner combined immense charm with visionary passion, an unswerving insistence on excellence and relentless attention to detail. Woe betide anyone who tied up a gate with blue baler twine. He was tough on his trustees, as all good museum directors should be, when he sensed compromise was in the air. But they knew inspiration when they saw it and gave him the backing he needed to create at Singleton a truly outstanding museum.*

Jonathan Bryant, a former chairman of the Association of Independent Museums, wrote in *The Guardian* in 2001: "A healthy preference for action over committee work ensured that Zeuner was a vigorous and forthright member of any activity to which he allocated time and energy".

Chris's hands-on approach to the task of developing and managing the museum was

obvious from the start, welcomed whole-heartedly, and was instrumental in enabling the museum's many achievements. When he was appointed director, he was described as being as capable of driving a tractor as of steering the organisation from an office. He felt a 'bottom-up' style of management was essential to what was ultimately a rural attraction, and followed what West Dean agent, Tim Heymann, who also practiced it, called "management by walking about". Staff and volunteers were drawn into the heart of the museum's development, becoming part of what former senior warden Keith Bickmore has called "the museum family". Empire-building and bureaucracy were not Chris's way: he led from the front, never deviating from the museum's purpose.

He also developed what Richard Harris described as: "a formidable ability to identify and extract money from a wide range of donors". His "fearsome tenacity was often masked by a charming informality of style," Richard recalled in the museum magazine about their 25-year partnership. "Chris always involved himself in practical matters … His speed and efficiency were legendary – any request was dealt with immediately, however busy he might be with other things."

Chris was interviewed by the media countless times, taking every opportunity to promote the museum. In a film made in 1992, *Kingsbury Square*, he was asked about the museum's philosophy. He painted a picture of the buildings at the museum as failures of the preservation and planning systems. Yet their importance was that they "shed light on buildings which are on their original sites and that

Above *Preparing to unload one of the encapsulated walls of the Redford pugmill house.*

Below *Livestock and archaeology – two life-long interests reflected from Chris' father's books,* A History of Domesticated Animals *and* Dating the Past.

clear up fallen trees off-site in the local area
Jon Roberts becomes honorary librarian

1988 Formal Collecting Policy adopted
Re-erection of the medieval barn from

Cowfold and the cattle shed from Goodwood
Visit of HRH Princess Alexandra
Chris Zeuner becomes chairman of the Association of Independent Museums

(until 1991) and president of the European Association of Open Air Museums (until 1992)
Geoffrey Godber becomes the museum's president

Above *Chris and Diana Zeuner at the Association of Independent Museums (AIM) Conference at Ellesmere Port in 1991.*

Below *Working horses became a deep interest; here Chris is with the museum's horse and timber wagon at an event on the Isle of Dogs.*

enabling it to be shared with others. "This is the key to what has been done at the museum over the last 20 years or so. Our founder believed the key to conservation was knowledge. We treasure things that we understand – we very rarely care for things we don't understand. People come and enjoy the museum and are inspired by what they see. They then look at their own buildings or others and understand."

As a teacher Chris always gave education a high priority at the museum and in 1990 the first steps were taken in the establishment of the Joint Centre for Heritage Conservation and Management, working with Bournemouth University as a partner. Out of this came the MSc in Timber Building Conservation, taught by Richard Harris for the university at the museum, and an extensive lifelong learning programme which was ahead of its time and remains one of the best examples of adult education in museums.

Chris's family life and the museum were completely intertwined. He had met Diana Sharp, who had volunteered following an inspirational meeting with Roy Armstrong at a college lecture at the age of 18, and they married in 1975. Diana's volunteering was to span all areas of the museum, from thatching the recreated woodman's bothy to making paths and planting trees, to car parking and site tidiness, house stewarding, interpretation and livestock care. As a journalist and writer, her skills were used to write news releases and exhibition texts, as well as undertaking photography, and in the production of the twice-yearly museum magazine which she still edits. Diana is also editor of the Association of Independent Museums' bi-monthly magazine. Daughters Francesca and Anna grew up at the museum, and were soon deeply involved in it too. Working draught horses had become an important element of interpretation at the museum and in 1987 Chris and Diana became joint publishers of the only specialist magazine in the UK covering working horses, *Heavy Horse World*, which Diana continues to produce. Her books, *Working Horse Manual* and *Heavy Horses* are sold in the museum shop. After Chris's death and to ensure the continuation of the heavy horse stables at the museum, Diana undertook its part-time management for two years working alongside a team of volunteers led by Derek Hilton.

go on being used, undergoing change and contributing to the economic and social life of the community they belong to". The process of dismantling had allowed the museum to learn about the buildings, using the disciplines of the archaeologist or the pathologist, building up a fund of knowledge, adding to our understanding and

Bakehouse from Newdigate and forge from Great Bookham dismantled

Neil Wilkins becomes the museum's miller

More than 5,000 people visit the Rare

Breeds Show in July, a record for a special event

1989 Bayleaf Medieval Farmstead research and furnishing project and *Historic Farms & Farmsteads* exhibition opened

Museum's first historic garden opens at Bayleaf farmhouse

Museum wins the Times/Shell Community Museum of the Year Award

Museum receives record visitor numbers, 186,000

Chris's interests and influence extended beyond the museum itself. He was a founder member of the Association of Independent Museums (AIM), formed in 1977 to represent the new type of museums sprouting all over Britain, serving as treasurer and chairman. He was deeply involved with the Association of European Open Air Museums, where his ability to speak German and natural affinity with the country of his parents won him many friends among museum colleagues; he became its president for four years in 1988. From 1996 to 1998 he was institutional vice president of the Museums Association, to which he was elected a Fellow in 1997. In 1990 he was appointed OBE for his services to museums, and was delighted to receive an honorary MA from Southampton University in 1998.

> " *Chris's style of management was hands-on. On a typical day he would take Rufus, his dog, on an early morning walk around the site, and notice anything out of place. At 7.00am he would meet the site staff and discuss plans for the day. I would often arrive at 8.00am after a drive from London, and before I had even turned off the ignition he would be at my car window with something urgent to discuss. Later in the day he might have an appointment in London and would hurtle up to take the train from Haslemere, then use the evening at home to finish the day's work and phone calls. He hardly ever seemed tired. He had his ear permanently to the ground and seemed to know everything before anybody else.* "
>
> **Richard Harris,**
> **then research director, 2001**

In 1981 he became a founding trustee of The Vivat Trust, which rescues derelict historic buildings and finds new uses for them, including holiday lettings; he was its chairman twice. He lectured on heritage interpretation and museum management in the UK, Europe and the USA, and was a member of several national working parties on museum matters. He became a trustee

of the Museum of Kent Life in 1992. In 1999 he was instrumental in promoting a re-consideration of the role of rural life and open air museums which led to a Museums & Galleries Commission report, and in turn to a study which was eventually to launch the Rural Museums Network.

Chris steered the museum through two major new initiatives as the century closed. With the advent of the Heritage Lottery Fund (HLF) money became potentially available to bring building conservation and the rural life collections onto the museum site. The chance was taken to commission an innovative new building from one of the country's foremost architects, and the museum was successful in receiving one of the earliest HLF grants. Then in 1998 the museum became one of the few (at that time less than 50) museums throughout England to become designated for the pre-eminence of its collections, opening up a new source of funding primarily directed at the care and interpretation of historic artefacts.

Richard Harris wrote that in the last three weeks of his working life at the museum Chris "worked with amazing energy and focus, spurred by his illness". At his funeral, Chichester Cathedral was packed with some 800 people. His obituary appeared in all the national daily newspapers. A light had gone out at the museum, where his dedication had been absolute and his imagination and vigour had known no bounds; it had become his life's work. His career as museum director was commemorated with a portrait commissioned from local artist Annie Rolls (which hangs near the portrait of Roy Armstrong in the upper hall from Crawley), a slate memorial on an oak plinth made by Roger Champion, and three hornbeams – representing one of his favourite trees – planted close to the Downland Gridshell.

Chris Zeuner, far left, attending a committee meeting of the Association of European Open Air Museums in Romania in 1992. With him, from left are, Jan Vaessen, Carl Ingmer Johannessen, Gunnar Elfstrom, Claus Ahrens and Stefan Baumeier.

Chris Zeuner's memorial overlooking the breathtaking view which he cherished.

	1990	
John Warren relinquishes his post as honorary architect	The museum's collections move to the new stores at the Charlton Barns complex	Bob Powell appointed curator
House from Godalming dismantled	Chris Zeuner appointed OBE	Re-erection of the brick-drying shed from Petersfield
First Food Fair held	Heather Champion retires (but continues to volunteer)	Richard Pailthorpe appointed as chairman of Chichester Visitors Group

Richard Harris, during the removal of Winkhurst to its new site at the museum.

Richard at the re-erection of Poplar Cottage in 1998.

Richard Harris

Research Officer 1977–1979, Research Director 1979–2001, Museum Director 2001–2010

The reputation of the museum for the quality of its historic building interpretations and reconstructions rests largely with Richard Harris, whose interest and work in building restoration and repair makes him one of the country's leading specialists in the field.

Working closely with Roger Champion as master carpenter, and steered by founder Roy Armstrong until his death and Chris Zeuner as museum director, the individual building restoration projects undertaken by Richard have attracted wide attention from others in the field, notably English Heritage and professional architects, engineers and commercial timber-framers.

In addition, the priority placed on education at the museum and Richard Harris's own career teaching his subject has led to the museum becoming a notable provider of practical training in its fields of interest, especially in timber building conservation, with Richard Harris teaching Bournemouth University's MSc in the subject on the museum site from 1995.

In the early 1970s, after reading economics at Cambridge, Richard studied for an AADip at the Architectural Association. At the same time he was working as a volunteer for Avoncroft Museum of Buildings at Bromsgrove, Worcestershire, which had been launched a fraction earlier than the Weald & Downland Open Air Museum and was chaired by Richard's father, managing director of the family firm, LG Harris & Co, manufacturers of Harris brushes. Richard was gaining experience as architectural assistant to Freddie Charles, Avoncroft's architect who specialised in the conservation of timber buildings, and with whom Richard had first worked on the vernacular buildings of Coventry. In 1973 he went on an extended tour of European and Scandinavian open air museums, meeting the directors and developing his ideas.

Meanwhile Chris Zeuner was volunteering at the Weald & Downland Open Air Museum, and they met a couple of times at conferences. However, it was not until September 1974 that they came to know each other better at the European Open Air Museums Association Conference at Graz, Austria.

Later that year Richard met Roy Armstrong at a timber seminar at the Institute for Advanced Architectural Studies in York. Also lecturing on that occasion was the eminent vernacular architecture historian Cecil Hewett. Richard was fascinated by Roy, and at the course dinner they sat next to each other locked in conversation for

Publication of *Weald & Downland Open Air Museum: The Founding Years 1965-1970* by Kim Leslie
More than three million people have now visited the museum

1991 Joint Centre for Heritage Conservation and Management launched in partnership with Bournemouth University
Museum wins Gateway Interpret Britain Award for Bayleaf Medieval

Farmstead project
Re-erection of the medieval house from Sole Street, and opening of the new catering facility

the whole meal, speaking mostly about European open air museums. The next time Roy, Chris and Richard met was at the launch of the Hereford & Worcester Architecture Record Group, which Richard founded.

Early in 1975, Chris and Roy asked Richard to undertake a study of the timbers of a hall from Boarhunt, recently dismantled. Richard had just finished his studies so it was perhaps natural that the prospect of his working for the museum arose.

As founder, Roy Armstrong was given the title 'research director', but in 1977 he was ready to pass it on. When Chris and Roy interviewed Richard for the post, Richard remembers he was not required to appear before a selection panel. "Chris and Roy talked to me sitting on the grass, just below Hambrook barn. Roy was chiefly concerned about the long-term future – would I maintain and protect his vision? But Chris gently reminded him that no-one can be expected to sign away the rest of their life. The irony was, of course, that we both did exactly that."

Not everyone on the museum's council of management agreed about the proposed appointment, Richard remembers, adding: "Chris had made his mind up and I was treated to my first experience of his determination and powers of persuasion working in my favour". Richard was appointed assistant to Roy in his role as research

director, on a one-day-per-week basis, the rest of his time being employed in teaching (for Birmingham University's Department of Extramural Studies and the Architectural Association), adult education, writing and consultancy. In 1979 Richard formally became research director.

On technical matters Richard and Chris worked together with "complete mutual understanding".

Presenting the Duke of Gloucester with a framed drawing of the hall from Boarhunt, at the official opening of the building in 1981.

Above left *Richard drawing Cowfold barn, and* **above** *in Longport farmhouse.*

Opening of Historic Brickwork exhibition in brick-drying shed from Petersfield

Sir James Waddell becomes museum president

Dr Alan Hayes becomes museum chairman

The museum publishes *The Southdown Sheep*, by Valerie Porter, to mark the centenary of the Southdown Sheep Society

Museum Shire horse, Rosie, produces her first foal, Bayleaf Primrose

1992 Roy Armstrong receives honorary degree of Doctor of Letters from Sussex University at the age of 90

Discovering Timber-Framed Buildings, *which has sold some 130,000 copies to date and has never been out of print.*

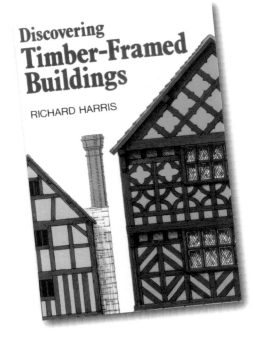

In the pugmill house from Redford in 1991 with Cecil Waters, the former foreman of the Causeway Brickworks, Petersfield. The museum's brick-drying shed, opened that year, came from this site.

Richard's first projects were Boarhunt and the Lavant building, both difficult as he had not seen them on their original sites. "For the first few years we seemed to be doing more dismantling than reconstruction," he says, a factor which reflected the need to rescue threatened buildings at that period.

In fact the museum was developing apace, with a constant flow of re-erections on site, amounting to one a year or one every other year in the period between the museum's opening and the end of the century. Dismantled buildings joined a 'queue' and very few were re-erected immediately after their arrival at the museum. A breakthrough came in April 1980 when the museum dismantled the house from Walderton. The BBC filmed the project for its *Chronicle* programme, so the repair and reconstruction process began immediately and the exhibit was opened by Neil Cossons in July 1982. "For the first time, we were able to spread our wings and invent something new and fresh, based around the idea of displaying the middle room of the house in two periods, the front half medieval and the rear half post-medieval. We expected to be criticised, but the project received mostly praise." It was through contacts with the BBC *Chronicle* team that Richard met his future wife, Judy Rich.

As research director, Richard's role incorporated overseeing the technical aspects of dismantling and re-erection of exhibits; research, planning and design of interpretative displays; undertaking lectures and conferences, and editing and producing the museum's guidebook. He was working across a number of disciplines, incorporating traditional carpentry techniques, manufacture and use of traditional building materials, building recording and analysis techniques, indexing and classification of building records, techniques of repair and conservation of timber-framed buildings, display and interpretation of buildings in museums, the theoretical basis for studies in vernacular architecture, and medieval and Tudor furnishing and vernacular interiors.

In the early 1980s when microcomputers first became available to hobbyists and businesses, Richard's enthusiasm for IT developed apace. He wrote his first program on a Sinclair ZX80, moving to an Apple II+ system that was installed at the museum. Taking advantage of the needs of the BBC *Chronicle* programme, he produced 25 simple line drawings showing a changing perspective view of the building which was incorporated into the film. Today such animations are commonplace, but then they were ground-breaking.

Working four days a week at the museum he pursued freelance work as well, including the

The museum is registered under the Museums & Galleries Commission's Registration Scheme to ensure high standards of museum work

Longport farmhouse from the Channel

Tunnel terminal site at Newington, Kent is dismantled, providing a solution to the need to improve visitor facilities

The European Home exhibition opens as part of the European Arts Festival,

celebrating the traditions of European domestic rural architecture

Getting to Grips, a hands-on exhibition exploring traditional building materials and techniques, opens

dismantling and recording of Elland Old Hall, Yorkshire, for the West Yorkshire Archaeological Unit; consultancy for the repair of the Hoop & Grapes, Aldgate, London, for Haslemere Estates, and advice on the reconstruction of the Globe Theatre, London, working with McCurdy & Co. He ran courses at the Architectural Association on vernacular architecture and held extramural and WEA (Workers' Educational Association) classes in Worcestershire and Sussex. Six weeks in 1982 were spent as visiting professor at Louisiana State University followed by a tour of US historic houses and museums and, at the Ulster Office, Richard presented a scheme for the relocation of a farmstead to a proposed new Museum of American Frontier Culture in West Virginia.

Many of his publications ran alongside his work at the museum, reflecting the research undertaken for exhibitions and displays. Examples include *Recording Timber-Framed Buildings for Buildings Archaeology: Applications in Practice* (Institute of Field Archaeologists) and *The Shallow Screen: Open Air Museums and the Heritage Crisis* (Institute for Advanced Architectural Studies, York). He was also involved in developing exhibitions, including *Traditional Building Materials* and *The European Home*. But the publication for which he is widest known is *Discovering Timber-Framed Buildings* for Shire Publications (first edition 1978), which has been published in three editions and has never been out of print. One of that company's best-selling titles, some 130,000 copies have been sold to date.

"It's the sort of job you could not ever dream could exist," he told *Ham and High,* the local newspaper for his London home in Primrose Hill. "It's very varied — from writing computer programmes for indexing the museum's artefacts to climbing on scaffolding to examine structure, to deciphering medieval documents."

Richard was embarking on a pioneering field of study within vernacular architecture. The house from Walderton and later Longport farmhouse

provided opportunities for innovation in the research and interpretation of traditional buildings. He described Walderton as "a textbook case of total archaeology, the most successful and satisfying job I have had".

When Chris Zeuner died, Richard Harris was appointed museum director. An operations director was appointed at the same time, splitting the role for the first time and redefining it. The new administration made a range of organisational changes, increasing staff numbers and expanding their portfolios. An immediate priority was to complete the Downland Gridshell project, and other initiatives during the first years of the new century included the further development of the lifelong learning programme with a new MSc in Building Conservation introduced, and the completion of a number of designation challenge fund projects. On Richard's retirement in 2010 he was appointed a visiting professor to the University of Chichester, recognition of the developing partnership between the museum and the university.

Richard with conservator Deborah Carthy inspecting painting on the fireplace stonework from the 17th-century town house from Reigate.

Death of Alderman James Farmer, the first chairman of the museum's council of management

1993 (19 October) Roy Armstrong dies at home in Storrington, aged 91

Cottage from Lodsworth dismantled

Museums & Galleries Commission visits museum during one of its regional tours

History Re-enactment Workshop begins annual visits, continuing for 10 years

Folk singer Bob Copper and his family stage *The Four Men* in tribute to Sussex author Hilaire Belloc

'Tuesday Gang' of volunteers established to work on practical site projects

Roger Champion at work on the timber frame of Longport farmhouse.

Repairing the roof of Longport farmhouse in the workshop at Charlton Barns.

Roger Champion
Master Carpenter 1968-2003

Roger Champion famously learned about the embryonic museum project from a publicity leaflet that caught his eye in a litter bin at Stedham, near Midhurst in summer 1968 when he was throwing away an ice-cream wrapper. "A bloody daft idea," he thought, but nevertheless penned a letter to Roy Armstrong asking if there was anything he could do to help.

Roger was a trained instrument and tool-maker with aspirations to carpentry. But before he began making furniture for sale, he took three years out, intending to tour the world by bicycle. He abandoned the bike in Afghanistan and then hitch-hiked to India, Nepal, Indonesia, Malaya, Australia and New Zealand before returning home to Easebourne. By now it was November and Roy's response was to suggest he should come along to the site of Pendean farmhouse, just down the road near Midhurst, which was in the process of being dismantled.

Roger was soon smitten, and spent his first months at the museum with no pay helping on numerous site jobs including fencing and path-laying. By April the following year German carpenter Gunolt Greiner was on site preparing to restore Winkhurst, the first of the saved buildings to be re-erected. Roger's first job was to make pegs for the joints. He had never tackled carpentry on this scale before and learned Greiner's techniques as he went, especially his central philosophy that new timber should never be made to look old: no attempt at 'distressing'. Modern sawmill marks were perfectly acceptable in a restoration. Indeed it was important to the integrity of the structure and in increasing people's understanding.

Roger went on to repair the frame of the Catherington treadwheel in the yard next to his mother's home in Easebourne. On the building's original site he discovered, while sifting through rubbish thrown down the well over centuries, the wooden bowling ball he was to fashion into a mallet, which has been one of his most valued tools ever since.

The majority of the museum's timber-framed buildings followed. With his relative inexperience, Roger was astonished to be asked by Roy Armstrong to re-erect Bayleaf farmhouse, which was to become the jewel in the crown of the museum's exhibits. "I had no particular difficulty doing Bayleaf, although there are some repairs I now would have done differently, or not at all. That is one of the disadvantages of being in the same place for 30-odd years: you're surrounded by your mistakes, or at least, different ways of doing things."

Roger's humour and anecdotes rapidly became a part of the museum's special ethos. Whilst dismantling Hambrook barn, an old man went past on his bike. His uncle who had re-thatched the barn had found a bayonet wrapped in a French

1994 Opening of renewed Plumbing & Masonry exhibition in Court Barn

Nigel Stephens becomes museum chairman, taking on the task for the second time

Lord Nathan becomes museum president

MSc in Building Conservation launched in partnership with Bournemouth University (with further Masters' courses launched in 1998 and 2008)

Chris Zeuner joins other charity representatives on a sponsored walk through the 31-mile Channel Tunnel, to raise funds for Longport farmhouse

flag. Sure enough Roger came across the bayonet wrapped in what could well have been a flag in the thatch. "We took it back with us and put it in the new thatch on the barn at the museum."

As time went on Roger adapted Greiner's techniques and developed his own. Under the influence of vernacular architecture historian Reg Mason, he began to save more timber and make more repairs rather than introduce replacements. Over the years he was to experiment with a variety of repair techniques which placed the museum at the forefront of timber-frame conservation and, along with its teaching activities, led to its high reputation in the field.

Roger married a fellow museum employee, and one of its greatest supporters, Heather Jackson. A former teacher and one of the earliest volunteers, Heather undertook a number of important roles at the museum. In 1974 she was appointed information officer and then education officer, becoming senior assistant to the director in 1978 and later, effectively, curator. She became increasingly interested in the conservation of historic artefacts in the collections, and through the late 1970s this work took up more and more of her time. Heather was responsible for the cleaning, numbering, cataloguing and labelling of thousands of items, including the important Plewis wheelwrighting collection, between March 1975 and January 1990. She also undertook research into the history of some of the building exhibits, including the West Wittering school, and supervised the move of the artefacts to the new stores at Charlton Barns.

Heather's interests in the natural world were a constant draw, and her love and knowledge of bee-keeping also benefited the museum, where she kept several hives, demonstrated bee-skep making and ran courses in hive management. After retiring from full-time work in February 1990 to pursue her ever-increasing honey production, she became a part-time shop supervisor as well as a volunteer.

An enormous asset on any building dismantling project, Heather developed a close understanding of the attention to detail required in taking a historic building apart, cataloguing finds and building parts systematically. She also had a prodigious strength, moving heavy timbers around with her slight frame with apparent ease. Back on

Heather Champion demonstrating bee skep-making.

site her knowledge and appreciation of the task ahead was invaluable in assisting Roger and the team with building re-erections. When the bakehouse from Newdigate, Surrey, was dismantled, Chris Zeuner chose Heather to lead the project.

Her very considerable contribution to the museum came to an end in December 2003,

Roger and Heather Champion pictured during the re-erection of the house from North Cray in 1984.

1995 Re-erection and inauguration of Longport farmhouse as the museum's new entrance facility and shop
Lyn Armstrong dies
Richard Pailthorpe leaves for a new post managing Syon Park

Richard Pailthorpe and Diana Zeuner revise and edit Roy Armstrong's *A History of Sussex* (fourth edition, published by Phillimore & Co)
Sue Shave joins the staff in the new post of interpretation officer, responsible for

interpretation and education
'Dovetail' arts programme launched

1996 David Tomlinson becomes museum chairman

Making oak furniture for Pendean farmhouse in 2001.

medieval and Tudor furniture enhance the interpretation of the historic buildings and draw much appreciation and social understanding from visitors. Between work on buildings and furniture-making Roger also undertook numerous general carpentry tasks around the site, from the repair of wooden agricultural machinery to shelving in the museum shop. After retirement he continues to undertake projects at the institution he had played such a large part in developing.

So was it such "a bloody daft idea" after all? "I think it's been worth doing," says Roger. "You would think we might be a relatively large organisation doing the sort of work we do. But we're a relatively small organisation, as regards finances and abilities to do things. Maybe we're a bit too ambitious. On the other hand, but for the likes of Chris [Zeuner] and Richard [Harris] we wouldn't have achieved what we have."

He might have added his own name to that short list. Roger was to become a consummate carpenter whose work has left its own distinctive mark of quality on the buildings at the museum. He brought a dedication, an idiosyncratic sense of humour, an appreciation of economy in the use of resources and most of all, an intuitive understanding of historic buildings and their builders which reached down to him through the centuries.

when sadly she died from cancer, aged 57. She had taken up bellringing three years earlier and on the day of her funeral a quarter peal was rung in her memory from Chichester Cathedral belltower. The museum had lost a warm-hearted and generous member of its team.

It was not just carpentry but Roger's great interest in joinery that was to prove especially significant for the museum. His carefully replicated

Roger erecting his scale model of North Cray hall house in the market square. The real building is to the right, out of this picture.

Visit of HRH The Prince of Wales
Chapel from Ovingdean dismantled

1997 Re-erection of Whittaker's Cottages from Ashtead

Museum celebrates 30 years since its launch in 1967
Museum wins Heritage Education Trust Sandford Award for excellence in education

Corporate plan re-states and enlarges on the museum's objectives
Virginia Lyon, trustee and former chairman of the Friends, dies

6

The Museum's 'Life-blood' – its Volunteers

Diana Zeuner

The museum's remarkable band of volunteers is often referred to as its 'life-blood', for without them the project could never have got off the ground or prospered.

Many of the new breed of independent museums of the 1970s relied totally or mostly on volunteers – the museums themselves had sprung from grass-roots preservation movements; people who were determined that significant elements of their history should not disappear forever.

People volunteer for many reasons and come from all walks of life. Some specialise in particular aspects of the museum's work, others are happy to help wherever they are needed. Some volunteer occasionally, others for most days of the week. Some practically live here.

Today volunteering is closely managed, albeit in a friendly way; a number of grant-giving funds require information on the value to museums of their volunteer force. In 2003 the museum estimated that its volunteers clocked up some 50,000 hours of work a year, worth up to half a million pounds.

Ted Nash, one of the museum's most stalwart volunteers, helped with anything; here he takes a break on top of the rick during steam threshing.

Chris Zeuner elected as institutional vice president of the Museums Association

Museum makes two Heritage Lottery Fund bids, for Poplar Cottage, and for a building conservation centre to be "housed in a greenwood timber structure"

Timber-framing from scratch annual workshop launched

Timber crane from Privett dismantled

1998 Museum accorded designated status in new government scheme to recognise pre-eminent collections

Chris Zeuner receives an honorary MA from the University of Southampton

Right *Volunteer Michael Farr with a group of school children on the bank above Poplar Cottage.*

Below left *A reconstructed woodcraft area was the centre of some of the earliest volunteer activity, with thatching and hurdle-making among the crafts on display. In the photograph is Jon Finch. Others involved with this project included two of this book's authors, Diana Zeuner (then Sharp) and Carol Brinson (then Hawkins), as well as Heather Champion (then Jackson) and Matti Denton, writer of the diary quoted in this book.*

Below right *It takes dedication to work as a volunteer with the museum's livestock. This is Ros Hart with the museum's working horses, Donald and Gym.*

> **❝** The morning begins with a sleeping museum about to be coaxed to life. The warden walks past the doors of Hambrook barn to the pathway cutting across the grass and waits quietly, looking down into the valley. Slowly a trickle of volunteers flows along each little path heading west to their day's destination. The warden goes unnoticed until a hand in the distance shoots up in joyful greeting and news that you are on the hill drifts across to all. The museum family has gathered and is awake for another day. **❞**
>
> **Charlie Thwaites, head warden and visitor and volunteer services manager, 2009**

But at the beginning of the museum's life, volunteering developed much more responsively. At first people interested in this pioneering new project, or who had been inspired by Roy Armstrong's and Kim Leslie's many lectures on the subject, turned up on site to help. They created paths, planted trees and built fences, dismantled buildings, moved timber and materials, donated artefacts to the museum site and stores – and spent much time in discussion and planning for the future. In 1973 Pam West, one of the earliest volunteers with her husband, Norman, was appointed to the museum's council of management to represent the volunteers.

One of the primary roles for volunteers has always been 'manning' the buildings, and these early volunteers were known as 'stewards'. Their task was to talk to visitors about the building they were in,

the earliest form of interpretation on the site.

In 1973 – then a record year for visitors (111,042) – museum warden Doug Bryant drew attention to the "heavy demands" made on the museum's embryonic infrastructure by the greatly increased influx of visitors:

Many hard and hectic hours were put in by stewards manning the ticket office and the shop, and those on the equally onerous but vital work of car parking. On a considerable number of days we had upwards of 1,500 visitors and were forced to use overflow parking, but happily managed to maintain smooth and efficient control.

Museum receives £250,000 legacy from the estate of Mrs Wilhemina Minet, enabling it to launch an Endowment Fund

Museum wins Interpret Britain Award for Formal Education Provision

West Sussex Countryside Studies Trust of which the museum is a partner, wins Sandford Award for Education

Diana Rowsell appointed training co-ordinator and Bob Easson appointed visitor services manager (formerly senior warden)

1999 Re-erection of Poplar Cottage as a memorial to Roy Armstrong

Mike Wall employed as collections manager under Designated Museums Challenge Fund scheme

Glazing & Leaded Lights exhibition opened

As the organisation of volunteers became more formalised an association was set up for them, with lectures and social events, and trips to other historic sites such as the one to the Tamar Valley in 1973. An early organiser of tours, mostly for the Friends of which he was at one time honorary secretary, was Bernard Johnson, Roy Armstrong's neighbour at Storrington.

Volunteers have a close relationship with the visitor services manager, or senior warden, as the post used to be called, and successive postholders have made an art of organising volunteer rotas, understanding the many different characters and personalities and their likes and dislikes, and developing an appreciation of their value both to the museum and to each other.

Doug Bryant was the first museum warden; he and his wife Marjorie were vital to the smooth running of the opening of the museum and they developed a close friendship with the early volunteers. They also ran the shop in the Littlehampton granary. In 1975 Alf Bryden, a retired carpenter, became Doug's assistant, remaining in that post until 1982 and continuing to volunteer for a further 10 years. Someone who could be relied upon to turn up in any weather or circumstance — "We never close!" he said during snowy conditions in 1978 — his carpentry skills were also much in demand. In particular he made scale models of the buildings displayed regularly in the museum's publicity caravan at shows.

In 1983 Doug retired, and a former police inspector arrived for interview. Keith Bickmore became senior warden and shop manager and, 27 years later, is still involved at the museum. Keith had been the prosecution inspector at Chichester

All hands on deck for the Rare Breeds Show. Jean Piggott and Ann Allen collating results in the secretary's tent.

> " Sunday 10 May. Susan and I worked together and alone all day at the woodcraft site. We managed to get two logs into position for use as seats for the public when the museum opens, which won't be long now. Sunday 23 May. I notice it hasn't taken but two weeks for someone to remove the two seats that Susan and I placed by the woodcraft. I wonder why they have been removed — perhaps they didn't realise how much toil and sweat went into that job. It was on Roy's instructions that they were placed in that position. "
>
> **Matti Denton's diary, 1971**

Reg Knight undertook a wide variety of voluntary roles over many years at the museum — here he is helping visitors experience daubing.

Pat Wilkins, steward and mother of miller Neil Wilkins, with a school group at Bayleaf farmhouse in the late 1980s.

Alf Bryden, assistant warden for seven years, outside Titchfield market hall.

Magistrates Court as well as being licensing and gaming inspector and in charge of the special constabulary. It was not long before his wife joined him. Keith and Beryl, a WPC, had met at West End Central Police Station, then the busiest police station in the western world. Beryl's activities included helping with car parking and ticket sales, with the horses and the harvest, in the mill and helping Keith open the exhibits. She gave guided tours to blind and partially-sighted groups,

became a Saturday shop supervisor and organised flower arrangements for weddings and daffodils into 800 bunches each year for Mothering Sunday.

"Little did I know then what I was taking on," says Keith of his first days. "The museum was still in its infancy with very little in the way of facilities for the administrative staff. The offices were in a portacabin and Chris Zeuner's office was in the nearby Goodwood granary where my interview took place. The shop was located on the ground floor of the building from Lavant. We had a very wet spring in 1983 and I wondered if I had done the right thing. But the sun eventually shone, and I stayed."

Keith's arrival coincided with a period when the museum was attracting very large numbers of visitors, some 180,000 a year, many responding to the BBC *Chronicle* programme on the dismantling and re-erection of the house from Walderton. "The numbers of school and college visits were also very high with daily numbers in the 500s and sometimes higher. On one occasion we had 800 in 18 coaches."

As senior warden, Keith's duties included the opening and closing of all exhibits and the lighting of fires in the houses. "This meant an

Richard Harris appointed museum director
Gail Kittle appointed operations director
Museum wins another Sandford Award from the Heritage Education Trust

Nationwide foot-and-mouth outbreak causes closure of the museum for two months

2002 Downland Gridshell opened by Sir Neil Cossons, and Chris Zeuner's

memorial dedicated
Julian Bell appointed curator. His first task is to move the collections into the Gridshell store
Re-siting and re-interpretation of

early start with a very fast run-round of the site in time to get back to the ticket offices to receive the volunteers and to greet and park the coaches," says Keith. "It was before we had the luxury of radios which meant a lot of walking and running to communicate messages, especially when the overflow car parks were in use." The ticket offices were in wooden kiosks at the entrance to the car parks where every car stopped and visitors were welcomed to the museum and paid their entrance fee.

Keith and Beryl Bickmore.

supply of refreshments for staff and volunteers across the site and he and Beryl, who have represented the museum for many years at the annual distribution of publicity leaflets to hotels and tourist attractions, have also manned publicity stands at shows.

The 1994 move of the offices, shop and entrance point to Longport farmhouse was a major change. The kiosks became redundant, with all visitors parking first and then paying their entrance fee. In 1998 Keith retired from his post, but remained involved, acting as assistant warden and running the shop until Paul Maxted took over in 2002, and eventually retiring from wardening duties in 2007. He continues to organise the

Keith's dedication to the museum, his natural eye for potential challenges and his instinctive nurturing of friendship with the volunteers, provided a crucial and steady rock for the museum at the time of its greatest development. For many years his assistant was Frank Knights, who became an indispensable member of the team, with his wife, Christine, eventually being appointed shop supervisor.

The main rota for volunteer stewards was drawn up to ensure there were as many people as possible manning the buildings and able to answer visitors' questions. But there is plenty of work for volunteers who prefer something more active.

> " *I was still commuting to Sandhurst and would look out for my first glimpse of Winkhurst through the trees on my way home. I was able to spend weekends helping Chris and Diana Zeuner do whatever was on at the time; tree planting, wood stacking, scrub clearing and much else. From March 1978 I was free, and soon involved in all the jobs available to amateurs. I can claim many of the original litter bins; getting them up the stairs from my cellar was the most difficult part of the job. Some of my bell yokes were still being worn by the museum's flock until recently. I've welcomed visitors in all the buildings. I've frozen in Hambrook barn, supervised young tilers in the hands-on exhibition. I've spent hours in Pendean. I've watched children galore posing for their photos on the garderobe in Bayleaf. I've listened to the electric man in Walderton thanking an empty room for listening more times than I can easily count. I've taken guided tours and had letters of thanks from children and I've even written to schools congratulating them on the behaviour of their pupils. There were days downstairs in Crawley which were so cold that we kept our feet in cardboard boxes during our book cataloguing tasks. But my main job for many years was the old ticket office, situated at the entrance to the car park. I was there on the day when there were six inches of snow and four visitors. It is I who have been the winner from my involvement with the museum. I owe a great debt to so many who have made my retirement into the happiest and most fulfilled part of my life. "*
>
> **Brigadier Walter Greenway, 2006**

Winkhurst Tudor kitchen completed (Designation Challenge Fund)

Furnishing and re-presentation of Pendean farmhouse completed (Designation Challenge Fund)

2003 'Gift Aid' on visitor admissions introduced

Roger Champion retires (but continues to

undertake some part-time carpentry work)

Heather Champion dies at the age of 57

Forward plan 2003-07 identifies need for 'Orientation Gallery'

With an increasing need for a more formal structure for volunteers tackling practical tasks, the 'Tuesday Gang' was set up in 1993, led by John Herniman, who had taken on the renewed role of volunteer co-ordinator. In its first season its 10 members redecorated the toll house, thinned and replanted snowdrop clumps, weeded around the buildings, refurbished the woodland exhibition panels, cleaned harness, helped re-organise the stores at Charlton Barns, prepared wood for charcoal burning, redecorated the shepherd's hut and prepared old horseshoes for sale in the shop. This particular task, which was originally undertaken by Bernard Rush, has continued annually for years, with an estimated total of over 50,000 horseshoes cleaned and sold, raising some £27,000 by 1994.

> **❛❛** As many volunteers who have spent merry hours in the car park, or in the middle of the overflow field, will know, there is a certain insane enjoyment in helping the public, most of whom seem to have forgotten or never really knew, how to drive. Two young volunteers added to the fun by parking the cars by colour: red in one bay, blue in another, and so on. **❜❜**
>
> **Carol Brinson**

Above *Candle-making is a much-enjoyed activity for visitors, led for many years by volunteer Brian Weekes, sitting on the left.*

Right *John Herniman, leader of the 'Tuesday Gang', working on the shepherd's hut in 1994.*

The curatorial department has long relied on volunteers to help with cataloguing and conservation. Nigel Westacott and Ray Ashdown were vital to the basic task of documentation for many years, and Mike Piggott and John Hurd were indispensable in the move of the collections from the Charlton Barns to the Gridshell. Many people have mixed volunteering and employment, happily working out of hours to finish off tasks.

Keith's post was renamed visitor services manager and the job passed to Bob Easson, not a policeman this time, but a naval officer. He had risen through the ranks to command one of the Navy's largest warships, HMS *Intrepid*, and in 1986 was elected Armed Services Man of the Year for organising the shoreside evacuation of British and foreign nationals during the civil war in South

Interpretation strategy and Volunteer support programme introduced (Designation Challenge Fund)
Diana Rowsell appointed head of learning

Jennie Peel appointed schools services manager

2004 Henry Warner appointed head of operations
Edward Cullinan Architects prepare

feasibility study on proposed sites for 'Orientation Gallery'
Conservation and access project for collections items stored off site (Designation Challenge Fund)

Above *Most staff members have acted as volunteers at some time during their involvement at the museum, while others began as volunteers and were later employed. Here are two: Carol Brinson (left) and Heather Champion.*
Above right *Bob Easson discussing the volunteer rota with Thelma Jack, who for many years led the Bayleaf stewards and worked with Bob Holman in the museum gardens. She still continues to help in the shop.*
Below *Stables volunteer Marie Merritt helps children understand working horse harness in 2002 by supervising cleaning activities. In the background are horseman Rob Dash and volunteer Patricia Wilkinson.*

Improvements to Lurgashall watermill carried out

Report on the museum's woodlands by Tim Heymann and Rod Stern

2005 Museum receives its five millionth visitor in September, 35 years after opening

Knowledge Transfer Partnership scheme with the University of Reading enables Dr Danae Tankard to research the social and

economic background to the museum's main exhibits

Hannah Miller (later Tiplady) appointed head of interpretation

Yemen, for which he was awarded the Queen's Commendation for Brave Conduct. The museum had succeeded in attracting a worthy successor to Keith. Bob continued the all-important task of nurturing the volunteers and oversaw a rise in their numbers from 200 to over 500. Bob's

Above *Volunteers' social events, at a barbecue in 1971, and* **below** *at an end-of-season party in the Downland Gridshell in 2005.*

leadership inspired others with confidence, enabling volunteers to develop and flourish in their many roles.

The museum has steadily increased its investment in volunteer training, reflecting a national trend. At first volunteers merely joined in with whatever was required, but by the 1990s museums were referring to 'Volunteers' Charters', and later to specialist training programmes for volunteers working on different tasks.

The first Volunteers' Briefing took place at the museum in spring 1982, offering an opportunity for museum director Chris Zeuner to focus on the hopes and plans for the forthcoming year and giving volunteers a formal chance to raise questions and make suggestions. A new development in volunteering occurred in 1988 when Thelma Jack was appointed as interpreter for the Bayleaf Medieval Farmstead project, assisted by a dedicated team of volunteers for that specific building group.

In 1993 the museum made a video about the history and themes of the museum as a way of

> " My friend and I had started on a bitterly cold winter's day in 1995, so we shut ourselves in the harness-room to clean the mountain of muddy leather. We had met nobody but after a while the door opened to a very surprised Chris Zeuner and his daughter, Francesca, who had come to give Shire horse, Baron, some work. At that stage we did not know one horse from the other and Chris was delighted to see us. They went off with Baron, and in a short time were back with two volunteers' badges emblazoned with our names. We must have been impressed as we served 11 years, enjoying every moment, talking to the visitors, cleaning the stables, making many new friends and trying to keep abreast of children's questioning minds. On one particularly hot weekend, I counted 90 children having a 'hands-on' drive with the working horses over two days. "
>
> **Marie Merritt, volunteer**

2006	Museum adopts northern boundary site for new visitor centre and car parking: outline planning application approved	Timber crane from Privett re-erected. Chapel from South Wonston dismantled	Challenge Fund)
	Marjorie Hallam, founding trustee and former honorary librarian, dies	'Hidden Histories' videos made showing the operation of animal-powered agricultural equipment (Designation	Historic Clothing Project launched
			Museum hosts the final of BBC's *Restoration Village*, in support of historic building conservation projects

briefing new volunteers; a highlight is an interview between museum director Chris Zeuner and the founder, Roy Armstrong. Made only five months before Roy's death this is the only known film of him in existence.

Periodically the museum has made special efforts to recruit more volunteers needed as the number of exhibits grew and visitor facilities expanded. "What do you need to become a volunteer?" was a question posed in the museum magazine in 1991:

Nothing particular — but the following are useful. A good pair of legs! Fire-lighting capability. Stamina to cope with school parties and occasional bad weather! A packed lunch. A warm approach to your fellow man. An enjoyment in chatting to people. A reasonable or good memory for facts to aid question-answering! And of course, you need time.

In 1996 the museum instituted a new structure. There were to be more closely defined groups of volunteers, working in education, conservation, gardening, the watermill and stewarding of the buildings, each led by a member of staff. Volunteers' agreements were being introduced, designed to make the task of the volunteer as rewarding as possible and setting out the parameters of their involvement. Volunteer Training Workshops were held later that year, led by Marista Leishman of the Edinburgh-based Insite Trust which had an established track record for training in customer care for museums and historic houses, including Buckingham Palace.

Three years later Bob Easson was busy establishing several fresh initiatives including a training programme to help new volunteers and refresh regulars, while Carol Brinson co-ordinated the production of a volunteer tour guides' handbook. New groups of volunteers were set up to assist in the library and with livestock. In 1999 the museum became the first heritage project to sign up to the new Heritage Volunteers' Handbook and Charter produced by the British Association of Friends of Museums.

In 2002 the volunteers' briefings evolved into the Museum Community Forum, with heads of department speaking about their proposals for the coming year. A Volunteer Support Programme was launched the following year, including videos and

written material, and in 2010 a further training programme was introduced with sessions taking place nearly every week.

Volunteering is a two-way process. On the one hand it is essential for the continuing operation of the museum, and it imbues people's visits with a richer, people-orientated experience. On the other, for volunteers it frequently has deep social and personal significance, often enabling them to fulfil dreams or to recuperate and thrive, following a life-changing experience. Their dedication is sometimes astonishing — from those who have devoted every weekend for years to their museum tasks, to the nonagenarian who came to the museum weekly by bus from Chichester. The museum is forever in their debt.

Above *Marista Leishman (standing centre), of the Insite Trust, providing volunteer training in customer care in 1996.*

Below *Sometimes volunteers arrive in ready-made teams, like this group of employees from The Body Shop, Littlehampton, who cleared undergrowth by the Gridshell and in the copse next to Poplar Cottage in 2009.*

2008	Paul Rigg becomes museum chairman Vehicle and Implement Gallery opened Museum awarded Learning Outside the Classroom Quality Badge Landscape Conservation & Management Plan for West Dean Park approved		Feasibility study and sketch design for 'Access Project' carried out		Friends contribution to the museum since its foundation stands at £1.7 million
		2009	Interpretation pavilions plan launched South Downs National Park announced	2010	Re-erection of hay barn from Ockley Museum celebrates 40th anniversary of opening to the public

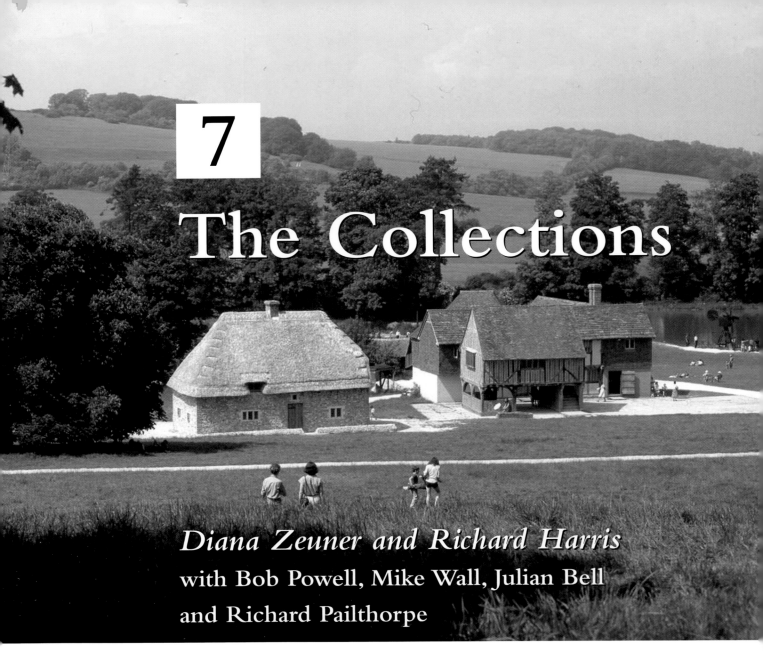

7

The Collections

Diana Zeuner and Richard Harris
with Bob Powell, Mike Wall, Julian Bell
and Richard Pailthorpe

The museum collects only those buildings which "cannot otherwise be preserved in situ", and structures that help to tell the story of vernacular architecture and rural life in the Weald and Downland region. The museum site has proved ideal, big enough to allow space between buildings, but small enough to comprehend.

In 1973, after the struggle to establish the museum and open to the public had been won, Roy Armstrong wrote about the aims of the museum in an article called *The Open Air Museum: Idea and Reality* which was published in the *Transactions of the Ancient Monuments Society*. It contained a simple, clear and easily understood statement of intent:

Our purpose is to create a museum of representative traditional buildings which it is impossible to preserve in situ, *rebuilt with associated crafts and furnishings for enjoyment, research and instruction.*

Somewhat earlier, probably in 1969, he wrote a paper that contains a more comprehensive declaration:

The aim of the committee is not to create simply a museum of buildings, but to illustrate the social and economic history of the area in as vivid and living a way as possible. … In the selection of buildings for re-erection and reconstruction the intention is not to give an idealised and false picture of the past by the choice only of technically fine examples. … For this reason the intention is to acquire only buildings which cannot otherwise be preserved in situ, *but which nevertheless represent the widest possible range from extreme simplicity, or even poverty, to high sophistication and technical perfection. From many points of view the humblest buildings are more appropriate to the study of social and economic history than are the more elaborate buildings.*

In its insistence on only acquiring buildings that would otherwise be destroyed – which was, and is, shared by all other English open air museums – the museum faced a serious problem: how do you collect if you never know what items you will be offered? How do you know whether to accept and re-erect a barn when a couple of years later a much better example might be offered? For most museums the cost of collecting is relatively low, but the cost of dismantling and re-erecting a building represents a serious investment.

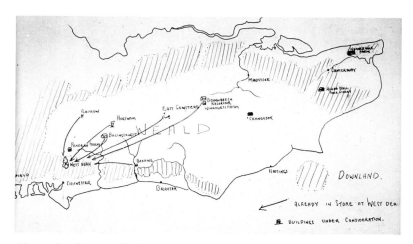

Above Roy Armstrong's first sketch of the Weald and Downland region, showing the original sites of the first buildings rescued and brought to the new museum site at Singleton. **Below** A more recent map; the red diamonds mark the original building sites.

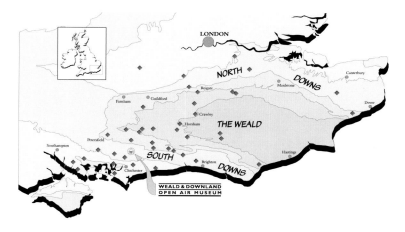

The answer is that every time we are offered a building as an exhibit, the decision must be based on two considerations. Firstly, is the building able to tell a sufficiently clear story? And secondly, does that story link in a coherent way with what we have collected already? So in a sense the collecting policy changes every time a new exhibit is acquired, because the story being told at the museum itself changes. Roy Armstrong recognised the problem in his 1973 article:

It follows that the scope of the museum itself must be limited by what buildings become available, and not by what it might be able to acquire, had it the means, in order to create an ideally balanced and representative collection. This means that the future content and shape of the museum can be planned at this stage only in fairly general terms capable of adaptation. If, for example, a much more determined effort were to be made at national or regional level to preserve in

Master planning   *Richard Harris*

The museum's master plans were drawn up to aid museum development and planning negotiations with West Sussex County Council's planning department and show potential sites for building exhibits. They were all produced by the museum's honorary architect, John Warren, who had extensive experience in conservation architecture and planning through his Horsham-based practice.

There have been four generations of the masterplan:

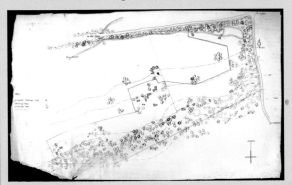

1) An undated plan showing some of the early ideas for the layout of the site. The village was to be on the downland slopes south of Gonville Cottage rather than in its present position, and ten buildings are shown sited near the edge of the woodland. The millpond site is already established in the north-east corner, and a stream is shown running from it to join the Lavant.

2) This plan was drawn in February 1971 and illustrates the start of the intense discussions in that year. Four possible sites for the village were under discussion and the matter was not settled until mid-1972. On this plan the dotted rectangle indicates a possible site for the village, and is the one that was finally adopted, but it was necessary for the Edward James Foundation to agree to move the site boundary westwards to accommodate it

(shown as a broken curved line) and part of the west end of the site was given up in exchange.

WEALD AND DOWNLAND OPEN AIR MUSEUM   MASTER PLAN '72

3) Once the village site had been settled it was possible to develop the rest of the masterplan. This plan dates from November 1972 and most of the main elements of the museum's final layout are shown, the main exception being an area at the west end marked as 'Area for detailed consideration'. In the event, this area was given up in exchange for an extension southwards into the woodland.

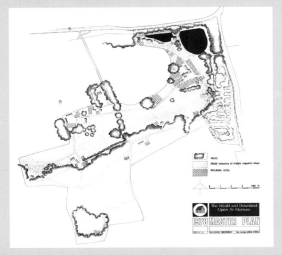

4) This plan dated 1978 was probably produced at the very end of the year and it shows the boundaries of the museum and the general areas for building that guided development for the next 30 years. A building site is shown in the southern woodland which was not subsequently thought practical to develop, and we have tended to reduce rather than increase the number of woodland-edge sites. Otherwise, however, the main areas for development have been closely followed.

situ *all buildings of medieval date at whatever cost, the planning of the museum would require drastic reformulation. Unfortunately this is a rather unlikely contingency. ... Because of this uncertainty as to what size or type of buildings may need to be accommodated, the master plan has to be conceived in terms which provide maximum flexibility.*

> ❝ *I always expect my first day on site [for a dismantling] to be devoted to tiles: either carrying them, or forming part of a human chain. This time I was too late for tiles, and it was bricks instead. Heather [Champion] and Andrew, a teenager from Newdigate, were on the scaffolding tackling the chimney; I was on the ladder; Val, Andrew's mother, was on the top of the oven; Alf was on the ground. Heather numbered the bricks in each course, and loosened them, Andrew lifted them off, and handed them to me, and I gave them to Val, who cleaned them and handed them to Alf, who put them in the barrow, and from time to time trundled them off to the pallet. It was slow going, but just fast enough to justify my position on the ladder.* ❞
>
> **Brigadier Walter Greenway reporting on dismantling the Newdigate bakehouse, 1989**

Another problem that Roy addressed in 1973 concerned the desirable size of the site – and the stamina of our visitors. Some early plans had envisaged a collection of as many as 80 buildings, but Roy saw clearly that that was too many:

> *My own view is that thirty-five acres and a limit of about thirty-five buildings is desirable for a number of reasons. ... Experience [on the continent] has convinced many administrators that there is a certain size which, if exceeded, leads to frustration, fatigue or simply boredom. ... Size also induces an element of impersonality ... destroying those very qualities of informality which we are particularly anxious to preserve at Singleton.*

Parts of buildings are also collected. Late 16th-century painted panels were discovered in Ivy House, Fittleworth in 1970, well preserved behind a later layer of plaster on battens. They are displayed in the entrance lobby of the upper hall from Crawley.

Why are the timbers painted red? *Diana Zeuner*

Museum volunteers and visitors alike were disturbed by the decision to paint the timbers of the re-erected house from North Cray in red ochre – just as they had been when the whole of Winkhurst was lime-washed across the timbers, removing its 'black-and-white' appearance. The museum was simply following the evidence. In the case of North Cray traces of red paint were found on both the inside and outside surfaces of the timber, where it could only have been applied before or during the erection of the building, including beneath the soot accumulated from smoke from the central fire. There was already evidence that many medieval buildings had red-painted timber in the Midlands and Yorkshire, so there were no qualms in

following the evidence in the case of the museum's structure. Pictured are (left) the hall house from North Cray, showing the red-painted timbers, and (right) Winkhurst, lime-washed across its timbers.

Above *The dismantled buildings store at Singleton railway cutting; all structures are brought here direct from their original sites.*

Below *Tiles, bricks, slates and other materials in store awaiting reunion on the museum site with the rest of the building from which they were dismantled. In the foreground is a game larder from Boarhunt, Hampshire.*

These views proved remarkably prescient. The museum's main site of 40 acres (16 hectares) has proved an ideal size: big enough to allow space between buildings, which visitors enjoy as it gives an opportunity to walk and chat, and with plenty of variety, but small enough to comprehend. The number of buildings will probably eventually rise to 55-60, but the number of groups and farmstead sites is rather lower than envisaged by the founders.

Starting in 1968 and continuing until 1990, the acquisition and siting of exhibit buildings was discussed and agreed by the sites and buildings advisory committee, and the minutes of its meetings form an invaluable record of how and why the key decisions on the museum's development were taken. For most of that period the chairman was Robin McDowall, senior investigator for the Royal Commission

> **"** *Over the 30 years of the museum's existence vernacular architecture has developed into an established discipline, but it is still hard to define. Essentially it means the common speech of building – ordinary buildings in which people share, or shared, a common understanding and experience. When we open a new exhibit people often ask 'what is special about it', and the answer is usually everything – and nothing. Everything, because every physical component and every aspect of the design can tell us something about ordinary people and their lives. And nothing, because if a building is unique or extraordinary it would find no place in our collections.* **"**
>
> **The museum's application for designation as an outstanding collection, 1998**

on Historic Monuments (he was later to be secretary of the commission) and one of the pioneers in the publication of high quality new research in vernacular architecture. Committee members included regional and national experts such as Reg Mason, Ken Gravett, Joan Harding, Stuart Rigold, Eric Mercer and David Martin, together with architects David Russell, who was a trustee from 1967 until his death in 2007, and John Warren, who was the museum's honorary architect from 1967 until 1989.

For many years the early reports and memoranda by Roy Armstrong formed, in effect, the museum's collecting policy. In 1988, however, the museum took steps to formalise a collecting policy which was adopted by the trustees, to ensure that it would be eligible for the museum registration scheme being introduced by the Museums & Galleries Commission. This took place in 1988 and in 1989 the policy was published in the museum magazine. Chris Zeuner wrote:

> *It is necessary to be very selective in building up our collections if we are not to accept too many items that will never be used for study or go on display, or indeed are irrelevant to our subject areas…. The [registration] scheme is welcomed because it will identify to visitors, donors, sponsors, public authorities and grant-giving bodies, those museums which set out to conduct themselves as*

Developing new building conservation techniques
Diana Zeuner and Richard Harris

An important element of the museum's work has been the development of new repair and conservation techniques, a source of interest and assistance to many other organisations concerned with historic buildings. The museum has made particular strides in the repair of timber-frames and in the authentic rebuilding of historic brickwork.

Carpentry

A section of timber-framed wall from Bayleaf farmhouse laid out on the ground prior to re-erection.

At Pendean farmhouse Roger Champion carried out half a dozen repairs using glass fibre. It was the first time the museum had not replaced missing wood with wood. "It was not 100% successful, practically or visually," Roger says.

The museum entered into a contract with the company, Renofors, whose material was being used on buildings *in-situ*. "On a rotten timber you would use shuttering and put in a liquid chocolatey goo. It didn't seem particularly appealing. It was no good for joints as it made them too rigid. We used it on Boarhunt in 1975 and on Crawley hall. Really, it was used as a filler."

The museum did not use this technique again until the repair of North Cray hall house. The elm timbers had been weatherboarded for 200 years, making their surface soggy, but the evidence showed it had been painted red from the beginning of its life. As it was impossible to paint onto soggy timber it was decided to consolidate the surfaces with a thin epoxy resin. "We were never quite sure whether damp would penetrate behind the resin. It was thought this would not occur for 30-40 years. Well, 20 years later, nothing has shown up as a problem. But the new timber we used for repairs has shown signs of decay."

The museum regarded experimentation with repair methods as an important part of its academic work. Commercial professionals were unable to do the same, but could gain from the results of the

Timber-frame repairs at the museum. 1. An early repair on Bayleaf farmhouse (1971) where a large oak patch has been inserted into a main post. By today's standards the dowels used for fixing detract from the pegging of the original joints. 2. On the repair to Poplar Cottage, carried out in 1999, the recessed patch has enabled more of the original timber to be retained. Poplar Cottage was the first building on which this type of repair was used comprehensively. 3. Another early form of repair used fibreglass, seen here on Pendean farmhouse. 4. A 'V' scarf repair in the bottom of a post in the Charlwood wagon shed with the original surface kept intact. 5. On Winkhurst, the main post shows a repair carried out in 1968 (at the bottom of the photograph) and a recessed patch repair to the mortice (top right), carried out in 2002 prior to the building's re-erection on its new site near Bayleaf farmhouse.

Above *The number on top of each individual brick as they were dismantled from Longport farmhouse together with the corresponding batten, and* **below** *bricks and battens arranged in order at the museum, ready for re-building.*

research. "Of the resin repairs we have done to date none has failed," says Roger, adding that the material enables the preservation of very much more of the original timber.

In an effort to find a repair method which would reflect the condition of the timber before the repair, experiments took place with patches beneath the surface of the old timber, rather than repairing from the front. Poplar Cottage was the first building on which this new technique was used comprehensively. The amount of original timber surviving was limited and it was important to retain the maximum amount. Resin-bonded oak patches below the surface made it possible. The original timber was bonded with epoxy resin rather than bolts or pegs. The same building was also the first in which original timber was repaired, not by mill-sawn timber but by timber that was pit-sawn and hewn in the traditional way.

"I don't know anyone who uses resin in the way that we do," says Roger. "Very few people have the understanding of its use as we do. English Heritage sends its carpenters on our courses."

Brickwork

Brick walls present very different challenges from timber. There are rarely more than a few dozen timbers in each component frame, so giving them all individual numbers is easy. With brickwork on the other hand, there can be thousands of individual bricks in a wall; giving them individual numbers is difficult enough, but how do you also record each brick's position so that the wall can be accurately rebuilt?

The museum's methods were based on pioneering work at the Black Country Living Museum, West Midlands. First, drawings produced by tracing rectified photographs gave a perfect place to record the number allocated to each brick. Then, when the top of each course had been cleared of lime mortar, an ordinary roofing batten was laid on the bricks and the positions of the joints were recorded on it. Each brick was marked with a number on its top surface, and the number was also recorded on the batten, so that when it came to rebuilding, the bricks could be accurately laid by simply following the batten.

"This simple system did away with any need for measurements, except for the overall dimensions of the wall and openings for setting out the work," Richard Harris wrote. "On the whole the system worked well, but we found that as well as the batten it was necessary to have large-size colour photographs of the wall for the bricklayer to follow the subtle variations in position and angle of the bricks." These techniques are now taught to students on the museum's building conservation courses.

Three buildings have been dismantled using these techniques: Newdigate bakehouse (1988), the house from Godalming (1989) and Longport farmhouse (1992). Of these only Longport has so far been reconstructed, but the re-positioning of the 7,618 18th- and 19th-century bricks was an outstanding success; the building looks and feels uncannily like it did on its original site.

museums (rather than heritage centres or leisure parks) in a responsible way, and which seek to meet necessary standards.

> 66 *It was 50p a cubic foot. Nowadays it would be £30, £40 or £50. Even in those days we were getting it cheap. Roy spent £250 on 500 cubic feet but more was needed so I spent £250 of my own money on another 500 cubic feet. That lasted until three-four years ago and was used on all the floors in every building in the museum, plus doors and furniture. That was a good buy, that was.* 99

Roger Champion on acquiring green oak from Charlton Sawmills when it closed in the late 1960s.

Ten years later the policy was incorporated into the application for designation as an outstanding collection with a small but significant change: as well as buildings, and building parts and materials, a section headed 'Building trades' was added, a response to concerns that we should be putting more resources into that area of collecting.

Registration has since developed, becoming known as 'Accreditation', with more stringent requirements for museums' collecting policies,

> 66 *The concept of the 'vernacular threshold' underlies the choice of buildings for the museum's collection. This is the idea – which is not undisputed – that there is a threshold, admittedly ill-defined, above which buildings are 'polite', not vernacular, and that this threshold moves down the social scale over time. Thus from the 15th century we have Bayleaf, a substantial farmhouse, but we are unlikely to acquire a similarly substantial farmhouse from the 18th or 19th century, because it would be too 'polite'. Some people think that even the 19th-century pair of cottages from Ashtead are uncomfortably near the vernacular threshold.* 99

The museum's application for designation as an outstanding collection, 1998

Daubing repairs under way at the house from North Cray, with Mick (left) and Ron Betsworth. Pete Betsworth, the first of the Betsworth brothers to be employed by the museum, is pictured on page 121.

now re-named the 'Acquisition and Disposal Policy', and incorporating regular policy review and information about legal title to acquisitions.

The timbers of Poplar Cottage laid out in an on-site workshop awaiting re-erection. Roger Champion's repairs to the original timbers with new material can be clearly seen; the diamond shaped holes on the three timbers to the left will take the window mullions once re-erected.

The building collections album

This album of the buildings at the museum lists them broadly in order of re-erection on the museum site, and is followed by a list of buildings and building parts not yet re-erected or on display.

Winkhurst Tudor kitchen

from Sundridge, Kent. Early 16th century. Dendrochronology date range – 1492-1528
Dismantled 1968, re-erected 1969

The first building to be re-erected at the museum, Winkhurst was one of the Bough Beech Reservoir houses which were saved from destruction and brought to the museum. An excellent example of late-medieval timber-framed building construction with a crown post roof, it was originally assumed to be a farmhouse. New evidence shows that it was probably a kitchen, part of a larger farmstead, and used for cooking, smoking, brewing and washing; a typical building of its period. In 2002, therefore, the museum moved it from its original position on the site to a new more appropriate place near Bayleaf farmhouse, building two modern extensions to represent earlier structures known to have been present. It is now presented as a Tudor kitchen, fully reconstructed and operational.

Left *Winkhurst Farm before dismantling.* **Top right** *Winkhurst on its original site at the museum, and* **bottom right** *the new site near Bayleaf farmhouse.*

Treadwheel

from Catherington, Hampshire. Late 17th century. Dendrochronology date range – 1670-93
Dismantled 1969, re-erected 1970

The treadwheel and its house were moved from the downland village of Catherington, north of Portsmouth, where it was in a very derelict condition. The treadwheel was designed to raise water from a well, thought to be nearly 300 feet deep, and was in use until about 90 years ago. It has been reconstructed in working order, with a demonstration well 12 feet deep. The wheel was covered for protection by a timber-framed building infilled with split hazel and left undaubed, typical of some farm buildings.

Top left *The treadwheel on its original site, and* **left** *in its new position at the museum with* **right** *detail of the treadwheel as reconstructed.*

Charcoal Burners' camp

Reconstruction, first carried out in 1969

The craft of charcoal burning is a very ancient one and was an important industry in the Weald, supplying fuel for iron-working. Because it was essential to watch the burning kilns night and day, the charcoal burner lived on site with his family. The original camp at the museum was built by Mr and Mrs A Langridge, retired charcoal burners from Kingsfold, near Horsham. In addition to the earth kilns, they created two huts, a day hut and a night hut, using turf and sacking over a pole frame, following a very old tradition.

Left *The camp in its first days, and* **right** *in the late 1970s.*

Toll house

from Upper Beeding, West Sussex. Early 19th century
Dismantled 1968, re-erected 1970

Toll houses were built as part of the system of road maintenance by Turnpike Trusts in the 18th and 19th centuries for the collection of tolls from passing traffic, the money being used to repair and maintain the road. Built on a newly turnpiked road established in 1807, the building became available after it was damaged by a lorry in 1967. It has been moved from its original site at the museum, and the opportunity taken to represent its construction more correctly.

Left *The toll house on its original site, and* **right** *at the museum.*

Medieval cottage

from Hangleton, East Sussex. Reconstruction of a 13th-century structure
Rebuilt 1971

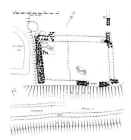

This reconstruction of a flint cottage was based on archaeological evidence obtained during excavation of the deserted medieval village of Hangleton, north of Hove, East Sussex. It was probably built in the 13th century and abandoned in the early 15th century. In spite of conjectural elements it was decided to rebuild it to represent a form of building in rough flint rubble once widespread over the chalk Downs. The reconstruction was led by Eric Holden who published descriptions of the Hangleton excavation in the *Sussex Archaeological Collections*.

Left *The plan of the cottage on its original site, and* **right** *the cottage as reconstructed at the museum.*

Bayleaf farmhouse

from Chiddingstone, Kent. Early 15th century. Dendrochronology date range (hall and service) – 1405-30
Dismantled 1968, re-erected 1972

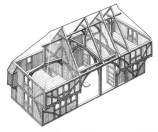

Bayleaf is perhaps the most iconic structure at the museum, with its image widely reproduced. A timber-framed hall-house dating mainly from the early 15th century, it is a typical example of a 'Wealden house', common in the Weald of East Sussex and Kent, with the characteristic feature of the recessed front wall of the hall and the two end chambers 'jettied' out at the front. The building has an open hall in the middle, entered from a cross passage, with the buttery and pantry service rooms at one end, and at the other, the parlour and solar. Surveyed by R T Mason and R Wood of the Wealden Buildings Study Group, it was the second of the Bough Beech Reservoir houses to be re-erected at the museum. In 1989 it was the subject of the museum's most ambitious interpretation project, the Bayleaf Medieval Farmstead, a ground-breaking attempt to recreate a medieval farmstead with farmyard, agricultural equipment and livestock, garden and curtilage.

Clockwise from top left *Bayleaf on its original site; during dismantling; during re-erection at the museum – receiving the craned timbers is Chris Zeuner, soon to become the new museum director; Richard Harris' drawing showing the structure and layout, and with livestock, farmyard and garden after the completion of the medieval farmstead project.*

> *Friday 27 August. Half a day off work yesterday to watch the great timbers of Bayleaf being jollied into place. It was a most fascinating afternoon. Rather like doing a man-sized jigsaw puzzle. A crane lifted the heavy beams and Roger, Chris and Olly guided them into place. Sunday, 5 September. Arrived on the site before the other folk. I sat alone on the last remaining timbers of Bayleaf, with a rising sun and heavy dew – it all seemed so unreal. If only these timbers could talk to me. On to do my bit at the charcoal area, and return to have lunch 'in' Bayleaf. 'In' in inverted commas as the roof isn't all up yet.*

Matti Denton's diary, 1971

> *Roy asked me if I would like to make Bayleaf my next job if I felt confident to do so. 'Nothing I'd like more' was my answer. So away we went. Lurgashall shed was now sheathed in polythene and became the workshop for Bayleaf with the main laying-out area where the garden now is. They were exciting times for me, working long hours, long days and long weeks, but learning all the time: couldn't keep away. Longleys, converting West Dean House into the College, loaned a carpenter, Keith Jenner, who was responsible for the reinstatement of the dragon post and bracket. Work progressed largely without mishap and erection day arrived. We played to quite a large audience, with Roy and General Hawes front of house. I am pleased to say every single timber dropped into place without any embarrassing mis-fits, much to my relief! Among the volunteers on the erection team was Chris Zeuner, soon to become the museum's full-time and successful director. New oak timber for Bayleaf was supplied by West Dean Estate. Wattling the completed frame was carried out by Ernie Austin, hurdle maker, of East Dean.*

Roger Champion

Windpump

from Pevensey, East Sussex. Mid-19th century
Dismantled and re-erected 1972

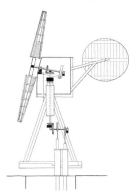

A rare survival of a wooden wind-powered pump – once a common machine – the museum's example comes from an old clay pit near Pevensey. The centre post carrying the windshaft and sweeps is hollow, and within it is an iron rod, which transmits power to the water pumps below.

Left *A section through the windpump showing the mechanism, and* **right** *the windpump on its lake-side site at the museum after a fall of snow.*

Granary

from Littlehampton, West Sussex. c1731
Dismantled 1969, re-erected 1970

Thought to have been built in 1731 – as incised on one of the bricks – the timber-frame is mainly of elm infilled with brick, and the building is raised on 16 stone staddles to protect the grain from damp and vermin. Threatened with destruction due to a

road scheme, it is an unusually large example, measuring 20 feet square. Used at one time as the museum shop, it is now presented as a furnished granary.

Left *The granary on its original site, during dismantling, and* **right** *at the museum.*

Granary

from Goodwood, West Sussex. 19th century
Dismantled and re-erected 1973

Donated by the Goodwood Estate, this granary was transported intact to the museum where it has been in use as an office.

Left *The granary on its original site, and* **right** *being craned into position at the museum.*

Cattle sheds

Late 18th-19th century
*from Rusper (dismantled and re-erected 1970); Lurgashall (dismantled 1970, re-erected 1971);
Kirdford (dismantled 1971, re-erected 1973, but burnt down in an arson attack in 1981);
Coldwaltham (dismantled 1973, re-erected 1974), and Goodwood (dismantled 1986,
re-erected 1988)*

Open-fronted sheds provided shelter for cattle kept in yards, forming part of a farmyard group with barns and other sheds around a foldyard. Five have been re-erected at the museum: the small three-bay shed from Lurgashall with its own yard near Bayleaf farmhouse; the seven-bay shed from Kirdford (which was burnt down in an arson attack in 1981); a shed from Goodwood (Redvins Farm), which has a shepherd's room at one end and a display of horse-drawn implements and an exhibition about the geology of the Weald and Downland; a shed from Rusper (now used in conjunction with the working horse stables) and a shed from Coldwaltham (now in use as part of the museum's woodyard).

Clockwise from top left *The Rusper, Lurgashall, Kirdford and Coldwaltham cattle sheds on their original sites, and the Lurgashall and Goodwood sheds at the museum today.*

Smithy

from Southwater, West Sussex. c1850
Dismantled and re-erected 1971

Typical of many village smithies, the museum's example was built using inexpensive but sturdy construction. The smith's work included making and repairing tools and

equipment for farmers and craftsmen, as well as shoeing horses. It was given to the museum by the son of the last practising smith and wheelwright to work there. A wheel-tyring platform is installed outside. Demonstrations of smithing have taken place regularly since its reconstruction at the museum.

Left *A photograph taken of the smithy during its working life, and* **right** *at the museum.*

Aisled barn

from Hambrook, West Sussex. c1771
Dismantled 1971, re-erected 1973

Built in the mid-18th century the barn is of a type common in West Sussex and eastern Hampshire. Tall main doors lead onto the threshing floor, on which sheaves of corn were hand-threshed by flail. The rest of the barn was used to store the unthreshed crop and threshed straw. The most characteristic feature of the barn is its aisle, which continues round the ends as well as the sides of the

building. A date found scratched on a rafter during repair of its oak timbers, 1771, is likely to be the date of construction. The barn houses the museum's introductory exhibition showing traditional regional building materials and methods.

Left *The barn on its original site, and* **right** *as it is today.*

Wagon sheds

18th-19th century
from Selsey, West Sussex, (dismantled 1973, re-erected 1974, but damaged beyond repair in a gale in 1975) and from Pallingham Quay, West Sussex (dismantled and re-erected 1980)

Wagon sheds were another typical building of traditional farmyards.

Left *The Selsey shed was partially re-erected when it blew down in a particularly severe gale.* **Right** *The Pallingham Quay example has been converted for use as the museum's café. Both are pictured here on their original sites.*

Market hall

from Titchfield, Hampshire. Dendrochronology date – 1619
Dismantled 1971, re-erected 1974

Typical of many market halls built in the 16th and 17th centuries, the market hall has an open arcade at street level where goods could be sold or stalls set up by traders, while the room on the first floor served as a town council chamber. Under the stairs leading to the chamber is a lock-up for offenders. Many of these timber-framed market halls were demolished having

outlived their useful purpose, and the Titchfield example became derelict and deteriorated rapidly in the 1960s. The museum assisted local efforts to save it, but these failed, and a dangerous building notice was served by the local council which insisted on immediate demolition.

Left *The market hall on its original site, and* **right** *as it is today.*

Pendean farmhouse
from Midhurst, West Sussex. Dendrochronology date – c1609
Dismantled 1968, re-erected 1976

A small yeoman farmhouse built around 1609, Pendean represents the next stage in house building in which the open hall has given way to a brick chimney. This revolutionary change in house planning started in the mid-16th century. Pendean, nevertheless, retains some medieval features such as unglazed windows. Now furnished, the opportunity has been taken to paint the internal brickwork of the chimney, a fashionable practice in the 17th century. Documentary evidence reveals that the owner in 1609 was Richard Clare, with the property including 40 acres of land, a barn, and herbage and pasture for 100 sheep and 14 bullocks on common land at Woolavington manor.

Left *Pendean on its original site.* **Top right** *Furnishings and the painted fireplace in an interior room, and* **bottom right** *as it is today.*

Stable
from Watersfield, West Sussex. Mid-18th century
Dismantled 1974, re-erected 1976

This timber-framed and weather-boarded stable contained standings for four or five horses or oxen. In its lower end the museum has

installed a horse-powered chaffcutter. At one time the Plewis wheelwrighting collection was displayed in the building, but it is now furnished as a working stable.

Left *The building before dismantling, and* **right** *at the museum.*

Upper hall
from Crawley, West Sussex. Early 16th century. Dendrochronology date range – 1494-1513
Dismantled 1972, re-erected 1978

The main feature of this building is the hall on the first floor, a long open room thought to have been a communal meeting place, its use today at the museum. The ground floor is divided into separate rooms and at the museum is used for the Armstrong Library. The surviving structure was originally the centre of a longer building, and modern ends have been added to replace what had disappeared. Its importance was discovered after Crawley New Town Commission decided on demolition.

Left *The building on its original site, and* **right** *as it is today.*

Building
from Lavant, West Sussex. 17th century
Dismantled 1976, re-erected 1978

Demolition of this building had already begun when it was realised that it was of considerably earlier date than the date stone (1773) set in a blocked window in the front wall. A good example of early 17th-century brickwork, the interior was destroyed by fire in the

late 18th century. The original use of the building is unclear, but it is thought to have been used as an upper meeting hall, with store rooms below. At the museum its

lower rooms were used as the museum shop for a number of years; today it is the base for the museum's schools and interpretation services.

Left *The building on its original site, and* **right** *at the museum.*

Court Barn
from Lee-on-Solent, Hampshire. Late 17th–early 18th century
Dismantled 1977, re-erected 1979

This handsome barn had to be demolished to make way for a housing development. Similar in form to the one from Hambrook, the barn is earlier in date with different roof construction. At the museum it houses an exhibition on building crafts, including plumbing and leadwork (established by the Worshipful Company of Plumbers),

stone and masonry, and glass painting and glazing.

Left *The barn on its original site, and* **right** *at the museum.*

Wagon shed
from Wiston, West Sussex. 18th century
Dismantled 1976, re-erected 1980

This small shed was built close to the farmyard to house carts and wagons needed on the farm, and incorporates open ends for ease of storage. It was one of many timber-

framed buildings surveyed by Roy Armstrong and others on the Wiston Estate, Washington, West Sussex.

Left *The wagon shed on its original site, and* **right** *at the museum.*

Watermill   *Diana Zeuner and Robert Demaus*

from Lurgashall, West Sussex. 17th century
Dismantled 1973, re-erected 1977. Operational 1981

Lurgashall watermill on its original site.

The dismantling and re-erection of Lurgashall watermill, the installation of the machinery and the construction of upper and lower ponds to enable full-scale flour production was a very ambitious project for the museum, especially at such an early stage in its development. It took eight years to bring it to fruition, and cost £50,000.

The task began in 1973, with the survey of the structure on its original site and the construction of two millponds with a 12 feet (3.6 metres) height difference to incorporate the overshot waterwheel. It was officially opened in April 1981 by Mr and Mrs Hugh Anstey, whose family had operated the mill before its decline and removal to the museum. Two of the museum's early buildings project staff were heavily involved – Geoff Kent, an experienced bricklayer, whose wife, Dorothy, helped in the office for many years, and John Friar, a builder and amateur archaeologist who was one of the museum's earliest members of staff.

Dismantling under way, with the wheel being removed by a crane.

The watermill was built in the 17th century at Lurgashall, four miles north of Petworth, West Sussex. It used water from streams which flow into the River Rother near Halfway Bridge. Rebuilt and modified at least once during its working life, the remaining machinery dated mostly from the 19th century. The mill served not only the village and its locality, but also the residents of Petworth House and park, at one time having two waterwheels each driving independent sets of machinery; one set survives. There were two sets of grindstones to each waterwheel, thought to be used for flour, animal feed, and oak bark for the leather tanning industry. It continued in use until 1935,

Major stones were numbered, to ensure their correct replacement during rebuilding.

by which time it was mainly grinding animal feed. In 1968 autumn rains caused the millpond to flood, carrying away part of the road and flooding the mill building, heaving the floors apart and disturbing the millstones, which crashed through rotting timbers. The museum was interested in including a mill on its site and was delighted to be presented with it by the Leconfield Estate in 1973.

Over the eight-week dismantling project, the museum raised over 100 tons (101.6 tonnes) of stone from the watermill walls to the top of the dam and loaded it onto a lorry for removal to the museum. Major stones were marked and drawn, and although no archaeological excavation of the site was possible, Paul Simons, a final year student at the Architectural Association, prepared detailed drawings for use in the re-erection of the structure. Paul was later to be involved in the foundation of the building conservation body, The Vivat Trust, of which both he and Chris Zeuner were trustees and chairmen.

Roy Armstrong and Chris Zeuner (centre) during the dismantling, with Paul Simons to the far left and John Friar and Geoff Kent to the right.

Meanwhile, back on site, the museum was undertaking a considerable earth-moving project to construct the two ponds necessary to bring the mill into operation. Howard

Humphreys & Sons gouged out the pond profiles with earth-moving machines and over the whole surface of the upper pond, a soft layer of clay and sand was applied over which a substantial polythene lining and 12 inches (30 centimetres) of soil were laid.

The ponds represent an important environmental resource in themselves, attracting wildfowl, plants and other natural life. Heron and Canada geese have been welcome arrivals – the 30 cormorants who had their eyes on the carp and young Mallard, less so. Both fish and wildfowl have been the subject of occasional culls to ensure healthy populations.

*The excavation of the mill ponds was a major undertaking. **Left** the pond profile is lined with heavy duty plastic, while a bulldozer continues excavations, and **right** the central island entirely surrounded by water. Pevensey windpump is already in position. The lower millpond had yet to be excavated.*

By 1976, John Friar was involved in the "very laborious task" of building the watermill walls, the wheel pit and the sluices. John had considerable expertise in moving and lifting, gained from his career in the Royal Engineers. He had useful experience with dynamite (invaluable during the creation of the car park terracing for despatching tree roots), but his chief contribution was in dismantling and re-erecting buildings. As well as the mill these included Redford pugmill house, the Pevensey windpump, the dovecote from Milton Street, the house from Walderton, and several timber frames.

Meanwhile, millwright Peter Stenning restored the machinery, and the 12 feet (3.6 metres) diameter cast-iron wheel was repaired by Geoff Boxall of Binderton, West Dean. Invaluable help was received from James Lee of Midhurst who had been involved with its installation in the watermill in 1911. The wheel had been cast by Chorley, the Cocking iron-founder, originally for Costers Mill in West Lavington.

Unlike the original site at Lurgashall there is inadequate natural surface water to maintain the level in the upper pond when the mill is working. To overcome this a powerful electric water pump re-circulates the water from the lower pond back to the upper pond. A borehole was sunk to ensure that sufficient water is available to achieve the circulation. Today the mill runs as long as possible each day for the benefit of visitors, whereas during its working life the miller would have produced flour as quickly as possible, so the mill works much longer hours than in the past, but under a much lighter load.

John Friar rebuilding the mill stonework. John took equal pride in the quality of his flint wall construction. "Flint walls should never look like a pudding studded with almonds," he would tell visitors.

In 1980, to complete the restoration of the machinery, the museum engaged an experienced miller, Robert Demaus, who had run the working cornmill at Newcastle Emlyn, South Wales. But his story begins four years earlier.

It was the long hot summer of 1976. I was 22 and had gravitated to West Wales to learn the trades of corn miller and millwright. I was working at Felin Geri, near Newcastle Emlyn, one of the first water-powered flour mills in the UK to be returned to serious working production. The restoration of the mill had resulted in a prestigious European Heritage Award presented by The Prince of Wales, and much coverage in the national and specialist press. This must have caught the eye of Chris Zeuner, who travelled over from Sussex to see what had been achieved. The conversation turned to the mill from the Leconfield Estate that the museum was starting to re-erect at Singleton. Chris was intrigued by the possibility of running Lurgashall mill regularly and producing flour commercially, and I was attracted by the possibility of setting up a working mill within the museum complex. Chris and I parted, agreeing to remain in touch.

At the time, many people did not believe that the mill could operate successfully as a commercial venture within the museum;

*Robert Demaus dressing the mill's stones, a vital maintenance task to ensure the efficient production of flour, and **below** repairing the timber work at the mill leet.*

it was still a fairly novel idea then, and I will always be grateful that Chris had the drive and vision to bring the idea to fruition. At the time of our conversation, the mill was little more than a large hole in the ground, and there was no suitable stream on the museum site. For a working mill, this was quite a major problem. As I was struggling to find enough water to run Felin Geri during the 1976 drought at the time of our first meeting, I knew just how much water a working mill needed. The 'rough-guide' maths is quite simple – 40 buckets each holding about 3 gallons turning at around 5rpm is 600 gallons a minute which is over a quarter of a million gallons a day – and that is just to run gently. It rises to about 4,000 gallons a minute (40 x 8 gallons x 12rpm) at full chat, which is nearly two million gallons in a working day. A surprisingly small stream can supply this volume, but without one available a very big pump is needed to recirculate the water.

When I moved down to Sussex in November 1980, the shell of the building and most of the machinery had been completed, but there was still a huge amount to do to get the mill ready for the proposed opening at Easter 1981. The mill had not been through its 'shakedown trials' or even run at all, as there was still no water supply, and floors, stairs and safety barriers had yet to be installed. The mill had to comply with health and safety requirements and legislation regarding food production, and the museum needed to source wheat supplies and flour bags.

The opening on Good Friday was a great success, and in that first weekend the mill was so busy that visitors were queuing out through the door, waiting to buy the flour as soon as it was milled and bagged. By the end of Bank Holiday Monday, I worried that we would never be able to keep up with demand, but then on the Tuesday it rained and I sold just three bags of flour.

Keeping the mill open and running on its own for the six days a week on which the museum was open proved quite a challenge, and volunteers were brought in to help. Peter and Ruth Stock and Peter and Heather Vincent were the first to volunteer in 1984. Both couples made considerable contributions to the watermill both as an exhibit and in the regular production of flour, including representing the museum at Traditional Cornmillers' Guild meetings.

Robert Demaus started to take a back seat, and Neil Wilkins took over some of the day to day running of the mill, supported by volunteers, eventually becoming miller in 1987, followed by Mike Tighe in 1989. Since 1998 it has been run entirely by volunteers with the support of permanent museum staff. Robert, however, has remained in charge of the regular and scheduled maintenance of the machinery and the occasional unscheduled repair.

Maintenance is vitally important to keep the mill running. In the first season the main

Heather Vincent, pictured here attending to the mill machinery, and her husband Peter were key volunteers in the mill, eventually retiring after 20 years' service.

> " *From my own experience as a novice baker, I can say that the wholemeal flour produced by Lurgashall mill will produce a very tasty loaf – nutty, light, and full of wheaty flavour, together with vitamins, protein, starch and digestible fibre. Nothing extra is put in and nothing is taken away.* "
>
> **John Herniman, 2000**

water shaft failed and had to be replaced. In 1997 the mill race needed major repairs following a leak which had undermined the structure. And in 2005 a small waterproof section within the lower pond was created to reduce water leakage, along with new access for disabled visitors and the rebuilding of the launder (the timber channel that carries water onto the top of the wheel). The next major anticipated works will be re-cogging the gears (in the next two to five years) and sourcing and making a new oak main shaft, which although not yet needed, should be prepared in advance. "The cogs will have lasted around 35 years, not a bad record," says Robert.

Today the mill grinds wheat flour for human consumption. Although not producing the tonnage it used to, it is now working and producing flour almost every day of the year. "It is testament to the robust and simple machinery and the skill of the band of millers that it scarcely misses a beat from one year to the next," Robert says.

The flour is sold from the watermill itself and in the museum shop, as well as at a number of outlets in the local area. Several booklets of recipes have been produced and biscuits made with the flour are sold to visitors. The flour is also used in food produced for the museum's café.

Visitors enjoying the mill – surveys have shown it is one of the most popular exhibits.

By 1995 the watermill was producing some 32 tons (33 tonnes) of flour annually, contributing around £11,000 to the museum from sales on and off the site. Mill volunteer Peter Stock found that it took 10.38 hours pump-running time to produce 0.98 tons (one tonne) of flour. Wheat sold to visitors for duck feeding that year amounted to 7.87 tons (8 tonnes), and a total of 3,000 cookies were sold, along with 562 recipe books.

In 2009, 19.68 tons (20 tonnes) of flour were milled, with a retail value of £18,000. The watermill is consistently cited in visitor surveys as the most popular exhibit at the museum.

The mill in the foreground of a wintry scene.

Saw-pit shed

from Sheffield Park, East Sussex. 19th century
Dismantled 1976, re-erected 1980

This structure provides cover for a permanent saw-pit and is typical of many such buildings in villages and on estates. The successor to the medieval method of sawing using trestles, the shed is designed to enable timber to be unloaded from a timber wagon and rolled on top of the pit. The museum's example houses a range of tools used in the handling and conversion of timber.

Left *The saw-pit shed on its original site, and* **right** *at the museum.*

Carpenters' shop

from Windlesham, Surrey. Late 19th century
Dismantled 1978, re-erected 1980

Typical of the small workshops which were once common in towns and villages, this example came complete with the benches and many of the tools and materials the carpenter needed for his trade.

Mr Dale, carpenter and undertaker, was the last to use the building.

Left *The building on its original site, and* **right** *at the museum.*

Pugmill house

from Redford, West Sussex. 19th century
Dismantled 1979, re-erected 1980

This brick and stone structure was built to house a horse-powered pugmill, in which clay was prepared for brick-making in a small rural brickyard. All other traces of the brickyard at Redford have disappeared. The pugmill itself came from a brickyard at East Grinstead.

Nearby at the museum is a horse 'gin' (engine) from Patching, near Worthing, used for pumping water from a well, and one of the museum's earliest exhibits.

Left *A drawing of the pugmill house in use.* **Top right** *A section of the walls arrive at the museum, and* **right** *as it is today.*

Brick-drying shed

from Petersfield, Hampshire. Dendrochronology date – 1733
Dismantled 1979, re-erected 1980

This 80-feet long brick-drying shed came from the Causeway Brickworks, near Petersfield. The shed's purpose was to cover 'green' (freshly moulded) bricks while they dried before being fired.

A brickmaker's bench is included at one end, and it houses an exhibition on the history of brick-making.

Left *The shed on its original site.* **Top right** *During re-erection (Roy Armstrong is standing to the right), and* **right** *as it is today.*

Hall

from Boarhunt, Hampshire. Late 14th century
Dendrochronology date range – 1355-90
Dismantled 1970, re-erected 1981

A small but well-built example of a medieval open hall, the main feature of the building is the central roof truss of 'cruck' construction (a long curved timber which rises from the ground to support the roof timbers). It has a service room at one end, and at the other, a conjectural reconstruction of a medieval solar (missing at the time of dismantling).

Typical of cruck buildings in eastern Hampshire, the positions of doors and window openings were uncertain and have been conjectured.

Left *The hall on its original site.* **Top right** *During re-erection at the museum, and* **right** *as it is today.*

House

From Walderton, West Sussex. 15th and 17th century
Dismantled 1980, re-erected 1982

Constructed of flint and brick, this building appears externally to be of 17th-century date, but in fact contains the remains of a medieval timber-framed building with an open hall. The living room has been furnished in 17th-century style, while the middle room has been designed to show the transition from a medieval to a 17th-century dwelling. The house and grounds were the subject of an archaeological investigation, with an article published in the *Sussex Archaeological Collections*, and its dismantling and reconstruction was the subject of a BBC *Chronicle* programme transmitted in 1982.

Left *The building on its original site, and* **right** *at the museum.*

Animal pound

from Walton Heath, Surrey. 19th century
Dismantled and re-erected 1983

Near the smithy is this simple fenced enclosure in which animals found straying on Walton Heath were impounded until claimed by their owners. This example was on the line of the M25 motorway.

Left *The pound on its original site, and* **right** *at the museum.*

Joiners' shop

from Witley, Surrey. Late 19th century
Dismantled 1982, re-erected 1983

Another building typical of workshops to be found in towns and villages in the late 19th and early 20th centuries, this joiners' shop was the workplace of 12 men employed by the Mullard family's general building firm. At the museum its understorey is used for materials storage, and the workshop for the hands-on exhibition *Getting to Grips*.

Left *The building on its original site, and* **right** *at the museum.*

School

from West Wittering, West Sussex. 18th century
Dismantled 1981, re-erected 1984

For some years before 1851 this building was used as a school for "six poor children from the parish of West Wittering", financed and run by the Oliver Whitby Charity, which also ran the Bluecoat School in Chichester. Originally it appears to have been an open-ended cartshed with a hipped roof, possibly dating from the 18th century, converted to a school in the late 1820s. Outside is a yard and a stable, possibly used for the schoolmistress's horse. When the museum dismantled the building it had been empty and unused for many years and was on the verge of collapsing into the road. Today it is furnished as a school, and used for school sessions.

Left *The building during dismantling, and* **right** *at the museum.*

Medieval house

from North Cray, Kent. 15th century
Timbers arrived on site 1975 (dismantled by Kent authorities in 1965), re-erected 1984

A classic medieval hall-house of four bays with a central open hall between service and solar ends, this building was dismantled to make way for road widening. No progress in its planned re-erection in the borough of Bexley was made, and the timbers, all of elm, were donated to the museum. The external timbers have been painted red, following evidence on the timbers and from other sources that red paint was often used on the timbers of medieval buildings (a tradition which survives in French and German towns today).

Left *The house on its original site (photographed in 1928 by the Royal Commission on the Historical Monuments of England).*
Top right *During re-erection, and* **right** *as it is today.*

Granary

from West Ashling, West Sussex. 19th century
Dismantled and re-erected 1985

This granary came from behind West Ashling House and has been re-erected near Lurgashall watermill where it is used for the storage of grain to be milled.

Left *The granary on its original site, and* **right** *at the museum.*

Plumbers' workshop
from Newick, East Sussex. Late 19th century
Dismantled and re-erected 1985

Part of the premises of W R Fuller, Plumbers & Decorators, this building had a plumbers' workshop on the ground floor and a glaziers' workshop on the first floor. The building was moved intact, rather than being dismantled, and its lower floor has been fully furnished as a plumbers' workshop.

Left *The building on its original site, and* **right** *at the museum.*

Medieval shop
from Horsham, West Sussex. 15th century
Dismantled 1968, re-erected 1985

Originally part of Butchers Row (latterly known as Middle Street), Horsham, the medieval timbers were rescued from demolition when the site was needed for redevelopment. The building contains a pair of shops side by side, one of which has access to the jettied upper chambers. At the back of each shop is an open hall or 'smoke bay'. Dramatically altered during its life, many original timbers had been removed, but there was sufficient evidence for the reconstruction, which was one of three building projects at the museum carried out by specialist historic timber-framed building conservation company, McCurdy & Co. Like its neighbour, the upper hall from Crawley, the roof is covered with Horsham slabs, heavy laminated sandstone found only in the Weald clay and quarried extensively in a triangle formed by Horsham, Crawley and Steyning.

Left *The building on its original site, and* **right** *as it is today.*

House extension
from Reigate, Surrey. Early 17th century
Dismantled 1981, re-erected 1987

Dating from the early 17th century, this building was a rear extension to a house in Reigate High Street, owned from 1587 to the mid-17th century by brewers named Cade. It contains two main rooms with fine carved fireplaces and the upper room

includes the remains of high quality contemporary decorative wall paintings. Due for demolition to make way for a shopping centre, it was presented to the museum by the developers. The basement walls and chimney were built of Reigate Stone quarried from the Upper Greensand formation in the hills north of the town. The lower room of the building is currently in use as the Volunteers' Resource Room.

Left *Richard Harris' drawing of the building, and* **right** *the structure at the museum.*

Barn

from Cowfold, West Sussex. Dendrochronology date – 1535-36
Dismantled 1980, re-erected 1988

A typical late-medieval barn from the Weald, the roof is of crown-post construction, the walls are weather-boarded and the roof thatched. Mortices in the posts indicated lean-to structures on one side and one end, which have been reconstructed as open-sided shelters. The barn is linked with Bayleaf farmhouse to form a typical late-medieval Wealden farmstead.

Left *The barn on its original site, and* **right** *at the museum.*

Medieval house

from Sole Street, Kent. 15th century
Dismantled 1970, re-erected 1991

Originally from the small village of Sole Street, this building's historic

importance lies in the fact that it includes an aisled hall, which has survived intact. Usually a feature of early houses, dating from the 13th and 14th centuries, this example is more likely to date from the 15th century, and is one of a number of single-bay aisled halls in the North Downs near Canterbury. The aisled hall was open to the roof and had a central open hearth, with a later cross wing at the service end. The building is currently in use as a tea room.

Left *The building on its original site, and* **right** *at the museum.*

Longport farmhouse

from Newington, Kent. 1500-1900
Dismantled 1992, re-erected 1995

Longport is a typical Kent farmhouse, but complex, with several periods of construction and alteration from 1500 to 1900. It was moved from the site of the Eurotunnel terminal, near Folkestone, after the museum agreed to accept it for re-erection and won the contract, with the Canterbury Archaeological Trust, to undertake the dismantling within a demanding schedule laid down by Eurotunnel. It is in use as the museum's entrance facility, shop and offices.

From top left *The farmhouse before dismantling; the complex structure of the farmhouse is apparent in this photograph as the roof of the oldest section of the building, dating from 1554, comes down; two images as the farmhouse rises on its new site at the museum; and completed, as it is today.*

Whittaker's Cottages
from Ashtead, Surrey. Mid 1860s
Dismantled 1987, re-erected 1997

This pair of cottages, to be demolished for a housing development, are from Ashtead, Surrey, and were built in the 1860s facing the newly-opened railway line between Epsom and Leatherhead. The foundations and chimneys are of brick, but the rest of the building is of timber. Each cottage is 12 feet wide and 20 feet long (3.6 x 6.09 metres), with two rooms on each floor. At the museum they have been presented differently, one furnished at a late 19th century date and the other left unfinished inside, to expose the timber-framed structure. Although very different in appearance from the older timber-framed buildings at the museum, they were built using traditional carpentry and timber-conversion techniques.

Left *The building on its original site, and* **right** *as it is today.*

Poplar Cottage
from Washington, West Sussex. Mid-17th century
Dismantled 1982, re-erected 1999

Poplar Cottage was probably the home of a landless labourer and occupied a small plot of land on the southern edge of the common at Washington, near Steyning, West Sussex. Its historical importance lies in the existence of a 'smoke bay', an early form of chimney in which smoke from the fire is taken out of the house from within a bay about four feet long. It represents an intermediate stage of development between the open hall, as in Bayleaf farmhouse, and full chimneys, as in Pendean farmhouse. Smoke bays were first identified by researchers in Surrey and are common in 16th- and 17th-century houses in the Weald and Downland region. The cottage was re-erected as a memorial to Roy Armstrong, founder of the museum.

Left *The cottage on its original site, and* **right** *at the museum.*

Horse whim
from West Kingsdown, Kent. 19th century
Dismantled 1981, re-erected 2000

This three-bay structure covers a horse-driven mechanism for raising water from a well – a 'horse whim'. Removal of a pin in the shaft allows the drum to revolve freely when lowering the bucket, with the speed of descent controlled by a brake. The power is provided by a small horse, pony or donkey.

Left *The horse whim before dismantling, and* **right** *the interior at the museum.*

Open shed
from Charlwood, West Sussex. 18th century
Dismantled 1999, re-erected 2000

This building came from the perimeter of Gatwick airport. Originally open on all four sides, its purpose is likely to have been as a cart and wagon shelter. However saw cuts on the tie beams suggest that is was also used as a saw-shed, with the

balk to be sawn placed on the tie beams instead of on trestles or over a pit. It is currently used to display hop equipment.

Left *The building in its original position, showing its close proximity to the airport site, and* **right** *at the museum (left) with the horse whim opposite.*

Timber crane
from Privett, Hampshire. 1911
Dismantled 1997, re-erected 2006

This hand-operated timber crane dates from 1911 and comes from Basing Home Farm, Privett, Hampshire. Designed to lift 10 tons (10.16 tonnes), it has been restored to working order for use in the woodyard to transfer incoming logs from the timber wagon to the hewing area, the sawpit or the

racksaw bench. The shed from Coldwaltham, Sussex has been moved within the museum to a new site in the woodyard and is used for demonstrations of other woodworking machinery.

Left *The winding gear of the crane on its original site, and* **right** *at the museum.*

Hay barn
from Ockley, Surrey. Dendrochronology date – 1805
Dismantled 1985, re-erected 2010

This oak-framed hay barn with a tiled and hipped roof stands on eight posts and is almost square in plan. The sides are open to allow air flow, with the exception of four-feet deep weather-board fixed at the top of two opposing sides.

Left *The building on its original site, and* **right** *at the museum.*

Buildings and building parts dismantled and not yet re-erected

Wealden-house roof truss from Billingshurst, West Sussex.
Dismantled 1968

Little Winkhurst from Sundridge, Kent.
Dismantled 1968

Granary from Yapton, West Sussex.
Dismantled 1969

Roundhouse from Bersted, West Sussex.
Dismantled 1970

Roundhouse from Binsted, West Sussex.
Dismantled 1971

Granary from Chilcomb, Hampshire.
Dismantled 1972

'Tindall's Cottage' from Ticehurst, East Sussex.
Dismantled 1974

Granary from Ashurst, West Sussex.
Dismantled 1977

Woodsheds and pigsty from West Dean, West Sussex.
Dismantled 1978

Barn and cattle shed from Kirdford, West Sussex.
Dismantled 1978

Dovecot from Milton Street, East Sussex.
Dismantled 1980

Outhouse or shed from Shipley, West Sussex.
Dismantled 1981

→

'Folly' from Scadbury, Bromley, Kent. *Dismantled 1987*

Bakehouse from Newdigate, Surrey. *Dismantled 1988*

Forge from Great Bookham, Surrey. *Dismantled 1988*

House from Godalming, Surrey. *Dismantled 1989*

Cottage from Lodsworth, West Sussex. *Dismantled 1993*

Chapel from Ovingdean, East Sussex. *Dismantled 1996*

Church from South Wonston, Hampshire. *Dismantled 2006*

The Rural Life Collections

It was clear from the earliest years that it would be important for the museum to collect the paraphernalia of everyday life alongside its historic vernacular buildings. Largely this meant rural life, as even townspeople were dependent on the produce of the farms and countryside for survival.

As a specialist rural-life teacher, Chris Zeuner had a good working knowledge of agricultural implements and equipment. He was appointed honorary curator of crafts and equipment in 1971, and established the first cataloguing system for donated artefacts. Whilst the buildings' collection was to be curated by the research director (Roy Armstrong, followed by Richard Harris), the rural life collections were always curated separately.

When buildings were dismantled there were often other objects to be rescued from the site, notably artefacts relating to domestic and agricultural life. These were brought back to the museum and stored in one of a number of buildings and sites in and around West Dean and Singleton, as well as some further afield.

As news of the embryonic museum project spread, people offered to donate objects, and with a collection to build up from scratch, most were accepted. Many of the new museums being established in the late 1960s and 1970s were responsible for saving large numbers of historical objects ('the stuff', as collections are fondly called), which would otherwise have been discarded, preserving this knowledge base for future generations. It is for this reason, and to safeguard donors' gifts made in good faith, that museums operate stringent collections policies and will only rarely de-accession (offer for sale or

disposal) historic items. Today the museum's collecting policy has been refined and with space and funding issues playing a part, will not accept donations which replicate good quality artefacts already in the collection.

As Chris Zeuner became the museum's keeper and then director, it was to Heather Jackson (later

Above *The first accessioned item in the collection, a drawknife from Tamplins Brewery in Brighton, numbered 1968.001.*

> From its foundation the museum has always been part of the local rural community, and agriculture and rural crafts have always been major concerns, both in the buildings and the artefact collections which, as the collecting policy states, are intended to support the primary collection of buildings.
>
> **The museum's application for designation as an outstanding collection, 1998**

Below *Two restored wagons from the collection ready for use on site.* **Left** *The boat wagon, here with carter Les Whitecall and Shire horse Freddie, and* **right** *the Sussex wagon, used for many years as the museum's main promotional horse-drawn vehicle.*

open days were held to allow interested visitors access to those items the museum was unable to display on site. Heather was responsible for the cleaning, numbering, cataloguing and labelling of thousands of items and took charge of the display of the important Plewis wheelwrighting collection in the Watersfield stable on the museum site, where it remained for many years.

The museum was granted a lease on redundant farm buildings in the village of Charlton by the Goodwood Estate Company in 1980. The aim was to centre the museum's collection and the master carpenter's workshop in one place. Considerable work was needed to repair 'the barns', before they were ready to take the collections from Preston Farm, Binderton, a cottage in West Dean village and Roger Champion's workshop in the old railway cutting at Singleton. To meet costs some of the buildings were let to other craftsmen, including a wheelwright, a blacksmith, a jeweller and a potter. The museum's collections and workshop remained there until the completion of the Downland Gridshell in 2002, which enabled both to be brought on-site and be made regularly accessible to visitors.

It was spring 1990 when Chris Zeuner offered the job of curator to Bob Powell, providing him with the opportunity to be involved in many of his personal interests: rural life and crafts, farming, vernacular architecture, living history and, most of all, heavy horses. It was the start of the best six years of his professional career, he says, and even today, as curator at the Highland Folk Museum, Newtonmore, he "persistently quotes the Weald & Downland Museum for best practice and personal experiences".

Professional highlights were many. They included developing the children's hands-on exhibition, *Getting to Grips*, in the Witley joiners' shop, working with the Worshipful Companies of Plumbers and Masons on their displays in Court Barn, the research and mounting of an exhibition on the Women's Land Army (followed by a book on the subject written with Nigel Westacott), and the 'pinnacle' of his time at the museum, the dismantling of Longport farmhouse at Cheriton and its later re-erection.

Champion, after her marriage to Roger, the museum's master carpenter) that the practical curatorial tasks fell. Heather spent two years developing the education service but became increasingly interested in the cataloguing and conservation of donated artefacts, ranging from parts of historic buildings to rural craftsmen's tools, agricultural equipment and domestic items. Through the late 1970s this work took up more and more of her time and she became the effective curator and conservator; all the entries in the accessions register are in her handwriting from March 1975 until January 1990.

It was Heather who later supervised the move of the artefacts to the new store at Charlton where, in an initiative then unusual in museums,

Bob's additions to the museum's collections included many items connected with heavy horses, notably harness and horse-drawn implements, including spares. They all added to the treasures within the Charlton Barns complex where Bob contributed to the early stages of the collections' revision before the move to the Gridshell. Bob accompanied Chris Zeuner to off-site

heavy horse events with the museum's own Shires, including the London Heavy Horse Parade and Portsmouth Parade and struck up a valued friendship with Rob Dash, the consummate Surrey horseman who was a keen museum supporter and part-time horseman after Chris Zeuner's death.

By 1998 Julie Massey was curator, and she described her profession in the museum magazine:

Objects not necessarily of use for display today may well be required in the future. If they are not collected when they become available they may be more difficult or even impossible to find. Whittaker's Cottages are a good example of where forward collecting is important. Furniture, clothes and domestic items have been added to the museum's collection with the intention that they will be used in the furnishing of these Victorian cottages. Some items are intended as replacements to those used on site, which, due to their very nature, will eventually deteriorate.

She pointed out that some objects were not suitable for display because of their poor condition, or duplication with another object already on display, or simply lack of room. Some were collected principally for researchers, such as the museum's collection of building parts and materials. Objects accepted become the responsibility of the museum to conserve and store forever, she pointed out: "a huge undertaking, especially for large items, such as wagons and farm machinery". Chris Zeuner took on the additional role of curator for a short time when Julie Massey left.

A quarter of the museum's lifetime had taken place when the Designated Museums Challenge Fund Collections Management project began in 1999. It was Mike Wall's first formal involvement with the museum although he had been a frequent visitor over the years. In the late 1960s he was working at the Science Museum as assistant to the keeper of agricultural implements and machinery, but on visits back home to Harting would often be treated to an enthusiastic update on the creation of 'The Open Air Museum' from fellow Harting resident and one of the earliest trustees, Major General Hawes.

By the 1980s Mike was working as manager/curator at Amberley Chalk Pits Museum (now Amberley Museum & Heritage Centre) which owed much of its genesis in early planning to the Weald & Downland Open Air Museum. The Downs Steam Show held at Singleton provided Mike with his first meeting with Chris Zeuner. Two months later, Mike had a new job and was

Conservation in the Charlton Barns workshop, with, left to right, Mike Piggott, John Hurd, Lara Band and Ray Ashdown.

on a tour of the stores in the old railway cutting at Singleton station and at Charlton farmyard before being handed the keys. Mike recalls the cornucopia of rural life artefacts which awaited him:

Tin-roofed sheds in the cutting covered a mass of ancient farm machinery and the dismembered timbers, bricks and tiles from buildings awaiting re-erection. At Charlton the main barn and many of the outbuildings in the two adjacent yards were packed to capacity with what appeared to be every conceivable rural artefact. Once the eyes had become accustomed to the gloom, it became increasingly apparent that there really were farm wagons stacked three deep with some of their wheels suspended from beams! A menacing array of spike-rollered barn machinery, cider-apple scrutters and leather-lunged blacksmith's bellows lurked in dark recesses alongside the aisles of steel shelving which retained mysterious crates of building materials, iron window frames and stacks of ornamental plaster patterns.

As its name implied the 'Small Items Store' housed smaller objects. Teetering piles of fruit and vegetable boxes, some wearing Dymo accession labels dating back 20 years or more, contained domestic paraphernalia, axes, handbills, planes and plumbers' bobbins from a host of once common rural trades and industries. A massive clutch of 'long-handled tools' – pitch-forks, hay-rakes and ditching scoops – were bound together with the ubiquitous string, like giant spillikins about to be spilled!

In preparation for Mike's arrival a computer system had been set up by Richard Harris who had also incorporated the accession register. Thanks mainly to Heather Champion, the

The winding engine from the West Kingsdown horse whim is carried out of the workshop after repair by Roger Champion, Mike Wall and Mike Piggott.

Charlton outbuildings for a basic conservation workshop; another became a curatorial office.

As the surveys progressed the team was often able to add further information to that already recorded, in rare instances even making contact with donors from some 30 years previously. Farmer Ron Peel from Forestside had made several gifts of agricultural items to the museum in the 1960s and after a visit from Mike the museum was given more of Mr Peel's gems including copies of a delightful series of watercolours depicting farm work at Forestside during the last war.

The extensive Stevenson collection of agricultural bygones had been purchased in the mid-1980s at a farm sale after the death of Mr Stevenson, with funding from the museum Friends. At the time of accession little had been known about the family farm in a remote part of Ashdown Forest,

> **❝** *The Weald & Downland Museum collections project was undoubtedly one of my most memorable working experiences, an exceptionally rare privilege shared with such a committed and companionable team of colleagues. All too soon the time allocated to the project was drawing to a close and the impressive state-of-the-art industrial racking was finally being installed in the Gridshell basement. At last the long-anticipated removal from Charlton began and some of the museum's best-hidden secrets emerged blinking in the daylight.* **❞**
>
> **Mike Wall, collections' manager**

documentation on the 10,000 objects was exceptionally complete. In the former dairy Mike found volunteer Ray Ashdown steadily working his way through the most recent acquisitions. Mike formulated a strategy to survey every item in each of the museum's collection categories, including families of related sub-collections. Each object was to be assessed for its relevance within the museum's stated collecting policy, its condition and provenance. To bring the museum's records in line with collections' classification used nationally he oversaw their transfer to the MODES software system.

Heather Champion was often able to solve mysteries surrounding some of the earlier accessions, with Roger adding some priceless ingredient to the tale. Independent funding brought in David Viner for a preliminary heritage merit survey of the carts and wagons, and former curator Bob Powell came down from Scotland to give useful assistance with the harness collection.

Much-valued team members who contributed to building the knowledge base included Mike Piggott, Jon Roberts and Guy Viney, a group of NADFAS (National Association of Decorative & Fine Arts Societies) ladies who appraised the smock collection and other costume items, and Philippa Edom who analysed the museum's collection of sheep bells.

Remedial conservation was assisted by East Anglian conservator George Monger's manual of first-aid practice, with space created in one of the

and the objects, ranging from an early Marshall's of Gainsborough threshing machine, various carts, wagons and implements, to harness, hand-tools, domestic items and furniture had all been dispersed into their various sub-collections in store. It was the often-recurring name 'Stevenson' which alerted Mike to the importance of the collection as a whole.

The Stevensons had continued to employ several archaic farming practices long after most of their neighbours. They had used horses until the 1970s; the harness was still fit for use and the much-patched vehicles and well-maintained tools showed signs of recent wear. There were rare examples of horse-drawn sledges for transporting hay-cocks, a very scarce Sussex foot-plough complete with all its parts, and wood-framed harrows in good order, all as if they had recently been put aside from work. Lara Band undertook research into the family and their farm, vastly improving the museum's knowledge and even uncovering photographs of some of the artefacts in use.

The late Tony White had been a good friend to the museums at Singleton and at Amberley and had stored bulky items for both on his farm at Yapton. Having read about the collection survey in the museum magazine, Tony telephoned in the hope of retrieving some framed examples of Victorian wheat samples which he had loaned to the museum many years earlier. The treasured cereals were eventually unearthed and returned and Tony was glad to re-establish contact with the museum, subsequently making several generous donations, including the very rare Carter Brothers of Billingshurst wagon and later, on Tony's passing, the beautiful little Hayter van – and, again, the Victorian wheat samples.

Julian Bell's arrival as curator coincided with the transition of the collections between Charlton Barns and the Downland Gridshell. His role has been to exploit the extensive development of the artefact collections since the museum's early days, making use of the advantages and new opportunities offered by the Gridshell.

"Very few curators in any museum have the opportunity to fill a purpose-built artefact store, but this was the first task I faced," Julian said. "The prospect was both exciting and daunting, due to the large amount of material involved." Rudimentary resources were available for transferring the artefacts the short way to the museum. They consisted of three people, himself, Guy Viney and Jon Roberts, the museum's horsebox, and a large number of bread crates. "It was oddly reassuring, given the state-of-the-art nature of the Gridshell, to have my other foot firmly planted in the reality of 'make do and get on with it', and a deadline which dictated the move be complete by the end of the year."

Once the artefacts reached the Gridshell they had to be stored, according to type, size and subject matter. But the painstaking groundwork carried out by Mike Wall and his predecessors in building up and maintaining a high level of artefact documentation, was to stand Julian in good stead. Documentation is not the most exciting part of a curator's job, but definitely one of the most important. "My predecessors had the foresight to start recording these gifts, noting who had given them to us, where they were from and most vitally in many cases, what the item actually was,

then linking this information to the artefact itself via a unique number."

The ability to find an object from a collection seems a very basic task for a museum but one which relatively few can do comprehensively, Julian says. But the diligence of his forerunners and a location audit carried out immediately after the collections' transfer to the Gridshell mean that virtually all items within the store can now be found from their associated documentation. When, for example, a visitor asks to view an item donated many years ago by a relative, the museum is able to locate it, giving donors confidence in the custodianship of their cherished items. This makes it possible to show visitors the first ever accessioned item in the collection, a drawknife from Tamplins Brewery in Brighton, numbered 1968.001.

The thorough background information proved invaluable when organising artefacts within the new Gridshell store. The surveys established by

Above *Mike Wall finding a new home for the museum's extensive collection of horse team, or latten, bells in the Gridshell store.*

Below *Tony White's framed display of 19th-century wheat samples from the Brighton area, given to the museum in the 1970s, returned at his request, and bequeathed again on his death in 2007. The case includes four different varieties with a sample for each year from c1860 to the 1890s – a valuable record of cereal growing in the region.*

The main barn at Charlton farmyard, empty of artefacts following the move to the new Gridshell store.

Mike Wall gave structure to the task of physically arranging the items, one which fell largely to long-standing volunteers, John Hurd and Mike Piggott, who were, Julian says, chiefly responsible for the stunning visual impact the store has today.

Awaiting their new home: forks of various types, scythes and yokes.

Mike Wall's paper-based surveys remain a useful tool today despite an increasingly comprehensive computer database of the object collections, a resource which continues to be updated. They have provided the core system for organising the collections within umbrella subject headings, and the list provides an insight into the wide range of subjects covered by the museum's collecting policy.

Survey headings

Agriculture – hand
Agriculture – powered
Animal husbandry
Architectural ironmongery
Blacksmithing
Brick and tile-making
Builders, decorators, stone-working
Building materials
Carpentry
Cider and brewing
Coopering
Costume
Dairying
Domestic
Doors, windows, shutters and panelling
Fire furniture
Furniture
Gamekeeping, trapping and field-sports
Harness
Illumination
Land management
Leatherworking – cobbling and footwear
Leatherworking – harness-making
Leconfield Estate Workshops Collection
Millwrighting
Plewis Collection
Plumbing
Shepherding
Stable furniture
Stevenson Collection
Thatching
Tinsmithing
Well fittings
Wheelwrighting and vehicle parts
Wood processing

The museum's policy is generally to engage in the *conservation* of items where historic materials are retained and preserved, rather than their *restoration,* but sometimes where much of the original has disappeared or is badly damaged, partial replacement is the only option to prevent wholesale instability of the object.

Presenting and interpreting artefacts from the

Gridshell stores in an increasingly interesting way is possible through projects and activities aimed at 'doing' rather than simply 'seeing'. The museum believes visitors should have as much close access as possible to the physical history in its collections rather than being kept at a distance. The generally robust nature of the items helps; visitors usually respond with great surprise when told that they are welcome to touch items in the store, but to beware as the artefacts will probably do them more harm than they will do to the artefacts!

The development of the woodyard embodies this approach: woodyard weeks are held periodically, demonstrating traditional woodland and timber-related skills such as hewing, pit-sawing, hurdle-making and timber movement and conversion. Visitors show great interest, and members of the collections team have further developed their own timber skills.

In the late 1990s the museum's entire collections were awarded designated status, recognising their outstanding national and regional importance. With the transfer of the rural life and building trade artefacts to the new store in the Downland Gridshell they are able to occupy a more central place in the museum's activities and their conservation and greater use has opened up new opportunities.

Above left *John Hurd and Mike Piggott arranging horse collars in the new Gridshell store.*
Above right *Guy Viney fixing cross-cut saws to the Gridshell store's roller-racking.*

Curator Julian Bell at work in the Singleton railway cutting store for timbers and large objects.

Most items have been donated in single or small numbers, but on rare occasions large numbers of objects are received. The collection donated in the 1970s by the late Arthur Plewis, wheelwright of High Halstow, Kent, constitutes not only the largest donation the museum has received, but stands out for its quality and the comprehensive history it provides of the life of a village wheelwright. There are around 700 recorded items from the workshop of Mr Plewis, and together with his immensely detailed diary which he kept from the beginning of his apprenticeship aged 14, they provide a rounded history of a once commonplace village activity. **Top left** Arthur Plewis, and **right** a sketch he made of his workshop. **Bottom left** The tools on display in the stable from Watersfield where they remained for some years, and **right** stored in the Gridshell.

In 2006, June Knight donated a shepherd's crook. This donation demonstrates well that the object is only half the story. The crook, an excellent example of the Pyecombe style, was given to Mrs Knight by Josie Oliver, with whom she worked as a Women's Land Army (WLA) girl during the Second World War. Josie came by the crook through her relation, H P 'Shep' Oliver, a renowned South Downs shepherd who subsequently looked after the Southdown flock at the museum until the mid 1980s. June provided information relating to her work with the WLA which built into an engaging history of her life at that time. In this instance the crook, despite being a very good example, becomes almost a

secondary part of the donation; a hook on which to hang a fascinating story. Pictured **left** is June Knight in her Land Army days. **Right** a display of crooks in the Gridshell, including Pyecombe examples.

Conserved artefacts are focal points in demonstrations, displays and at special events across the museum site, used in conjunction with the schools service department, and via the developing outreach programme in which groups of artefacts are loaned to recipients across the region. One of the more unusual of these is the loan of a shepherd's hut to Bosham Primary School in December 2008 (**left**); most loan items are somewhat smaller. **Above** Julian Bell and John Hurd preparing another newly-restored shepherd's hut from the Best collection on its new site by the museum's sheepfold.

The Gridshell facilities, together with the broad skills base of the collections' team members, have led to an increase in the number of specialist conservation projects. Larger artefacts such as agricultural machinery, carts and wagons can be widely used across the museum, increasing visitors' understanding and far outweighing any resulting potential damage to the artefact. Pictured is the Blackstone hay turner, restored and in use on the museum's hay crop, with Pete Betsworth at the reins.

The threshing machine acquired from the Stevenson collection in the mid-1980s was repaired, conserved and researched by Ben Headon and Paul Pinnington following a successful application to the Museums, Libraries & Archives Council/PRISM Fund.

Manufactured in 1862 by Marshalls of Gainsborough, it is one of the oldest, fully-working threshing machines in the country, and can perhaps be considered as the centrepiece of the rural life collections. It is pictured before restoration, **above**, and **left** afterwards, being drawn by a visiting steam engine which is also towing a living van.

During 2006/07, again with a PRISM Fund grant, the collections team led a project which involved a high level of restoration and material

replacement. The timber crane had been collected in August 1997 from Basing Home Farm, Privett, Hampshire, where it had been used since its manufacture in 1911. A fixed, hand-powered crane built by John Smith of Keighley, and designed to move up to five tons (5.08 tonnes), it was operated with two winding mechanisms, one to manoeuvre the jib and the other to lift the load. Although once a very common piece of equipment in timber yards, quarries and other places where heavy lifting was required, such cranes, especially working examples, are now very rare. Preparing it for use on site involved the complete replacement of the original timbers although nearly all the ironwork was retained. It now forms the centrepiece of the museum's working woodyard, where a sawpit and powered racksaw bench have also been installed, along with the relocated Coldwaltham shed to provide a covered working area. **Above** the crane in place in the museum's new woodyard.

The Armstrong Library

From the outset a principal objective for the museum was that it should become a recognised centre for research into, and the recording of, traditional buildings within its region. The re-erection of the upper hall from Crawley in 1983-84 was the essential step in meeting this aim, providing the museum with a lecture and meeting room on the first floor and a library on the ground floor.

Roy Armstrong wrote in 1988:

The library should do what the exhibits by them-selves do not. Whereas the latter can provide a few selected examples of buildings typical of a limited area and period, the library provides details and explanation of their setting within a larger context.

Based mainly on donations, a remarkable library developed, containing over 11,000 printed works, personal archives and specialist collections (such as those of the Worshipful Company of Plumbers), and a huge photographic collection, with Roy Armstrong's 75,000 transparencies at its core. The library focuses on three areas: buildings and archi-tecture, especially vernacular architecture and build-ing trades; local studies, especially the social and economic background to the museum's exhibits; and museum theory and practice, especially open air museums worldwide. It is thought to be the only specialist library of its kind in the country.

Jenni Leslie had acted as the museum's hon-orary librarian since 1975, and in 1982 Marjorie Hallam took over the position. One of the earliest museum supporters, sometimes described as 'deputy founder', Marjorie was a key figure in the establishment and development of the museum. A member of the promotional committee for the

museum since 1966, she made an important contribution to the rescue and interpretation of some of the earliest buildings to come into the hands of the museum in the 1970s and during its rapid development in the 1980s.

Her particular interests lay in social history (she was related to Elizabeth Fry, the Quaker reformer) and the development of the library. She researched the background to some of the buildings, notably the Bough Beech houses (Bayleaf, Winkhurst and Little Winkhurst), Pendean farmhouse and the hall from Boarhunt. She also organised study tours for museum supporters, in the UK and overseas, includ-ing Poland in 1986 and Normandy in 1993. After her retirement from the post in 1987 (when she was replaced by Jon Roberts), Marjorie continued as a trustee and in 1991 was appointed a vice president. On her death in 2006 her collection of books and papers on vernacular architecture was deposited with the museum. A group of trees and a bench have been sited near Pendean farmhouse in her memory.

The library was named after Roy Armstrong who with his wife, Lyn, worked many hours there towards the end of his life. It was open to Friends, volunteers and researchers, and the public was able to visit on special open days. With the completion of the Horsham shop more space was made available to the library, almost doubling its size. Working with volunteer Annelise Fielding, Marjorie Hallam used her knowledge of botanical classification to devise a hierarchical system for published works, which is still in use today.

Among new deposits in 1984 were the Royal Commission's English county inventories, including microfilm of out-of-print volumes and equipment for reading microfilm, achieved with the help of a £500 grant from the Chichester branch of NADFAS (National Association of Decorative & Fine Art Societies). Marjorie Hallam said:

Having such material readily available on the shelves and being able to produce immediately detailed descriptions and drawings of significant vernacular buildings in such places as Salisbury, York or Cambridgeshire is a very heartening experience and bolsters our confidence that we are becoming one of the foremost libraries in this country for the study of vernacular architecture.

Starting in 1984, a series of Manpower Services Commission teams spent three years working

A major figure in the museum's development, and for many years honorary librarian, Marjorie Hallam is seen here, right, watching the re-erection of Poplar Cottage with Dr Annabelle Hughes, of the Wealden Buildings Study Group.

Volunteers working in the Armstrong Library. **Left** *Bernadine Saunders and,* **right** *Jane and Charlotte Murgatroyd.*

alongside volunteers in the library under the guidance of Marjorie Hallam and a succession of supervisors including her daughter Caroline. Using a computer program written by Richard Harris, this project established the catalogues for printed books and Roy Armstrong's slides on Apple computers. Thanks to excellent hardware support, the data produced then has been success-fully migrated through several further systems, and is still in use today.

In 2002 Roy Armstrong's transparencies and the museum's archive of photographs and material relating to its collections – some 20,000 items – were moved to the Mitford Foulerton Studio in the Downland Gridshell, easing space constrictions in the library and enabling greater security and accessibility.

In 2003 the museum became a partner in a Heritage Lottery Fund-aided project to develop a West Sussex Photo Heritage Database, which included seven local museums, the county's Library Service and West Sussex Record Office. 50,000 of the best photographs, prints, drawings and paintings in the county were to be digitised and made available to search free of charge via the internet and on CD-Rom. Volunteers selected 5,000 slides from Roy Armstrong's Sussex collec-tion and in June 2004 the resulting website was launched at the museum.

In 2010 the library catalogue contains over 27,000 entries, including over 11,000 mono-graphs, and is maintained by a volunteer team.

*Mill authority Frank Gregory (**left**) was a frequent visitor to the museum as part of his life-long interest in wind and water mills. His knowledge and experience were drawn on by the museum for its own mill projects. When Frank died in 1998 he left his considerable collection of images, books and documents to the museum, and they are now fully catalogued and integrated with the library. In 2009 the Heritage Lottery Fund provided a grant for the Frank Gregory Online collaborative project between the museum, the Mills Archive and the Sussex Mills Group. This enabled his most important records to be available via the internet for the public to access. A well-attended Frank Gregory Symposium reporting progress on this unique project took place that year. **Right** Museum director Chris Zeuner with Frank Gregory's mill archive shortly after its arrival at the museum.*

8

One Building – the Story of the House from Walderton

Richard Harris

with Fred Aldsworth and Diana Zeuner

The dismantling and re-erection of the house from Walderton – known as Walderton cottage, although it was too big to be a cottage – was probably the most intense and formative experience of my professional life, certainly of my career at the museum. In response to a phone call offering materials from a house soon to be demolished, I made my first visit to the 'Old Post Office' in Walderton on 13 September 1979. Two weeks earlier I had taken over from Roy Armstrong the title of research director, and was now working two days a week for the museum.

My first memory of the house involves butterflies. On 9 November 1979 – a cold, hard day with the distant sound of the hunt – I sat in the roof doing my first drawing of the medieval timbers. As I shone my torch round I became aware of a gentle but persistent noise, a bit like someone breathing in and out through pursed lips. Mystified for a moment, I soon saw

The front (north) view of the building before dismantling; the right hand section beneath the corrugated iron was in a ruinous condition.

Richard Harris, left, and Roger Champion discussing roof timbers during the dismantling of the house from Walderton. Behind them are members of the BBC Chronicle *film crew.*

that it was the noise made by the peacock butterflies that were hibernating in the roof; they had been disturbed by my torch and were opening and closing their wings.

The sites and buildings committee met on Sunday 2 December in the newly completed Crawley hall, and agreed that the building should be accepted. By Christmas the owners of the two ends of the building, Mr J G Hurst and Miss Mills, had given formal permission to take possession. Mr Hurst had already obtained listed building consent for demolition, and he planned to (and eventually did) build a new house on the site.

Work re-commenced as soon as Christmas was over, and on 3 January 1980 Chris Zeuner, the museum director, and I met Fred Aldsworth, the county archaeologist for West Sussex, and John Friar on site. Fred and John were to be the two key players in the project, Fred surveying the site and carrying out the archaeology, and John dismantling and re-erecting the flintwork. I wrote a draft programme for dismantling and Chris made funding applications to West Sussex County Council (WSCC) and the Margary Fund. Both were successful, WSCC for £250 and Margary for £600, sufficient to get the dismantling under way.

Before it could take place, the building needed to be surveyed, and on 8 March I started an intensive programme of survey work alongside Fred Aldsworth. Fred set up a site grid and a system for

recording the external surfaces of the brick and flint walls, while I concentrated on very precisely measured plans and sections, and drawings of the timbers and internal features. Once the dismantling started we would always be rushing to keep up with the work, so this initial period was extremely important and intense. Fred also opened up a preliminary trench to see what the sub-floor layers might have to offer — and struck gold: a large part of the original 17th-century brick floor had survived under later 19th-century paviors.

I had established the basic interpretation of the building in my initial survey. There were two main phases: a timber-framed building with an open bay in which an open fire had deposited soot on the timbers; and radical improvements carried out in the 17th century involving the insertion of a brick chimney and rebuilding the outside walls in flint with brick quoins. But many details within this broad outline were not at all clear, and there were subsequent phases of alteration that needed to be unpicked. Throughout the dismantling we would be looking for clues, following leads and investigating the evidence. Archaeology involves continual observation and questioning — it is never a matter of simple recording.

Dismantling

The seed for a vital part of the project had been sown the previous July when the BBC showed

Staff, volunteers and film crew on site at the beginning of the dismantling of the house from Walderton.

still covered Mr Hurst's end of the building, and they set about the task with enthusiasm. The BBC filmed the huge bonfire, with the shots eventually used at the opening of the programme. What we had failed to appreciate, however, was that the base of the thatch had probably been there since the 17th century. It is now widely acknowledged that thatch is a priceless historical resource because it was normal practice every 20 to 30 years to add a new top coat but not to remove the base layers. These therefore contained seeds, pollen, weeds and straw taken straight from a 17th-century field. Today this would be carefully sampled and analysed.

The rest of the dismantling, however, was carried out with meticulous care. For 51 days from 14 April, when the first rafters were removed, until 3 June, when the building finally reached ground level, the work proceeded in almost perfect conditions. The weather was fine, and the site perfect for picnics. A small team carried out the work. Roger Champion was in charge of dismantling the timbers and his wife, Heather, did all the numbering and bagging up of samples. John Friar dismantled the flint and brick walls, and Martin McCurdy and Louise Jaggard helped with whatever was needed. Chris Zeuner came out to see us as often as he could, made sure everything was going according to plan, and discussed with me the interpretation and the practicalities of getting the building re-erected. If

interest in featuring our work in the *Chronicle* series of history programmes. Negotiations started just in time and by 24 March we knew that a BBC documentary would be made. The next day I met Anna Benson-Gyles, the producer, and on 10 and 11 April the first two days of filming took place – it all happened extremely fast. The BBC eventually paid us £100 "as a token of our appreciation"!

The first day of dismantling, Saturday 12 April, was a disaster, although we didn't know it at the time. Museum volunteers removed the thatch that

A high level view, looking south, during the process of removing the roof timbers.

he had time, he'd roll up his sleeves and help. For the first five weeks of the dismantling I worked almost without a break, seven days a week, and his encouragement and support were vital.

Some moments stand out in my memory. As an amateur archaeologist as well as an expert builder in flint, John Friar had a close rapport with Fred Aldsworth and me. Important clues to the development of the building lay in the changes of mortar from one area to another, which were visible but could be more positively identified by mortar analysis to extract the sand aggregate. John had a wonderful way of doing this involving a huge jar of concentrated hydrochloric acid, an old

army mess tin, and a plastic coffee filter – and one unforgettable shot in the film shows him bare-chested in the sun, carefully pouring the lethal acid into the tin and chortling with glee as the frothy reaction got going. Definitely no personal protective equipment!

Another moment occurred late in the job when the walls were only about three feet high. John called me over to a miraculous find: he had removed a layer of flints but underneath had found a mortar bed with the imprint not of flints but of bricks. What had happened was that an original window had been totally removed and the resulting aperture filled in with flint, but the

Below left A course of brickwork in the chimney exposed ready for recording. The large flue of the ground floor fireplace rises behind the chamber fireplace, which has curved jambs typical of the 17th century. Below right A record drawing of a course of brickwork from above.

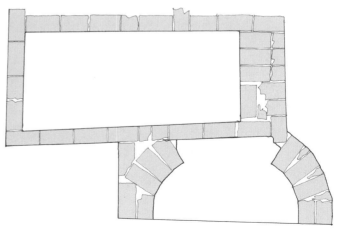

The archaeology *Fred Aldsworth*

As an archaeologist with a developing interest in the close study of the fabric of standing buildings – a discipline now often referred to as buildings archaeology – I welcomed the opportunity to become involved in the Walderton project. I had already been involved in some pioneering research of this type at Winchester in the late 1960s and at St Mary's Church at Deerhurst, Gloucestershire, in the early 1970s. But the opportunity to record a building in great detail, to observe its dismantling, and then to excavate what remained of it at, and below ground level, had previously escaped me. The sites of several medieval and post-medieval buildings have been excavated in the past, but seldom has this taken place immediately after dismantling and with the knowledge of what had stood above.

The first stage of the archaeological recording involved the production of elevation drawings recording every brick and piece of flint, extending a metric site grid up onto the walls, with vertical strings at metre intervals and horizontal strings also at metre intervals, above ordnance datum. A planning frame, with wires at ten centimetre intervals, was then fixed to the walls in order to allow information to be transferred to a gridded drawing sheet at a scale of 1:20. Information was recorded concerning the type of brick or flint used in construction and the nature of the mortar with which different parts of the walls had been laid. The result was a very detailed understanding of the original arrangement of the masonry elevations and of the alterations that had been made to them during the life of the property.

The west end of the house was in a ruinous state. This photograph shows the grid of horizontal and vertical strings used by Fred Aldsworth in his survey of the external elevations of the building.

A trial dig had already indicated that part of a 17th-century brick floor survived under a 19th-century brick floor with linoleum laid on top, so it was no surprise to find, after the building had been removed, that many of the floor surfaces had simply been laid one on top of the other. This was in sharp contrast to our experience at Poplar Cottage some years later, where all the earlier floor levels had been destroyed when the entire building was underpinned in brick in the 19th century, at which time the new floor levels were dug down to a lower level in order to increase the height of the ground floor rooms. The dig was mainly conducted at weekends using local volunteers, together with John Friar.

It has always surprised me that so much domestic refuse, such as pottery sherds and small finds, is found within dwellings when one might expect rubbish to have been discarded outside. In the event, we discovered that an earlier building had stood on the site, and the pottery sherds lying stratified between the floor levels, and indicating medieval occupation from about 1270 to about 1400, were probably associated with that earlier building. Two post-medieval pottery groups of about 1400 to about 1550 and 1550 to 1620 were associated with the surviving timber-framed structure; and some 17th- and 18th-century material was associated with the flint and brick walls. Other items found included part of a Neolithic stone axe made of granite from Devon/Cornwall or Cumbria; a medieval spindle whorl, used for spinning wool; two coins, one of 1736/1756 and the other of 1844; and two tokens, one of which had been issued by the Parys Mine Company of Anglesey between 1787 and 1791.

Local volunteers excavating the early floor levels.

Documents held by the latest owners of the cottage allowed the ownership of the property to be traced from 1614, when it was owned by John Catchlove, to the present day, and West Sussex Record Office holds a probate inventory for John Catchlove, produced in 1634, which lists many of his possessions.

brick imprint had remained from the brick sill of the window.

Most of the dismantling of the timbers and the brick and flint had to involve taking them apart, but we also looked for opportunities to remove sections of the building intact. Some soot-blackened wattle and daub panels were carefully reinforced and removed in one piece, as was the 17th-century partition frame in front of the chimney. The original plank doors of the cup-boards by the chimney survived with their dovetail hinges – and one even retained its squeak until an over-enthusiastic volunteer steward later gave it a drop of oil!

The BBC crew filmed for at least a dozen days, covering all the stages and keeping up with our discoveries. With the constant pressure of survey work it was sometimes annoying to have to spend time talking to the camera, so I became adept at doing things in a single take. The team saw the first rushes at Wood Lane on 23 April and it was clear that as a record of the dismantling and the interpretation of the building it was going to be excellent.

The element that took longest to dismantle was the 17th-century chimney. I insisted on not only

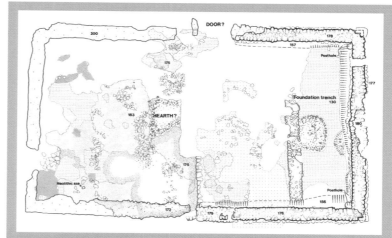

Above *Two of Fred Aldsworth's archaeological drawings superimposed. Periods I (1270-1400) and 2a (15th century) are shown in red; period 2b (late 15th century – c1550) is in black.*

Below *One of the record drawings from the dismantling, taken at the level of the upper floor and showing the soffit of the medieval timbers in reflected plan.*

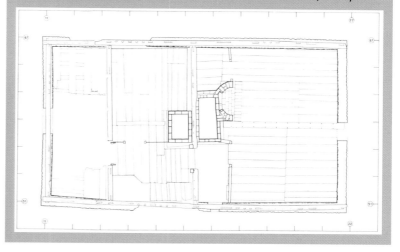

The joint lines of a row of bricks in a mortar bed revealed after removal of overlying flints, giving the position of a previously unsuspected window.

taking it down course by course, but making an accurate record drawing of every course in order to follow the twists and turns of the flues and openings within it. But eventually, on 3 June, we reached ground level, and for the next three weeks Fred Aldsworth and his team had the site to them-selves to carry out a thorough archaeological investigation of the site of the building.

On 27 June 1980 my diary entry reads: "Last visit to site. Empty at 5.05pm."

Reconstruction

Because of the BBC film, the Walderton project had to be pushed forward, and on 25 September Chris and I were already setting out and taking levels on the site for the reconstruction. In mid-October I

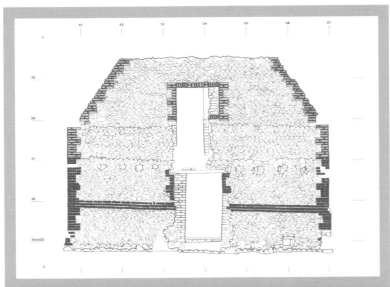

Record drawings by Fred Aldsworth showing, **top** the flint and brick elevation of the east end of the building and **bottom** the plan at ground floor level.

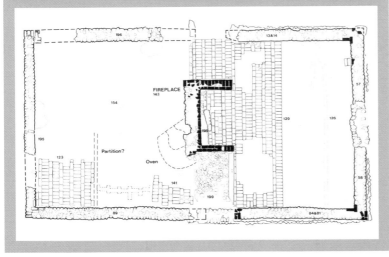

from which the reconstruction would be built, working from nearly 200 sheets of survey drawings and hundreds of colour slides.

To keep to schedule the reconstruction was going to have to start in the middle of winter – a nightmare for building flint walls with lime mortar, which must be protected from frost at all costs. To deal with this problem John Friar built a plastic-covered tent that covered the whole site of the building. In early February 1981 he started work on the walls, and on 22 May he and I set out the base of the chimney. Meanwhile Roger Champion – in amongst numerous other projects, including dismantling the 17th-century house extension in Reigate in June – had been carrying out the necessary repairs on the medieval timbers.

Eventually the tent was removed and on 25 and 26 August 1981 the timbers were hoisted into position on top of the flint walls – a public spectacle for August holiday crowds and a source of good shots for the film. As always, Roger's planning and preparation were immaculate and by the end of Wednesday 26 August the house had acquired its roof, complete with a celebratory flag.

The main challenge in reconstructing a building with a mixture of masonry and timber is that the timber frame has a size and shape which is immutably fixed, which the masonry has to follow. With a full timber-framed building it is easiest to insert the plinth wall after the main frame is erected, but that was not possible with the Walderton house because the frame sat on top of the full-height walls. Accurate setting out was therefore absolutely essential. Internally there were also timber fittings such as the original 17th-century winding stairs behind the chimney, and it was a great moment when they fitted perfectly in place between the chimney and the rear wall.

One of the challenges of the dismantling had been the rescue of the original 17th-century floor paviors that had survived beneath a later 19th-century floor in the living room. The bricks were very worn, eroded away by hobnail boots, and most of them were broken. John Friar made careful plans for lifting them, holding them together by pasting hessian on the top surface and carefully transferring strips of the floor onto metal shelving. This was successful, and back at the museum a volunteer, Matti Denton, patiently removed the hessian and bonded the broken bricks back together. By July 1981 they had been re-laid and make a big contribution to the accuracy and authenticity of the reconstruction.

The next main stage was thatching the roof, and for that to happen the chimney had to be

prepared the drawings for the planning application. Although our site has overall outline permission for use as an open air museum, each individual project requires a full planning application, and permission was granted on 13 January 1981.

My system at the museum has always been to draw in detail every individual timber after a building has been dismantled. This gives the opportunity to come to as full an interpretation of the building as possible, and provides a solid base for planning the conservation and repair of the timbers as well as the form of the eventual exhibit. I drew the Walderton timbers in November and December, using the museum's new workshops at Charlton, and then started producing the drawings

completed. This turned out to be the most problematic phase of the reconstruction. Despite my best efforts, drawings were misunderstood, and part of the work had to be taken down and done again, but it was eventually finished in early November and the thatching took place in December and January 1982. The original thatch was tied to the rafters with an organic material which Chris sent to Kew for identification, and it turned out to be old man's beard. Rod Miller was the thatcher, and the BBC crew filmed him and other finishing work such as wattle and daub on 7 December. A E Holden and Sons carried out the internal plastering of the flint walls, Andrew Breeze made the iron casements at Amberley Museum and Cox & Barnard of Hove provided the leaded lights using glass with the 'movement' and sparkle of crown glass. By April 1982 the reconstruction was complete, just two years after the start of dismantling.

Publication

Fred Aldsworth has an excellent record of prompt publication of archaeological reports, and he inspired me to collaborate in producing an article under our joint authorship for *Sussex Archaeological Collections (SAC)*[1], the venerable journal for Sussex archaeology first published in 1848. The 48-page article appeared in volume 120, 1982 – my first publication in an archaeological journal.

Fred had carried out research into the documentation for the building, using deeds in the possession of Mr Hurst and Miss Mills and other documents in West Sussex Record Office, so the report included documentary history as well as details of the building and the archaeology. The dismantling of the building had been a groundbreaking piece of buildings archaeology – an established discipline now, but almost unheard of then – and the *SAC* article did justice to it as a comprehensive account of a fully investigated building and its site, still a rarity even today.

Furnishing and interpretation

As soon as the re-erected building started rising slowly from the ground in April 1981, Chris and I started thinking about its interpretation: how were we going to present it to the public and explain its complex history of development?

The most fundamental decision had, of course, been taken at a very early stage: the building would

1 F G Aldsworth and R Harris, 'A Medieval and Seventeenth-Century House at Walderton, West Sussex, Dismantled and Re-erected at the Weald and Downland Open Air Museum' in *Sussex Archaeological Collections* 120 (1982), pp. 45-92.

be reconstructed as it looked in the 17th century, and would therefore incorporate two phases of construction – the original timbers from the 15th century and the flint and brickwork from the 17th. This was a big step for the museum to take; all previous (and most subsequent) exhibit buildings had been reconstructed to show only their original form, later alterations being recorded but discarded.

As yet the museum had included very little furniture in its domestic exhibits. Roy Armstrong had, since the early days, spoken and written of his support for furnishing in principle, but very little had taken place. The toll house had been used for an exhibition; Winkhurst, Bayleaf and Pendean had some token tables, benches and stools, and the medieval hall from Boarhunt was left empty.

So with the house from Walderton we had to strike a balance between explaining the building's development, with the contrast between its two main phases, and making the interior come to life

Above *The first view of the original 17th-century brick floor concealed beneath the later floor.*

Below *John Friar pasting hessian onto the original 17th-century brick floor in preparation for lifting and conserving the bricks.*

Two John Catchloves   *Diana Zeuner*

The museum's Knowledge Transfer Partnership associate, Dr Danae Tankard, carried out further research on the house from Walderton as part of her study into the social and economic background to the museum's main building exhibits.

As Fred Aldsworth and Richard Harris identified in their *Sussex Archaeological Collections* article there were two John Catchloves living in the parish of Stoughton in the early 17th century, evidently related. The John Catchlove who lived in the house from Walderton was an illiterate husbandman of poor means, but the other John Catchlove was a tailor and acted as the parish clerk. From tithe dispute depostions of 1625 we know that 'our' John Catchlove was aged 55 at that time and was therefore born in 1570, the son of William Catchlove. The other John Catchlove was younger, 28 in 1614, and lived in nearby Stoughton.

The 17th-century alterations to the house had made it into a substantial property, yet husbandmen typically lived in smaller houses; John Catchlove's probate inventory lists only two rooms. One conclusion is that at the time of his death in 1634 he was living in two rooms of what by then would have been a decaying medieval hall house. So who rebuilt the house and when? Perhaps it was the husband of one of his two daughters, or another family member, William Catchlove, who acquired the property between 1634 and 1646. At the museum the house has been rebuilt as it was immediately after its refurbishment. The service end of the house, which includes an oven, is disproportionate in size to the eastern half, pointing to its possible use as a 'victualling house', or public eating house. Like alehouses, they had to be licensed by justices of the peace at quarter sessions. Coincidentally, in 1638 John Catchlove, the tailor, applied to quarter sessions for a licence to keep a victualling house. The association of the Catchlove name with a victualling house may hint at a possible new interpretation of the building – perhaps the house was a bakery or eating house for the community?

The site during excavation which followed the dismantling of the building; Louise Jaggard is drawing, with the BBC film crew in the background.

with furniture. The strategy we adopted was to furnish the well-preserved living room, with its inglenook fireplace and original brick floor, and to use the middle room of the house to show its structural development. This was largely a pragmatic decision, a response to the qualities of the exhibit and the extent of survival and authenticity of the various elements of the building.

To fit with the reconstruction of the building as it looked in the 17th century, the interior would have be presented at the same period, and the museum had already recognised that furniture for its exhibits – at least, the early ones – would have to be replicas. We sought assistance from James Ayres, director of the John Judkyn Memorial at the American Museum near Bath, and author of *The Shell Book of the Home in Britain: Decoration, Design and Construction of Vernacular Interiors, 1500-1850* – just published, in March 1981. He entered into the project with great enthusiasm and was

soon sending me drawings and notes. I gave myself a crash course in 17th-century oak furniture, visiting numerous collections and talking to Peter Thornton at the Victoria & Albert Museum. Roger Champion had made the furniture that was already in Bayleaf, so he became involved in the discussions as well, and eventually he completed the basic pieces necessary for the main room of the house – a table, bench, chair and cupboard. We also commissioned ironwork for the fireplaces and some pewter to stand on the cupboard. The experience we gained on this project was to prove invaluable a few years later when we undertook the furnishing of Bayleaf farmhouse.

The other problem we had to solve was how to explain the structural development of the building from a timber frame with an open fire to a 17th-century house with a chimney and masonry walls. I saw this as a great opportunity to explore a simple theme, the invention of the modern house, as a radical change from black to white; from blackened timbers to white plaster. As it happened, in the middle room of the house, which had originally been open to the roof and therefore contained the sooted timbers, the inserted 17th-century floor was well preserved in the rear half of the room but not in the front half, so we developed the idea of showing both periods in the same space, medieval at the front, 17th century at the back, by the simple expedient of omitting the inserted joists and plaster ceiling in the front half.

Such an arrangement would have to be explained, and the best way to do that was through a recorded commentary. We enlisted the help of Michael Quinion, a museum consultant with experience as a BBC radio producer, and actor Mark Wing-Davey, to read the script for the recording.

The BBC *Chronicle* film

Anna Benson-Gyles and her team had done an excellent job of filming the dismantling and re-erection. Working with her and the editor, Tariq Anwar, we saw the need for some animated graphics to help viewers understand the relationship of one end of the building to the other. Nowadays, computer graphics are commonplace in TV archaeology programmes, but in 1981 it was a new field – so new, in fact, that I had to do it myself. Working long hours against the clock I produced 25 simple line drawings showing a changing perspective view of the building. The animation was incorporated into the film. It takes less than a second; blink and you miss it!

The film was transmitted on 24 March 1982, and gave rise to momentous consequences for the museum. A week after transmission it was Easter: the programme generated such interest among viewers that the museum received huge numbers of visitors, clogging the main road and with overflow parking on the site.

Opening

After so much effort it seemed appropriate for the building to be formally opened, and the obvious choice to officiate was Neil Cossons. He and Chris knew each other well as founder members of the Association of Independent Museums, and he had built a formidable reputation as director of Ironbridge Gorge Museum. At that time he was also president of the Museums Association. He agreed to come, invitations were sent and on 6 July 1982 the opening took place.

We thought at the time, and I still think now, that the Walderton project took the museum through a step change in the quality of its work. In part that was a consequence of having more resources; in the early days there simply wasn't the manpower available. In part also, we were building on the experience gained in previous projects. But it felt that the museum had found its stride. The pace was fast, furious and exciting. We had the wind in our hair and the future was all to play for!

9

Bringing the Museum to Life

Richard Harris and Diana Zeuner

The twin planks of the museum's interpretation policy – stewards and the guidebook – were in place from the start. Here, Joan Brooks, a long-standing volunteer steward, holding the guidebook, talks to visitors in the early 1980s.

Whilst the structure of vernacular buildings is an absorbing subject in itself, a museum of buildings open to the public would need to find ways of explaining their wider significance – a factor which was uppermost in Roy Armstrong's mind from the project's inception.

In August 1968 he wrote:

There are a number of buildings all of interest and condemned for reasons of road widening or re-development in Surrey, Kent and Sussex which,

regretfully, we have had to abandon to the fires of demolition contractors because there are not yet the means to meet the costs of careful dismantling, essential if re-erection is contemplated.

Buildings, however, are only one aspect. Furnishings, forgotten local crafts and early agricultural equipment and techniques are all part of the aim of such a museum and a great deal of material has already been collected.

'An Open Air Museum for the Weald and Downland', typescript 11 August 1968

Milestones in interpretation   *Richard Harris*

The museum's development has been marked by many minor improvements to presentation and interpretation, but there are six significant projects which represented major steps forward:

1972 Bayleaf farmhouse – when first re-erected it was not fully furnished and had a very limited curtilage, but nonetheless established a high standard of presentation, and was always stewarded.

1981 Lurgashall watermill – when the machinery was completed the building was put to productive use and has been running continuously ever since.

1982 The house from Walderton – radically raised standards of accuracy, authenticity and interpretation.

1989 The Bayleaf Medieval Farmstead project – for the first time one of the museum's exhibit buildings was fully furnished and given a realistic and appropriate curtilage.

1998 Whittaker's Cottages – interpretation of the interior in two different ways in the two cottages: building construction in one and social history in the other.

Dramatic interpretation in one half of the house from Walderton, 'cut-away' to show the juxtaposition between the 15th-century open hall phase, indicated by smoke-blackened timbers and later improvements, including the insertion of a floor in the 17th century.

2003 Winkhurst Tudor kitchen – established as a working kitchen, in which the food is real and the cooking methods authentic, and formed the hub for development of domestic interpretation at the museum.

By 1975 the purpose of the museum was stated clearly as: "to create a museum of representative traditional buildings which it is impossible to preserve *in situ*, rebuilt with associated crafts and furnishings for enjoyment, research and instruction".

But how would the museum help visitors to understand what they were seeing? In practice the twin planks of the museum's interpretation policy were put in place right from the start; volunteer stewards and the guidebook. Stewards give the museum a distinctive atmosphere and are on hand to answer visitors' immediate questions, while the guidebook provides orientation for the visit and a deeper level of information through text and pictures – for reading over a cup of tea or afterwards at home.

Then, in 1979 Chris Zeuner presented the museum's council of management with a paper, 'Keeping the Museum Alive', in which he says:

From its inception the museum was intended to be a museum of buildings, but this concept was not intended to be too restrictive. Buildings, to be of interest, need to be explained. The best way of doing this must be to use them for their original purpose, and where this is not possible to suggest the atmosphere and provide interpretation. The central theme of vernacular architecture must remain the dominant factor [author's underlining]. *… The emphasis to date has been placed on structure and plan and this is of first importance. However it leaves unexplained and almost ignored the social and economic aspects of the buildings, a subject of great interest and significance to many visitors.*

The 'essentially static' nature of the exhibits could be brought alive in various ways, he suggested, including furnishing some of the buildings, increasing the number and variety of craft demonstrations, the introduction of special events based on appropriate themes, the exploration of agricultural history using the museum's collections and the introduction of farm livestock, and a gallery covering the development of buildings.

All but the last of these elements have been put into place, with the major projects at Bayleaf farmhouse and Winkhurst Tudor kitchen taking the museum's interpretation to a new level.

Explaining historic domestic life: Bayleaf and Winkhurst   *Richard Harris*

Two projects represent significant developments at the museum in the authenticity of the interpretation of domestic life, Bayleaf Medieval Farmstead and Winkhurst Tudor kitchen. Coincidentally, both buildings came originally from the same part of Kent, having been dismantled to avoid sewage contamination of the Bough Beech reservoir.

The Bayleaf Medieval Farmstead project was completed in 1989. Previously the house had been essentially unfurnished, with only a few pieces of furniture, and a small and unrealistic garden. It had no barn, farmyard, orchard or fields; no well, wheelbarrow or cart; it lacked the atmosphere of a furnished household. The Bayleaf project was a ground-breaking attempt to recreate a medieval farmstead with not only buildings but furniture, farming equipment and an appropriate curtilage.

The first step in 1985 was the decision to site Cowfold barn behind Bayleaf to create a farmyard: it was re-erected in 1988. Garden historian Dr Sylvia Landsberg researched and reported on proposals for the garden, which was laid out in 1986. Other proposals for the exterior were made by Ruth Tittensor who wrote a report on the 'shaws' (narrow belts of woodland which were a typical Wealden feature), and medieval bee-keeping. Stephen Hall of the Cambridge Physiological Laboratory assessed the potential for displaying livestock appropriate for the target date (mid-16th century), a report which still underlies the museum's livestock policies; and Roy Brigden, director of the Museum of English Rural Life, reviewed the sources on

The replica medieval cart made for the Bayleaf Medieval Farmstead project by Emsworth wheelwright Keith Randall, scaling off measurements from the Luttrell Psalter. The 14 hands high Dales stallion, Babar, fitted perfectly between the shafts – practical proof of the size of horses prevalent at this period.

which replica farming equipment could be based. Victor Chinnery, an expert on oak furniture, wrote the key report on furnishing the house and the museum carried out its own research into probate inventories and contemporary illustrations.

Other experts wrote reports or gave advice on specialised aspects of the interior, such as the iron and brass (Ian Goodall), treen (Carole Morris) and textiles (Frances Pritchard). Many individuals gave time and effort to help the museum achieve as accurate an interpretation of a Wealden farmstead as possible, including weavers, potters, blacksmiths, coopers, wheelwrights and artists. In-house, the most important contribution was that of Roger Champion, who made all the replica oak furniture based on his own examination of original pieces. All the important steps and evidence in the project were illustrated in a panel-based exhibition in the service chamber, and a special guidebook was published, *The Bayleaf Medieval Farmstead: The Research – A Road of Discovery.*

The timbers of Winkhurst arrived at Singleton in 1968 and were re-erected the following year. The building had been recorded and analysed by R T Mason and R H Wood and interpreted as "a largely complete and well-preserved example of a small hall house dating around 1370".

In 1986 the museum carried out a major programme of repairs to the building during which observations were

The solar, furnished for the medieval farmstead project, including the principal bed and trundle (or truckle) bed beneath and the painted cloth on the wall.

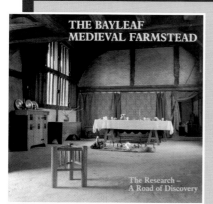

The Bayleaf Medieval Farmstead: The Research – a Road of Discovery *was produced to accompany the Bayleaf furnishing project in 1989.*

made that led to a completely different interpretation; that it was originally built in the early 16th century as a kitchen or service block, attached to – and functionally part of – a larger house. Originally it was attached to other structures on two sides. Its site at the museum was inappropriate both in topography (set high up on a Downland slope rather than in a low-lying Wealden pasture) and orientation (the building's original east wall was turned to face south at the museum), and its steeply sloping site precluded the addition of structures to represent those to which it had originally been attached. It was therefore moved to a more appropriate site close to Bayleaf farmhouse and is presented to the public as a Tudor kitchen, fully reconstructed and operational.

Used almost every day for cooking, its significance for the museum's interpretation lies in its authenticity. Food

preparation, often by costumed interpreters, includes vegetables, herbs and eggs from the museum's gardens, flour from the mill, ham and bacon from the museum's pigs, and even occasionally a carp from the lake. It established 'field to feast' as an important underlying theme at the museum.

Dawn Stevens, the first interpreter for Winkhurst Tudor kitchen, cooking on a trestle table in 2003 following the furnishing project in the building on its new site.

❝ *In the early summer of 1989 I was fortunate to spend a month in the museum on a work placement as part of a Master's degree in Heritage Management at the Ironbridge Gorge Institute. I arrived just after Bayleaf was dressed with replica furniture, wall hangings and household goods. The makeover was widely publicised and attracted huge crowds, especially schools. I was assigned to Thelma Jack, the part-time steward, to help her deal with visitors' questions and make sure that children didn't use the four poster bed as a trampoline. So many of them wanted to know what sleeping on a palliasse was like that the only way to answer them honestly was to try it out. Roger Champion was also keen to test out the beds he had made and when Chris Zeuner approved the suggestion, Thelma fell in with our plans.*

On the chosen day we kept the fire in the hall going after closing time. Heather Champion had researched 16th-century recipes and prepared some pottage which we

warmed up in a clay pot borrowed from the displays in the buttery. We had decided against using modern forms of lighting, so when night fell we took to our beds; Thelma opted for the trundle bed in the solar and I was allowed the four poster. Roger, ever the gentleman, kept guard over us with his dog from the bed in the parlour. We all slept soundly until the resident cockerel sounded the alarm at 3am. And yes, one of us did use the garderobe.

The experience was a useful if unusual form of research which enhanced our understanding and interpretation of the building. It was very peaceful without the background noises associated with modern technology, and very dark when the shutters were pulled up. And we were able to tell children that, although the straw was a bit noisy it didn't scratch, and the beds were very comfortable. ❞

Christine Beresford, 'The First Bayleaf Sleepover'

Guidebooks and the website

The museum's earliest guidebook started a long tradition that has lasted to the present day. It was written (mostly by Roy Armstrong) in July 1969, more than a year before the museum opened, and was intended to explain the project and outline its progress. Open air museums were still almost unknown in England and the guidebook made reference to successful projects in Europe and Scandinavia, together with an account of the foundation of the museum and its first projects. Over the next 40 years about a dozen editions were published. At first the pace of development was so rapid that a new edition appeared every year or so, but from the mid-1970s the interval

increased to three to five years. The original format – a neat small size – was retained until 1977 when a new square shape was used, which in turn gave way to a larger portrait rectangle which, with minor changes, has been retained ever since.

The 1982 edition introduced an important change, whereby every exhibit was given a short 'header paragraph' as well as the main text, in recognition of the fact that visitors needed a quick summary of information while on their tour. In 1987, for the first time, a professional graphic designer (David Baker) worked on the layout, moving away from the basic Times New Roman typeface and greatly improving the guidebook's visual quality. In 1992 a new design was created by Robin Wade Associates, along with a new logo

which was used throughout all published material in the museum – a line drawing based on the front of the house from North Cray. This was the first edition to be created entirely electronically, and since then the museum has taken in-house the job of making revisions and additions for subsequent editions.

The guidebook is detailed and includes only black and white photos. Chris Zeuner's firm policy was to keep its cost as low as possible so that a full account of all the exhibits would be kept in print – tens of thousands were sold every year so the print runs were quite substantial. To avoid undercutting sales of the guidebook, the museum has never produced a 'miniguide', although in the early 1980s each guidebook included an inserted card with a list of the exhibits and a 'birds-eye view' of the site. More recently the Friends of the Museum financed the publication of a 'Welcome leaflet' to be given to every visitor, which contained a map and list of exhibits together with an invitation to join the Friends, which led to greatly increased recruitment of members. The needs of foreign visitors have for many years been met by French, German and Dutch miniguides produced in-house.

As the internet became part of our lives the museum created its own website which went online in 1999, created and run by museum trustee Jeff Houlton. By generating millions of online visits it brought the museum's presence to a new and wider audience. Now, ten years later, a new system has been introduced in which content can be easily changed or edited by staff as necessary. Eventually, perhaps, this will extend to volunteers and visitors, and include social networks and other facilities offered by the ever-changing internet.

Stewards

People have always been the greatest strength of the museum's interpretation, with volunteer stewards at its heart. Their dedication has been extraordinary, and their enjoyment communicates itself to visitors. Matti Denton, an early volunteer, noted in her diary in 1971:

31 May: I spent the day getting brown in the deck chair and swotting up on charcoal burning. I am supposed to be a labouring volunteer but if I am to watch over charcoal burning then I may as well join the stewards mob, for I can't beat them.

13 June: Susan, Sarah and I spent the day at the charcoal burning area. I took a few more photographs. The weather was glorious although after midday the sun doesn't shine directly on the

Bayleaf Medieval Farmstead has its own dedicated band of specialist stewards to explain its operation as a working and domestic household of its period. The steward on the left is John Goodfellow.

charcoal pad. From early morn until lunch time the sun comes over the hill and through a gap in the trees and it is beautiful. I am beginning to be more and more absorbed in this charcoal burning process. The visitors ask me many questions and I learn such a lot from them. I have to make many notes as the day goes on or I should forget which questions I could not answer.

After 40 years, volunteer stewards remain at the heart of the museum. Regular briefings, training sessions and social events have featured over the years, and more recently significant resources have been committed to supporting and strengthening them. In 2004 a grant from the Designation Challenge Fund was used to create a series of videos to help volunteers when talking to the public; 24 titles were produced, together with a lending library of books and other background information. In 2005 a head of interpretation and two assistants were appointed to support volunteers in domestic and craft demonstrations, and in 2010 a training programme was launched with three or four sessions a month open to all volunteers. The aim is not to provide a script but to help volunteers develop positive and creative conversations. People often assume that there are answers to all questions, but in many cases the most appropriate answer is a further question.

Daily lunch-time tours of the Gridshell workshop and collections store enable improved access to areas often hidden 'behind the scenes' at museums.

The Plumbing Museum & Workshop Trust

Edward Hopkinson, President, Plumbing Museum & Workshop Trust Ltd

The Worshipful Company of Plumbers has enjoyed a happy and constructive association with the museum for over 30 years from its base in Court Barn.

The topping out ceremony at Court Barn, with the timber-frame completed. In the foreground is museum chairman, Geoffrey Godber, and Mr W M Graham, master of the Worshipful Company of Plumbers.

In 1972, the master of the company proposed a display of tools from the traditional plumbers' trade, to meet the company's objective of improving plumbing education and skills and communicating the craft to the public, aims which had been in existence since 1365.

The Sussex branch of the then Institute of Plumbing introduced the Company to Chris Zeuner, who welcomed the idea of a plumbing display being established at the museum. He gave much help and encouragement, and the benefit of his knowledge and experience, to achieve its completion. The barn from Court Farm at Lee-on-Solent was identified as a suitable building.

The Worshipful Company of Plumbers began to raise the money necessary to re-erect the barn and to fund the establishment of its museum. With the help of the plumbing industry, a collection of suitable artefacts, tools, books and catalogues was begun. These are on display today in Court Barn and the Newick plumbers' and glaziers' workshop while books and other documents are housed in the museum's library. The collection grows steadily each year.

Once funds had been raised, Court Barn was re-erected and an inaugural ceremony held in May 1979. The plumbing museum was formally opened by Her Grace, Lavinia, Duchess of Norfolk, on 4 October 1980. Demonstrations of leadwork on that day were carried out by students from Chichester College. Craft demonstrations have been carried out in the barn continuously for the past 30 years, initially by students and teachers from colleges in the south-east of England, and latterly by volunteer craftsmen from the industry. At one time, 75 to 80 demonstrations each year were normal.

Liveryman Richard Murdoch was responsible for equipping and setting up the plumbers' and glaziers' workshop from Newick in the early 1990s. Richard, who also carried out demonstrations every Wednesday until 1998, and liveryman Phil Mead, who continues to demonstrate, have formed the backbone of the project.

The Plumbing Museum & Workshop Trust has enjoyed support from the plumbing industry and, as well as craft demonstrations, offers courses in leadwork skills that are still required particularly for work on historic and listed buildings.

Leadworking demonstrations under way in Court Barn in 2007.

These are held in the Downland Gridshell and in Court Barn. The Worshipful Company of Plumbers liaises closely with the museum's schools services department to support schools visiting the museum, and, wherever possible, arranges special craft demonstrations.

These efforts are rewarded by volunteers' commitment. In 2010 the museum has over 550 registered volunteers, of whom over 200 are stewards, and these numbers are growing all the time.

Stewards deliver what is known as 'third-person' interpretation to distinguish it from 'first-person', which involves role-play. The museum itself has never delivered first-person interpretation, but for ten years from 1993 the History Re-enactment Workshop (HRW) was welcomed to an annual residency. HRW is an outstanding re-enactment group and solved many of the problems of so-called 'living history' through the use of 'red T-shirters', mediators between the 20th-century public and the 17th-century re-enactors. Despite the success of HRW, however, the museum's policy now is to achieve excellence in exclusively third-person interpretation.

The provision of guided tours is a challenge for all open air museums; two hours is the minimum time that would be needed for a full tour, but few visitors are willing to stay with a guide for that length of time. Even tours provided for booked parties often end up with only a dedicated hard core still with the guide. In 2008 the museum introduced a new form of guided tour that addresses this problem: the 'ten minute talks'. On arrival visitors are advised that at specific times a trained guide will be at one of the main exhibit buildings to give a talk lasting only ten minutes, long enough to give good quality background information but short enough to retain people's interest. The guide can then engage in conversation with visitors before they move to the next spot. These talks have proved popular, with some visitors using them to structure their whole visit and others just 'dipping in'.

Interpretation through displays and demonstrations

With the guidebook providing a consistent level of basic information about the exhibits, and stewards on hand to discuss questions with visitors, the museum never felt it necessary to install large numbers of display panels in its exhibit buildings. The buildings themselves, and in some cases their contents, are the important thing, and too many panels and other displays can easily detract from them. Visitors do not come to read a 'book on the wall', but they do appreciate having background information available. Every case is different and it is necessary to be pragmatic.

Our interpretation of the Upper Beeding toll

house is an interesting case in point. On its original site it had been truncated, and when first re-erected in 1970 it was not restored to its original length. Originally it had two rooms and central chimney, but was re-erected with just one room, in which excellent display panels were mounted giving the history of toll roads and cottages, written by Kim Leslie. In 1981 it was moved to a more appropriate site and restored to its original form, together with toll gates and a garden, and some of the original display panels were reinstated in the front room. In 1988 the rear room was furnished as a bedroom, complete with a clothed figure of the toll keeper wearily getting out of bed in his nightshirt to attend to the gate. The contrast between the front room with its display panels and back room with its clothed figures is surprisingly

The History Re-enactment Workshop visited in the summer holidays for several years, based at Pendean farmhouse, and later also at Poplar Cottage. With rigorous historical accuracy the group's members use period clothing, replica artefacts and an appropriate story-line to portray domestic life at the beginning of the 17th century.

Tudor

Tudor clothing 1540 worn in 'Bayleaf Farmstead', a Wealden house from Chiddingstone, Kent.

In 2006 a Needlework Group was formed to produce historically accurate clothing to be worn by staff and volunteers working in particular exhibit buildings. With funding assistance from the Friends, the Historic Clothing Project was advised by social historian Ruth Goodman and historical costumier Barbara Painter. It concentrated first on clothing for the Tudor and Victorian periods (corresponding to Bayleaf farmhouse and Winkhurst Tudor kitchen, and the West Wittering school and Whittaker's Cottages). Pictured are Tudor clothing of 1540 and Victorian costume from 1890 made at the museum. An exhibition and booklet, Cutting your Cloth, were part of the project, and work continues on the production of Victorian and Stuart clothing.

Victorian

Victorian clothing 1890 worn in 'Whittaker's Cottages' from Ashtead, Surrey.

Rural trades and building craft demonstrations   *Diana Zeuner*

Gerard Lynch demonstrating lime-slaking outside Whittaker's Cottages. Dr Lynch also teaches the museum's courses on traditional and gauged brickwork.

John Lord flint-knapping at Titchfield market hall in 1996.

A wheel-tyring demonstration in the 1980s, with the museum's site manager, Jim Hampshire, left, and Gus Pollard of West Sussex Rural Engineering.

In 1973 John Lowe wrote: "There is no doubt that a major attraction is the craft demonstrations given at the museum at weekends. Crowds watched potters, spinners and weavers and woodcraft workers practising their crafts in a traditional way. Occasionally it was possible to work the blacksmith's forge and on one occasion a group of volunteers fired a charcoal kiln."

Demonstrations became a principal method of interpretation of the museum's building exhibits and rural trades and crafts, drawing particular interest from visitors and in many cases encouraging their continuation in a modern context.

Demonstrations over the years have included:

- Spinning and dyeing
- Drumming the bees
- Sheep shearing
- Steam threshing
- Blacksmithing
- Horse ploughing
- Medieval cookery and table manners
- Plumbing and leadwork
- Meat production from the museum's pigs
- Cider-making
- Open Weekends, when usually static exhibits were working, including demonstrations of pit-sawing, farriery, wheelwrighting, chaff-cutting, carpentry, milling, bread-making, charcoal burning, water-raising, hand-milking, pipe-making, candle-making, basket-making, cleaving and spar-making, brick-making, hewing and sawing timber, slaking and using lime, and flint-knapping

Demonstrating blacksmithing in the Southwater forge.

The production of hurdles and wattles has been a constant feature at the museum since its inception. Here the skill is demonstrated by Paul Clear in the early 1970s and by thatcher Rod Miller in 2010.

Jon Roberts pit-sawing — most timber for building was produced in this way until the 19th century.

Heather Champion and Dick Tutton demonstrating 'drumming' the bees in 1986.

effective and generations of children have squealed with surprise and delight when they see the figures. This is perhaps the ideal balance in interpretation – words and pictures are fine to browse through, but the unexpected shock of seeing a figure in night-clothes in a gloomy candle-lit room leaves an indelible impression. In 2005 it was felt that the figures had become rather old-fashioned and they were removed, which resulted in howls of protest and rapid reinstatement!

The effectiveness of contrast is evident in two other exhibits as well. At one end of the house from Walderton the living room is furnished and presented exactly as it was in the 17th century, while at the other end the space is used to explain the development of the house, complete with display panels and an audio commentary. Whittaker's Cottages presented an ideal opportunity for contrast between the two identical cottages, and one has been left unfinished to show the structure (again with panels and an audio commentary) and the other has been fully finished to show how the house was lived in. The twin interests of the museum – social history on the one hand, and the history of buildings as structures on the other – are neatly encapsulated by these interpretive schemes.

For most of the other houses in the museum the policy is to furnish them appropriately and they are occupied as often as possible by stewards.

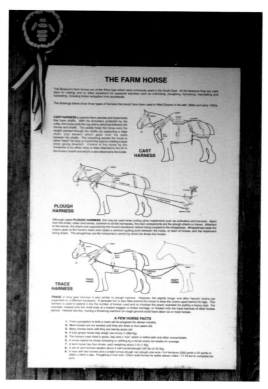

Display panels still have their place and can be seen in and around some of the exhibit buildings; this one is at the stables and explains working horse harness.

The first house to be fully furnished was Bayleaf in 1989 and this policy now extends to Pendean farmhouse, Poplar Cottage, the medieval hall from Boarhunt and the reconstructed medieval cottage

At Whittaker's Cottages (left), the interior of one of the pair is left at framework stage for visitors to see its structure and make comparisons with the older timber-frames on the museum site (right). An audio presentation (here activated by Anna Zeuner) and display boards help with interpretation.

The historic gardens   *Bob Holman and Diana Zeuner*

In 1983 the museum began to improve the historical accuracy of the curtilages around its buildings. Volunteers Ted Nash and Anne Beaumont had already recreated a small garden for the toll house and Ethel Buvyer was maintaining a herb garden at Bayleaf farmhouse. By 1986 garden historian Dr Sylvia Landsberg was drawing up plans for an appropriate historic garden for Bayleaf farmhouse as part of the museum's ambitious interpretation programme for the building.

The previous year a local man with a background in agriculture and horticulture was busy planting the shaws to the west and south of Bayleaf and laying hedges at various places on site. Bob Holman was asked to become the museum's gardener, setting out the proposed garden to Dr Landsberg's design. His initial reaction was one of euphoria, he recalls, but he knew little about gardening in medieval times. However, help was at hand in the shape of Sylvia Landsberg.

Bob Holman was to become a valued member of the museum team, creating seven period gardens for the houses, and was much in demand by the museum's learning and interpretation departments as well as film companies and media writers for his extensive knowledge. He retired in 2007, but continues to take an interest in museum activities.

Bayleaf garden in summer, an historic garden for the farmhouse as part of the museum's interpretation programme for the building.

At Bayleaf the basic layout was to be six beds with grass paths between them, sub-divided into six smaller beds with trodden paths used for weeding, a rough area around the perimeter and six herb beds of various sizes. The soil was thin, light brown in colour, a few inches deep over chalk and flint, and hungry for humus. This would not be a problem as the museum's livestock would provide a good supply of manure. Bob had vegetables to grow that he had never heard of, and herbs that he had little or no knowledge of, but he started reading everything of relevance that he could and the mist began to clear.

The bee skeps in Bayleaf garden, a vital source of nutrition for the occupants of the farmhouse.

Wattle fences were arranged around the herbs to give the impression of being grown in raised beds. Tall invasive strewing herbs were kept well apart from those being used for medicinal and other purposes, while gruit herbs (pronounced 'groot', such as hyssop, ground ivy – also known as alehoof – and germander), used to create bitterness in ale before hops were used for the purpose in the 13th century, were grown in the garden itself. Bob sowed the seeds, put the plants in and waited.

It wasn't long before a huge crop of fat hen, chickweed, speedwell, bristle ox tongue and every other weed ever recorded in Sussex emerged, swamping the carefully sown vegetable seeds. I had liberally sprinkled pot marigold seed amongst the onions, and every one grew; it looked beautiful and they would have been eaten as well as used medicinally. We had the only marigold bed with onions in. Sylvia Landsberg was delighted. Edible weeds she pronounced very nutritious, ideal for making pottage. Despite the weeds and marigolds we had good crops. I learnt an awful lot that year, not least how to manage edible weeds and the many uses to which marigolds were put.

Bayleaf flourished and thoughts turned to Hangleton cottage, Sylvia Landsberg again doing the research. This would be very different, set over a century earlier on very little ground and socially, well below Bayleaf. Hangleton had very little soil, was heavily shaded, and awkward to get at, with everything having to be transported by wheelbarrow. The garden was very simple; one small cultivated area of about 25 square yards (20.90 square

Museum gardener Bob Holman making a hurdle fence around the Poplar Cottage paddock.

The toll-house garden, with the pig sty beyond.

metres) for vegetables with two small beds for sweet and strewing herbs, together with a roughly constructed wood store for faggots or bavins. Soil and manure were barrowed up the steep slope; even soil from molehills was collected and dug in. But it was a losing battle; it was too heavily shaded, and with rabbits a constant problem, the Hangleton garden was abandoned in 2003.

It soon became clear that Bayleaf garden needed to be fenced; the free range hens were using the seed beds for dust baths. And the bees kept in traditional skeps were problematic with visitors, so had to be moved to the other side of the garden.

By 1995 new gardens at the toll house and the house from Walderton had been established. At the toll house vegetables were mainly grown, with some perennials and herbs. Shrub roses of the period were added, with a rambling rose and honeysuckle to clothe the fence. With a date of around 1860, seeds were not a problem, as varieties from that period were readily available.

Garden volunteers Jill Dickins, left, and Thelma Jack bringing in the apple harvest.

Walderton garden is set in the first quarter of the 17th century, a time of revolution in horticulture. Religious persecution in Europe had resulted in large numbers of people seeking sanctuary in this country, bringing not only their skills and professions but their plants and ideas about garden design, setting new trends in fashion, both for flower and vegetable gardening. The plant hunters were abroad and exotic flowers, fruit and vegetables flooded in to feed this growing appetite. The new trends gradually worked their way down through society to the artisans who would have lived in this house.

The hedge-lined path to the east of the garden represents a sunken track that would have been used to move livestock to and from pasture and for slaughter in the village.

The hard work involved could not have been achieved without the dedication of the garden volunteers, who give their time generously and are never daunted by any task. Bob Holman says:

We have tried to garden as the historical period we are working in dictates, so the volunteers' skills have to be many and varied – an understanding of social and garden history, hand weeding where seedling recognition is essential, a working knowledge of herbal lore, wattle fencing skills and, of course, how to make a good bonfire.

By 2000 the 16th-century Poplar Cottage garden, the 19th-century Whittaker's Cottages garden and the 17th-century Pendean farmhouse garden had all been researched and established. Poplar was particularly challenging as Bob and the volunteers set about taming a large area of former grassland; three semi-mature apple trees of the right period were moved from another site at the museum and re-established.

Bob Holman is interviewed in the Bayleaf medieval garden during the making of Tudor Times *for Channel 4 Schools.*

The gardens attract great interest from visitors, reflecting the current preoccupation with gardening as a hobby, a pause in a busy modern world, and in the production of home-grown food. According to Bob:

We did not set out to be organic gardeners but in the periods we were working with, pesticides were not used. An interesting array of predatory insects, as well as frogs and toads, inhabit the museum gardens; ground beetles prey on slugs, ladybirds and hoverfly larvae devour aphids, and hornets take young caterpillars. We have even seen the occasional wasp spider, usually associated with southern Europe, all adding to the rich tapestry that make the gardens such a fascinating part of the Weald & Downland Open Air Museum.

that was the catalyst for these public demonstrations, which previously had been delivered only as schools workshops. The creation of a new department of interpretation in 2005 stemmed from the realisation that to achieve consistent quality as well as quantity of live interpretation, additional resources would be needed.

Working buildings require a slightly different approach from houses. The ideal is that they should be used for their original purpose, and we are able to do that with two exhibits, the water-mill from Lurgashall and the blacksmith's forge from Southwater. The forge had been demonstrated on an occasional basis since the early days. In 1973, for example, John Lowe wrote that "Occasionally it was possible to work the blacksmith's forge …" and "The aim is to get as many professionals as possible for craft demonstrations in 1974", but it was impossible to achieve regular daily demonstrations. In 1982 Chris Zeuner announced an "action day to demonstrate those crafts and processes which aren't usually shown owing to lack of staff …" which included blacksmithing, and Keith Bickmore remembers that in the 1980s a blacksmith was at work on only one day a week – usually a Tuesday, so for weekend visitors the forge was normally a static exhibit. That situation persisted until the late 1990s, when more weekend demonstrations were achieved, and now volunteer blacksmiths on a rota keep the

from Hangleton. As well as stewards, the interpretation department has established regular demonstrations of domestic work such as cooking, cleaning and dairying. It was the re-opening of Winkhurst in 2003 interpreted as a Tudor kitchen

In 1999, to help bring furnished rooms to life, the museum engaged Peter Brears, a leading authority on the history of food and historic food consultant to Hampton Court Palace. He spent three days at the museum focusing on medieval and Tudor cooking and eating methods and table manners. It was an immediate success with visitors and Peter Brears returned in other years and taught courses on his subject as part of the museum's lifelong learning programme.

forge in use on a majority of weekends and week-days – but the story illustrates how difficult that can be to accomplish.

In Lurgashall watermill demonstrations were achieved in a different way. By setting the mill up for productive use the museum ensured not only that the building and machinery retained an authentic atmosphere, but also that there was an end product that could be sold. At first Robert

Volunteers Peter Stock and Beryl Bickmore preparing flour for sale in Lurgashall watermill. By working the mill, visitors see it in operation and there is an end product that can be sold.

Demaus and his successors attempted to make a living as full-time millers, but this is a formula that is rarely successful. Production from craft demonstrations can never compete commercially, especially when the demonstrators have to spend some of their time talking to the public, but by using well-trained and committed teams of volunteer millers the museum has shown that it is possible to achieve demonstrations seven days a week and also have the financial benefit of product sales – the museum's stoneground flour is popular with visitors and local bakeries alike.

In the other craft buildings at the museum realistic displays of tools from the collections have been included to show how the building appeared when in use, and in some cases the exhibit is enhanced by further interpretation by panels or audio. The carpenters' shop from Windlesham and the plumbers' and glaziers' workshop from Newick both have costumed figures to add to the atmosphere. The sawpit shed from Sheffield Park is sometimes used for demonstrations so has retained a 'lived-in' feel, and the more recent exhibit of a country woodyard centred on the museum's hand-operated timber crane is regularly used for demonstrations concentrated into 'woodyard weeks', usually at half terms or in the school holidays.

Exhibitions within buildings

The museum's buildings are chosen and painstakingly re-erected because they are of value in

A costumed figure adds to the atmosphere inside the furnished plumbers' and glaziers' workshop from Newick.

Steam sawing under way in the woodyard during the Steam Festival. Ash logs were swung onto the sawbench using the restored timber crane, where they were converted into planks for use in building restoration.

describing his ideas, Roy Armstrong proposed a village group of 30 to 40 buildings from the 14th century to the 19th, of which "most (if not all) would be open to the public and furnished appropriately to their original status and construction". But in addition, "one complete farm group might be set aside for use in connection with an exhibition hall, conference accommodation, museum offices, café and other public service facilities".

The earliest example of this was the barn from Hambrook. In January 1972, even before the building was dismantled, John Lowe suggested to the sites and buildings committee that it was most suitable for displays, and an exhibition was installed illustrating the history of building methods in our region, using models, samples and display panels. It was opened by Hugh Jenkins, Minister for the Arts, in June 1974, and in 1975 the museum won the National Heritage Museum of the Year Award for Hambrook barn and its introductory display. Ten years later the displays were modified with the addition of elements from a travelling exhibition, *Traditional Building Materials,* researched and designed by Richard Harris and funded by the Area Museums Service for South-East England and the Building Centre Trust. In 2010 the displays are again being modified to provide improved orientation for visitors, and an enhanced display about traditional building crafts is planned for a new Building Crafts Gallery in the space behind the upper hall from Crawley.

When the museum was offered a second aisled barn, known as Court Barn, from Lee-on-Solent, a similar decision was taken. In 1975 the Worshipful Company of Plumbers was seeking a site for an exhibition of traditional leadwork, and Court Barn seemed ideal for the purpose. The company formed the Plumbing Museum & Workshop Trust, to create and manage the displays, which were opened in 1980. From the start it was intended that there should be demonstrations as well, and this was achieved by inviting students and teachers at technical colleges to demonstrate their skills in leadwork. In 1993 it was decided to add displays relating to masonry supported by the Worshipful Company of Masons, and water supply supported by Southern Water, which opened in March 1994. In 1999 a new display about leaded lights was added with the support of another livery company, that of the Glaziers & Painters of Glass, and in 2004 the Masons sponsored the building of a new demonstration area for masonry, which is used by apprentices on the Cathedral Workshop Fellowship. Thus Court Barn has

themselves as exhibits, so in most cases they have been presented as such. Sometimes, however, space is needed for other purposes and in the absence of modern buildings, exhibits have sometimes been pressed into use. In one of the earliest memoranda

been the focal point for the museum's creative use of links to industry to achieve displays and demonstrations.

Another important aspect of the building industry is illustrated by a display in the brick-drying shed from Causeway Brickworks, near Petersfield. This building, 75 feet-long (22 metres), was dismantled in 1979, and was always intended to contain an exhibition about bricks, but it was ten years before funds were raised for its re-erection through sponsorship by Seaward Properties. The Redland Brick Company sponsored the exhibition, which was written by Richard Harris and incorporated both full-size mockups and panel displays illustrating the history of brickwork, with one end bay of the building kept as a demonstration area for moulding bricks. It was opened in 1991 and is still in place.

In 1982 a joiners' shop from Witley in Surrey was acquired, and its re-erection was completed in 1983. In 1989 the museum won the Times/Shell Community Museum of the Year Award, and the £10,000 prize was devoted to the creation of a new display in the joiners' shop. Called *Getting to Grips*, sometimes known as 'Hands-on', the primary aim was to give groups of school children an opportunity to handle and experiment with building materials and some of the techniques used in building construction. It was opened in April 1992 and at first was made available only to pre-booked parties of school children, as it needs constant supervision by trained volunteers. However, it rapidly became, and has remained, one of the most popular exhibits at the museum.

This display nicely complements the displays in Hambrook barn, Court Barn, and the other craft buildings by giving children an opportunity to get to grips – literally – with the building materials and processes they can see all around them. But building crafts and materials are not the museum's only interest; it occupies a fascinating historic landscape shaped by agriculture and social forces throughout the ages, and some of the displays have aimed to exploit that as a theme underlying visitors' experience of our site.

In the mid-1970s, the museum hosted a pottery project which aimed to achieve authentic practical re-creation of medieval pottery production methods, and for a short time the project was housed in a cattle shed from Coldwaltham that was re-erected in the woodlands for that purpose. That project came to an end in 1975 and in 1980 Chris Zeuner proposed that a new exhibition explaining the development of the local landscape should be installed there instead. The exhibition

was written by Ruth Tittensor and designed by Bruce Williams and opened in May 1982, with funding from the Countryside Commission and the Carnegie UK Trust. The museum's landscape is historical and multi-layered and it is important that visitors should be able to read it correctly. Some people make the incorrect assumption that the museum has attempted to re-create the landscape of the past, but that is impossible to do. Just as animal breeding can only move forward, not backwards, landscape changes can never obliterate the past. The exhibition in the Coldwaltham shed included an excellent set of paintings showing six different periods in the development of the Lavant valley, and while the exhibition itself has now been removed in order to release the shed for a new existence supporting the rural woodyard

The plumbing display in Court Barn, created by the Plumbing Museum & Workshop Trust.

The exhibition on historic brickwork in the Petersfield brick-drying shed.

exhibit, new interpretive displays on the landscape will undoubtedly be developed in the future.

Another exhibition created in the 1980s and now removed was *Historic Farms and Farmsteads*. Written by Richard Harris and designed by Ivor and Bridget Heal, this was opened at the same time as the Bayleaf Project in 1989 – British Food and Farming Year – and was supported by the NFU (National Farmers' Union) regional committee and other farming interests. The exhibition was based around the full-size reproduction of a series of historic maps, with associated details of farmsteads and agricultural practice. The shed in which the exhibition was housed, which came from

Redvins Farm on the Goodwood Estate, is now used to display agricultural implements from the collections, arranged to illustrate the farming year.

For many museums, mounting regular or 'temporary' exhibitions is a major part of their work. At the Weald & Downland these have been occasional; preference has always been given to displays as part of the interpretation of buildings. However, one or two stand-alone exhibitions have been mounted, usually displayed in the upper hall from Crawley, with some going on to tour other museums and institutions. Among these have been: *Biskupin: Poland's Iron-Age Village* and *Traditional Building Materials* in 1984; *The European Home* in 1992; the *Women's Land Army* in 1994; *Images of Bayleaf* in 2008, and *Cutting your Cloth: the Historic Clothing Project* in 2009.

In 2002 the artefact collections moved into their new home in the basement of the Downland Gridshell. Although the collections were very well documented, they had previously been stored off-site and it was therefore impossible regularly to access their richness and quality. Since the move there has been a consistent policy of putting as many items as possible on show to the public. The display of agricultural implements in the Redvins shed was part of that, and with the support of the Department of Culture, Media & Sport (DCMS)/ Wolfson Galleries Improvement Fund a simple shed, discretely tucked away but nevertheless at the centre of the site, has been built in which to display a number of wheeled vehicles and agricultural implements. An outshot added to the back of the Witley joiners' shop houses another three large vehicles, and the recently re-erected hay barn from Ockley shelters a threshing drum and elevator, two of the components of a threshing train. There is still a place for panel displays, but the emphasis has switched from the 'book on the wall' to showing the collections.

So for 40 years the museum has endeavoured to illustrate the twin themes of buildings and their social history, and rural life and crafts. Now there are plans to extend this by creating a series of interpretive 'pavilions' in which visitors can explore these topics. This idea came out of the feasibility study of 2008 which looked for ways to enhance intellectual and physical access to the exhibits. Each pavilion will contain displays on a particular theme, such as houses, local landscape, farming, woodland, artefacts and machines. In this way it should be possible to avoid using more buildings for that purpose and will provide places for visitors to pause in their tour and gain a context for their observations and impressions.

Livestock and farming

Most of the structures re-erected at the museum are from a rural environment and from a period in which every citizen relied on the produce of the countryside, including those living in towns. Chris Zeuner was a fervent believer in the power of livestock and farming to increase visitors' understanding of the historic buildings, and with a growing rural-life collection including agricultural implements and equipment, it was a natural step to introduce the complete range of agricultural tasks performed on farms from the date of the earliest building, 14th-century Boarhunt, to the latest, the 19th-century Whittaker's Cottages.

As a rural-life specialist, Chris already had considerable knowledge about farming practices, livestock and the ways of the countryside, and through contacts in the farming world, this continued to expand throughout his period as museum director. Many of the site staff were employed because of their knowledge of the rural scene. Albert Peacock, a former farm labourer with immense knowledge about the countryside, regularly made hazel spars for thatching, but he also imparted to staff a fund of information and experience about farming activities. Les Whitecall was a former carter who helped with the introduction of the draught horses. Horace 'Shep' Oliver was not employed by the museum, but as shepherd for David Humphrey in East Dean, cared for the first flocks of Southdown sheep. Nick Conway, the museum's site manager, was from a local family who had worked for generations on the West Dean Estate. Rob Dash, volunteer and later part-time horseman, had an encyclopaedic understanding of horsemanship techniques and farming history. All brought experience of a vanishing age, which stretched back through the centuries, and were happy to pass on their knowledge to visitors.

Although the introduction of livestock pre-dated the Bayleaf Medieval Farmstead research and furnishing project, it was this, in 1988-89, that focused further attention on presenting the 'correct' type of livestock for the late medieval/early Tudor period. By 1993 the museum was actively pursuing breeding programmes for its pedigree sheep, pigs and poultry, in tune with the work of the Rare Breeds Survival Trust which has successfully encouraged the preservation of many vanishing livestock breeds.

Livestock also serves as a resource for the teaching and development of traditional skills in today's rural economy. One example was the role the museum played in the late 1980s in the re-introduction of horses for timber extraction to reduce damage to the woodland environment.

Sheep

Sheep were the first animals to be introduced, with a small flock provided by David and Lady Elizabeth Benson, who farm at Singleton, to graze the museum pastureland during public opening times in the early 1970s. By 1979 Horace 'Shep'

People come first. A key strength of the museum is the way in which visitors can freely talk to knowledgeable staff and volunteers. Here Chris Zeuner describes the function of a horse's bit to visitors at the stables.

The traditional South Downs sheepfold and shepherd's hut, seen from the air.

Above left *Horace 'Shep' Oliver with the Southdown sheep from J & D Humphrey's flock at the museum in 1986.*
Above right *John Dewey shearing sheep in the mid-1980s.*

Below *Sussex cattle being trained for work at the museum in 1982 with Alan Waters, left, and volunteer Ted Nash.*

Oliver was caring for Southdowns from the prize-winning flock of J & D Humphrey of East Dean, a breed that was totally suited to the downland turf. Southdowns had been 'improved', however, particularly by John Ellman of Glynde, East Sussex in the late 18th century, and to better represent the sheep of an earlier age, Romneys were introduced – taller and rangier and more appropriate in the vicinity of farmhouses such as Bayleaf. A later group of three Southdown ewes and a ram came from the Moulton, Suffolk farm of Hugh Clark, whose flock was considered to be one of the purest-bred in the country. Today's flock comes once again from the Humphrey family.

The museum developed a considerable interest in sheep and the sheep economy of the Downs, with Richard Pailthorpe writing *The Downland Shepherds* (with Gordon Beningfield), incorporating the memories of downland shepherds collected by Barclay Wills in the 1920s. Valerie Porter's history, *The Southdown Sheep*, written on behalf of the Southdown Sheep Society, was published by the museum. When the traditional chestnut hurdles of the now-closed Findon Sheep Fair were threatened with destruction the museum rescued them to use for pens at its annual Rare Breeds Show.

The restoration of a traditional shepherd's hut from the museum's collections and the recreation of a typical downland sheepfold at the museum enabled further interpretation of the importance of sheep, with the fold used for lambing the museum's own flocks annually. Some of the sheep wore replica traditional sheep bells. In 2009 it was found that Gonville Cottage, the only *in-situ* building on the museum site, had been a shepherd's house in 1851. Archaeologists discovered the remains of a U-shaped range of buildings, thought to have been a sheep yard.

Working oxen

A pair of Sussex cattle was first introduced to work at the museum in 1982 when Alan Waters, Martin Bossom and volunteer Ted Nash were involved in their training and use. Hearty and Heedless came from Peter Clery's Upwaltham Farm and were a particularly appropriate addition to the museum's livestock, as the county of Sussex was one of the last places in the country where oxen were regularly used for farm work, finally disappearing from the land after the First World War. A second pair was introduced to the museum in 1984.

There was a gap before their reintroduction in 2002 when Chris Baldwin, shortly to become

farm manager, began training a further pair of Sussex oxen. After considerable research into their use on the Sussex Downs and with help from the few people available with specialist knowledge, such as Charles Martell of Dymock, Gloucestershire, Chris made a replica yoke based on one in the museum's collection. The museum's current two pairs of Sussex X Dairy Shorthorn cows are worked on the field strips and have recently been introduced to ploughing.

Working horses

Horses were first introduced in 1979. Chris Zeuner owned a Cob and used him for a range of site tasks before the decision was taken to move to heavy draught horses. The first Shires at the museum were retired ex-Whitbread's Brewery dray horses. Chris and Diana Zeuner's own Shire, William, an ex-coal wagon delivery horse, was unusually small for the breed and more typical of the sort of 'Shire-type' animals which would have been seen on the average farm in the horse era.

With William, a conscious decision was being made to replace tall town-based dray horses with more appropriate farm carthorses, although locating such horses, under 17 hands high, has become increasingly difficult nationwide as breeding trends change. Horses in use at the time of Bayleaf farmhouse would have been about 14 hands high, and the museum was fortunate for several years to have the black Dales stallion, Babar, on loan from the Duchess of Richmond.

However, the body of draught-horse working knowledge remained with heavy horses and it was felt appropriate to continue supporting the resurgent interest in the heavy breeds. After William's death the Zeuners replaced him with Radford Baron, bought from Shire breeder and wheelwright Mike Horler, from whom they also acquired Radford Gym, later buying Milnerfield Donald from Welsh horseman Will Williams. Rosie (Layston Bluebell), a Shire-cross was acquired from Richard and Angela Gifford, and kept primarily as a brood mare: she bred seven draught foals, with the first, Bayleaf Primrose, born in 1991. Neville, from Brookfield Shires, Huntingdonshire, was a strong, powerful horse any 19th century farmer would have specially valued, able to haul equipment all day long. From the original group he remains with the museum, now on light duties. His current stable mates are Mac, bought from Cotswold Cart Horse Society chairman, Dawn Large, and Major, bought from Fisher's Farm Park, Wisborough Green.

The horses were originally cared for by Les

Chris Baldwin training the new pair of working cattle, Sussex X Dairy Shorthorn cows.

Whitecall, and later Alan Waters, the museum's charcoal burner, who learned from Les and worked with William especially on logging in the museum's site and leased woodlands. John Chattaway and Peter Albon followed. Chris Zeuner became particularly interested in working horses, developing his own skills as a horseman over the years. He carried out horse work on the site himself when time allowed and at weekends, supported by his daughter, Francesca, who also undertook relief stockman duties. Rob Dash was employed as part-time horseman, continuing after Chris's death in 2001, and when he left shortly afterwards Diana Zeuner became stables manager working with volunteer Derek Hilton as part-time horseman. They were assisted by Pete Betsworth, the museum's stockman, and a team of some 10 volunteers, many of whom were able to develop considerable horsemanship skills as a result of a new training programme. The first full-time horseman was Lee Harrison, and he was succeeded in 2008 by Mark Buxton, who came to the museum from the Royal Parks.

At their zenith in the 1980s and 90s the museum's working horses undertook the whole range of farm tasks on the site, enabling visitors to see them in action on a daily basis and replicating their use as a source of power for those who would have lived and worked in the re-erected buildings. These included carting; hay-making; harrowing and rolling grassland and the arable fields; drilling and ploughing; harvesting with a binder and leading in the dried wheat sheaves, and logging. The horses were used to convey timbers of several historic structures from the museum's

(1) *Grazing:* The museum's working horses graze in front of six traditional ricks of wheat harvested to produce thatching straw. (2) *Carting:* a tandem of working Shires draws restored timbers on a timber carriage from the museum's workshop in Charlton through the village of Singleton to the museum site. (3) *Preparing the fields:* Chris Zeuner rolling the wheat field with a pair of horses. (4,5,6) *Harvesting arable crops:* Peter Albon with Neville and Gym cutting the wheat crop for thatching straw; loading the flatbed wagon with sheaves of wheat; horses deliver a load to the rick-building site in Lower Gonville field. (7,8,9) *Making hay:* Alan Wood mowing grass on the bank above Poplar Cottage; rowing-up and loading hay in 1992, Clive Kennett on the hayrake in the foreground, and Chloe Hill on the

workshop in Charlton for re-erection on the site; they became a regular sight in the village of Singleton, much to the residents' enjoyment.

In addition the museum played an important part in encouraging the interest in heavy horses and the rural crafts associated with them, such as harness-making and wheelwrighting, meeting

another of the museum's aims. Annual events in June and October enabled the public to see heavy horses in action across a range of disciplines, traditional and new, including the sport of cross-country driving with heavy horses. These events had their genesis in the horse-ploughing demonstrations by Bob Lomas and Rob Dash in

wagon; Rob Dash (right) making hay in the paddock below Pendean farmhouse assisted by his father-in-law, Bob Claydon (standing on the load), and site manager, Nick Conway. **(10) Ploughing:** Derek Hilton ploughing with Gym (left) and Neville, in this case at the NFU Ploughing Match at Chidham, West Sussex in 2002. **(11) Harrowing grassland:** Derek Hilton using horses to keep the museum's much-used grassland in good order. **(12) Grass-cutting:** Mark Buxton demonstrating a horse-drawn grass mower in the arena at the 2009 summer heavy horse event. **(13) Promotion:** the museum's horses have been useful ambassadors over the years. Here two tandem teams (the museum's own, right, and one horsed by Rob Dash) are taking part in Portsmouth Parade, leading two wagons loaded with wheat sheaves in the arena at Southsea Castle, a unique sight in modern times.

1981. Chris Zeuner was part of the British team which took part in the 1999 La Route du Poisson in France, which commemorates the use of heavy draught horses. The museum's horses were also contracted off-site to various logging jobs in the region, promoting the museum and the role of the heavy horse while at the same time bringing in income; using horses to clear felled timber on the South Downs at Cocking for the Society of Sussex Downsmen (now the South Downs Society) for example.

Off-site promotional activity also included regular attendance at events such as the annual Spring Working and All-England Ploughing

Match run by Southern Counties Heavy Horse Association (SCHHA), of which Chris Zeuner was the chairman; the South of England Show at Ardingly; the Portsmouth Parade and the London Harness Horse Parade. Bob Robinson and Rob Dash, both SCHHA members, entered on behalf of the museum, sometimes using vehicles from the museum's collection, and alongside the museum's own entry, for many years.

Pigs

Pigs were an essential source of food across the periods reflected in the museum's buildings. The first pigs to be introduced to the Upper Beeding toll house pig sty were Berkshire X Gloucestershire Old Spots weaners donated by the Ashdown Forest Farm at Wych Cross, East Sussex.

The museum's Tamworth sow and piglets grazing among leaf litter in the woodland, a scene which would have been familiar to farmers until the last century, but is now being reintroduced countrywide to provide conservation grazing on environmentally important sites.

Above right *The first pigs at the museum were Berkshire X Gloucestershire Old Spots from Ashdown Forest Park Farm, a rare-breeds centre at Wych Cross, East Sussex. With one of the two original piglets in the toll-house pig sty are Francesca Zeuner and Nicholas Pailthorpe, with Richard Pailthorpe standing behind.*
Right *Francesca went on to undertake relief stockman duties when she was older, and is seen right with a group of day-old Tamworth piglets.*

These were thought to be similar to the traditional Sussex pig that early 19th-century agricultural historian Arthur Young recorded as being a Berkshire or black and white cross. Gloucestershire Old Spots, then on the Rare Breeds Survival Trust's critical list, were also bred by Chris and Diana Zeuner at home and some of the piglets moved to the museum at weaning.

This breed was less appropriate for the Bayleaf Medieval Farmstead project as pigs at this time would have been smaller and rangier, and so another rare breed, the Tamworth, was introduced. Nellie, a pedigree Tamworth sow, was bought in-pig and produced nine piglets, a welcome addition to the farmyard.

In addition to the toll house, pigs have been kept at various times in Bayleaf yard, a new sty built at Pendean farmhouse, Hangleton cottage and in the woodlands demonstrating the centuries-old tradition of running pigs in woods.

From the start pigs were bred at the museum, with some gilts being sold on to breed and others butchered for pork and bacon. Paul Pinnington cared for them for a number of years after 2001 and the museum introduced the *Pig to Pork* events in Winkhurst Tudor kitchen, demonstrating to visitors how the carcases were prepared for meat. In 2010 they are cared for by Marc Odin.

Poultry and geese

Flocks of Light Sussex and Dorking hens have been acquired and run at various times at Bayleaf farmstead, Pendean farmhouse, Hangleton cottage and in the fields below the stables. Both of these breeds were considered appropriate for the Bayleaf project. Geese are kept in the orchard next to Bayleaf farmstead. Fox predation is a constant problem, but the sight of hens foraging in the

Domestic geese and Light Sussex poultry representing staple livestock for a medieval farmer.

The wheat crop stooked in Greenways field in 1980.

grassland and the honking of the geese as they welcome their food bucket would have been familiar to people across the centuries, and bring great joy to visitors.

Farming tasks

One of the museum's main developments in the 1980s and 1990s was its demonstration of agricultural tasks to produce food and other products vital to the survival of those who had lived and worked in the buildings. It was never intended to operate a working farm, since the museum's primary aim was the preservation and interpretation of historic vernacular buildings. But its farming activities enhance visitors' experience and promote the understanding of rural history.

Farming also has the effect of assisting in the care of the site itself, which has to endure the passage of many feet, bear the burden of extra use during special events and provide grazing for the museum's livestock. Grassland can be harrowed, rolled and mown; hay can be made for the livestock through the winter, and wheat, grown initially in partnership with West Dean Estate, provides grain and straw for thatching and the demonstration of traditional threshing.

The growing of thatching straw meets one of the museum's central aims, to assist rural crafts to flourish. Not only is the straw available for the museum's own thatched buildings, but for many years was sold to thatchers throughout the south. The crop has often been cut with a traditional binder drawn either by vintage tractor or the museum's own horses, which then lead in the

dried sheaves by wagon to the traditional ricks made ready for the autumn threshing demonstration. Albert Peacock knew how ricks were built and passed on his knowledge to site manager Nick Conway.

The museum's thatching straw has usually been grown on West Dean Estate fields adjacent to the museum site, but in 1980 the crop was grown in conjunction with South Western Thatchers on Greenways field, at the centre of the museum, the straw being used to thatch the buildings from Boarhunt and Walderton.

In 1998 a crop of two old local varieties, Chidham White and Chidham Red, was grown in the paddock in front of Bayleaf, after Chidham farmer and museum supporter Jonathan Bentall had spent some years gathering seed growing wild on his farm. As it was a relatively low-acre crop, Peter Albon scythed it in the traditional way, tying the stooks with straw withies, providing a sight which would have been familiar to the occupants of the house from medieval times. In both cases the crops were also useful in helping to regenerate the soil following many years as pasture.

Peter Albon scything Chidham wheat, an old local variety, grown in the Bayleaf paddock in 1998.

Harvesting and preparing the flax crop in 2007. **Top left** *the crop growing on the field strips,* **top right** *stooking the 'beets' of harvested flax in the field,* **bottom left** *carting it to the barn, and* **bottom right** *extracting the fibres by pulling the flax over sharp spikes.*

In 1985 the museum grew its second largest crop of wheat for thatching, 20 acres, yielding some 17,000 sheaves. The largest crop was achieved in 1996 by growing 10 acres on West Dean land and another 13 at Cucumber Farm, Singleton, through the generosity of trustee Lady Elizabeth Benson. Extra labour was brought in to help with the harvest, which became a central element of late summers at the museum for many years.

Rye was another crop grown specifically to order for harness makers who needed this cereal straw to make traditional English horse collars. Some was bought by The Countryside Agency for its harness-training courses in Salisbury.

On the neighbouring Goodwood Estate a new event was the annual Goodwood Revival meeting in September; the museum was asked if it would stage a threshing scene within the motor circuit, replicating photographs of the site in its motoring heyday. A crop of wheat was grown on the site, cut and stooked ready for the two-day event, with the museum bringing along its threshing tackle and labour to thresh the crop as historic racing cars enthralled visitors around the track.

In the immediate aftermath of Chris Zeuner's death and the foot-and-mouth outbreak in 2001 the scale of agriculture at the museum changed, and the museum revised the arrangements for crops in the fields which the museum leased from the West Dean Estate, growing less thatching straw, some potatoes and clover, and retaining the lower portion for sheep grazing, hay-making and parking for special events.

In one section Chris Baldwin developed a field-strip system to demonstrate pre-enclosure agriculture that existed at the period reflected in the Bayleaf Medieval Farmstead project. Six strips of 11 yards (10 metres) wide by 110 yards (100 metres) long (a quarter of an acre) were cultivated in pairs, each on a three-course rotation. Different crops and variations were the subject of experiments but those grown were mostly wheat, rye, spring barley, peas and beans. He also ran a market garden for a year, which was later given over to a hop garden, reflecting Bayleaf's original site in the Weald where hops were prevalent, and complemented by a display of hop-related vehicles and artefacts in the Charlwood wagon shed. In 2010, the hops were moved to the field in front of Bayleaf farmhouse, and the strips to the Bayleaf top paddock, where they are worked entirely by hand and working oxen.

The museum continues to use its arable areas to interpret elements of agricultural development across the centuries.

Drama in the Downs   *Carol Brinson*

The museum also became involved in drama away from its site. The museum's Shire horse, William, and Sussex wagon provided the 'stage' for a roving play through Chichester in 1986, The Spershott Version.

The museum's superb setting and its buildings are dramatic in themselves, but it did not take long for people to realise their potential as a venue for theatre, music and a variety of visual and literary arts.

One of the very first performances for the public at the museum was in 1984 when a group called the Medieval Players performed *The Great Theatre of the World* in the market square, but there was informal singing and dramatic action on the site long before that. There was certainly music at a Friends' social evening in the summer of 1975; as reported in the museum magazine "… the party brought Bayleaf to life in a memorable way, an effect heightened by the delightful singing of the Ladyholt Singers".

1993 was a lively year as it featured a performance by Amanda Waring and Robert Daws of *Sirius Dolphin* written by Robert specifically for the museum and staged in the aisled hall from Sole Street. Another magical evening with the couple was their performance of *The Education of Little Tree*, an adaptation from the 1976 book of the same name by Forrest Carter, under the trees near the same building.

The same year saw a memorable evening with the

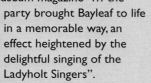

Actor Robert Daws appearing in The Education of Little Tree *beneath the pines and silver birches by the lake during the Penny Royal Theatre's season in 1991.*

The museum and Bob Copper

It was through the writing of The Downland Shepherds *that Richard Pailthorpe came to know the Sussex folklorist Bob Copper. Bob had actually met Barclay Wills whose writings were the basis for the book, and contributed the foreword. Bob and his family were renowned for their recordings of English traditional folk songs, and sang at the museum on a number of occasions. Richard Pailthorpe remembers visiting him at the social club in Rottingdean where he and the family regularly performed. He was a delightful person, inspired not only by the folk songs, but also his immense love and knowledge of the Downs and traditional ways of Sussex life. Bob was also a very talented author and eager to have published his personal account of how he followed in the footsteps of Hilaire Belloc and his* The Four Men. *Kim Leslie and Richard Pailthorpe found a publisher for Bob's work and saw it through its production stages. Bob and the Copper family (pictured) gave a memorable performance on a summer's evening to mark the publication of the book.*

Copper family in North Cray hall house with Bob Copper's adaptation of Hilaire Belloc's *The Four Men*. This was organised by Kim Leslie and John Godfrey of West Sussex County Council as part of the Belloc festivities that year. It confirmed a long, friendly association with the Copper family, which had started in 1991 with a 'Picnic with Sussex Songs' organised by Richard Pailthorpe and continued with wonderful candlelit evenings in the North Cray house over several years when they sang Sussex songs and told tales of old Sussex country life. It inspired museum charcoal burner Alan Waters to run a fund-raising 91-mile marathon across Sussex in the footsteps of Belloc, a journey which Bob Copper had himself also made. One of the many memories associated with the Copper family visits was the tradition for Bob to be supplied with a smart blue and white cushion to sit on, as he found the bench in North Cray a little low and hard as he got older. The museum was also proud to be the venue for the recording of a cassette, *Silly Sussex*, by the Copper family and Martin Muncaster in 1997.

The first Dovetail *arts events programme.*

In the early 1990s the museum was approached by John and Maggie Pollock who ran a very successful open-air theatre company called Penny Royal, with performances in their garden at Bosham. They had outgrown the garden, and their neighbours' patience, and were looking for another venue. Penny Royal moved to the museum for a couple of years and was popular with audiences, but the staging did not sit easily with the museum's own requirements and the arrangement came to an end. However, it had set the scene for open air theatre at the museum.

1995 was destined to be a national 'Festival of Arts and Culture'. It was also the year when the timber-frame of Longport farmhouse was to be raised – a dramatic event and traditionally a reason for festivities. The year before, Chris Zeuner asked me to organise a programme of arts events to coincide with the festival. With advice from South East Arts I sought out suitable performers, found the finance, and put the programme together, my contacts within The National Trust at the time proving fortuitous. We called the programme 'Dovetail' reflecting an irresistible play on the name of a ubiquitous carpentry joint as well as the intention for the events to slot into the scenery and ethos of the museum.

A programme of events continued under this title until 2000. We were grateful to the *Chichester Observer* for sponsorship for the first year and for grants from the Foundation for Sport & the Arts, West Sussex County Council and Chichester District Council. The museum hoped the programme would attract new visitors – and

so it seemed. The spring 1999 museum magazine stated that "80% of the audience over the last two years were not members of the Friends or volunteers" and "many had had their first experience of the museum and intended to visit during the day". It was also reported that "Dovetail more than paid its way".

Through the Dovetail programme the museum discovered Gail Duff, who still leads the Tree Dressing and other events at the museum, with her Rabble dancers and mummers players, and Illyria, an open air theatre company who visited for several years. A series of open-air barn dances were also popular. Folk groups Artisan and Lucky Bags also entertained the Dovetail audiences, together with a site-specific performance by Drip Action Theatre Company from Arundel.

The museum lends itself wonderfully to open-air theatre, particularly when the actors and audience move around the site. This was especially so during the performance in 2004 of *The Roses of Eyam* with a talented amateur cast of local people, and in 2007 when the museum's interpretation team worked with The Company, who presented a specially devised piece, *Centuries Apart,* and in 2009, *And That Will Never Be,* comprising a week of performances and drama workshops. In 2008 The Company Presents staged *Will at the Weald* featuring scenes from Shakespeare.

In 1995 I was introduced to the artist Gordon Rushmer who is now a regular visitor to the museum staging exhibitions of his work and as a teacher of painting classes. He follows a long-standing friendship with Gordon

'And That Will Never Be …' produced by The Company took place in 2009 both for general audiences and school groups. It was funded with grants from Awards for All *and West Sussex County Council's rural arts programme* Poems and Puddings.

The museum and Gordon Beningfield

The museum's association with Gordon Beningfield, the eminent countryside and wildlife artist, came about through a chance letter Richard Pailthorpe wrote to him in the early 1980s, inviting him to visit the museum which he thought he might enjoy. Richard had become an admirer of his work through his books and appearances on BBC TV's In the Country, *in which he featured with Bernard Price, the Chichester broadcaster and journalist, also a keen supporter of the museum. Gordon was instantly captivated by the museum and he and Richard struck up a close friendship until Gordon's death in 1988. He agreed to paint and donate three views of the museum which were made into prints for sale. A limited edition was made of the Bayleaf painting and over the next few years this raised several thousands of pounds for the Bayleaf Medieval Farmstead project. Gordon was passionate about the South Downs and shepherding, and this mutual interest led him to produce a book with Richard,* The Downland Shepherds, *based on the writings of Barclay Wills. Gordon was a great conservationist, much involved with the Countryside Restoration Trust. He loved Shire horses, rare breeds of livestock and traditional farming practices; whenever his busy diary allowed he would visit the museum. Pictured is his print showing the house from Walderton, the market square and the lake.*

Beningfield forged by Richard Pailthorpe in the early 1980s which led to his paintings of scenes at the museum, with prints of *Bayleaf Farmhouse* contributing to the Bayleaf Medieval Farmstead project.

Music has always played an important part in many activities at the museum. An Early Music Afternoon on a Sunday in July first organised by interpretation officer Sue Shave has been popular for many years, with musicians making use of the historic building exhibits. Each December supporters have enjoyed the magic of Christmas carols round the fire in a specially decorated Bayleaf farmhouse, and more recently in North Cray hall house, with home-bred musicians including Sue Shave, Chris Zeuner's daughters, Francesca and Anna, and my husband Malcolm.

In the 1990s the museum developed a good friendship with storyteller Pete Castle and his part-Romanian folk music trio, Popeluc. This led to an interesting link with Romanian tourism students, based for a few weeks at what is now the University of Chichester, who spent part of their course at the museum and on outings organised by staff.

In 2000 the museum took part in the first Museums & Galleries Month in May, with funding from the Millennium Commission for a programme called *Inspired by the Past* in which artists and craftsmen reacted to the buildings as inspiration for new creative work; it led to a series of water sculptures by Jonathan Froud. Sculptures of a different form resulted from a 'forge-in' by members of the British Artist Blacksmiths Association in 2008, when participants made signposts for the woodland trails in the museum, following an earlier year's creation of a 'totem pole' near the forge.

Film has also played its part, drawing in useful income. The museum provides an appropriate setting for a wide range of filming opportunities, from commercial advertising to fictional movies, but most importantly for documentaries on historical or rural themes and educational programmes. In 1984 museum staff took part in traditional rural scenes for a BBC Science Unit programme, *The Day the Universe Changed*, with James Burke, and local children and volunteer Ethel Buvyer were involved in a BBC Schools Service series *A History of the Kitchen*. Lighter entertainment filmed at the museum has included the Noel Edmonds Christmas Show and in 1999, a surreal fairy story, *The Tenth Kingdom*. In 2006 the museum hosted the final of the BBC's *Restoration Village*, which had highlighted important historic buildings at risk. The first film made at the museum in its earliest days after opening was *Life in Medieval England*. In 2009 Lucy Worsley, curator of the Royal Palaces, was at the museum filming for a BBC4 series *If Walls Could Talk*.

Poetry and literature, too, are inspiring and inspired within the museum. Christopher Fry, the celebrated poet and playwright who lived in East Dean, wrote a poem in 1991 dedicated to the museum, copies of which were sold on behalf of the Friends as a fund-raising venture. One hangs in the Partridge Inn in Singleton.

→

The museum was involved with local history publishers Phillimore & Co and Alan Sutton on two book projects. Phoebe Somers, sister of Juliet Pannett, the acclaimed Sussex artist whose portrait of Roy Armstrong hangs in the upper hall from Crawley, had for many years published a weekly series of articles on rural life in Sussex in the *West Sussex Gazette*; in 1993 the museum published *A Time There Was* in association with Alan Sutton. The following year Phillimore invited Diana Zeuner and Richard Pailthorpe to edit and update Roy Armstrong's classic book *A History of Sussex*.

More recently the museum has enjoyed the company of Jane Borodale as Leverhulme writer-in-residence. She wrote a group of fictional stories called *The Visitor* published in 2010, and her novel, *The Book of Fires*, inspired by Poplar Cottage, was short-listed for the Orange New Writers prize in the same year.

The two Fire Events held at the museum in 2000 and 2007 have contributed dramatic and magical activity, particularly as lanterns and a fiery dragon take on eerie shapes as darkness falls. Similar activities are planned for the 40th anniversary celebration weekend in September 2010.

Filming at the museum. **Top left** *Filming for television on the museum site in 1970; interviewing Mrs Langridge about life in a charcoal burners' hut.* **Below** *The Prebendal School choir from Chichester was filmed in the house from North Cray for ITV in 1996.* **Top centre** *Chris Zeuner being interviewed by broadcaster Julian Pettifer in 1977.* **Top right** *Working horses were a popular subject in the early 1980s, here being filmed for ITV.* **Below** *Staff in costume for The Day the Universe Changed in 1984.* **Bottom left** *A Ferrari seems incongruous in the market square, for a commercial promotion.* **Bottom centre** *Shire horse Rosie and her foal, Blair, filmed for regional BBC on the day Labour came to power in 1997 (Blair was later re-named).* **Bottom right** *Night falls on the final of the BBC's Restoration Village, which highlighted important historic buildings at risk.*

10 Learning at the Heart

A school party passes Poplar Cottage on a sunny day in 2009.

Diana Zeuner

with Kim Leslie, Diana Rowsell, Richard Harris, Sue Shave and Elizabeth Newbery

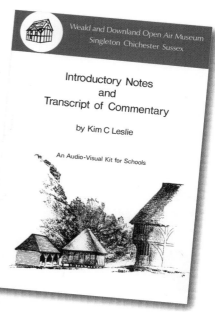

Bringing the museum to life in the classroom, 1974 – with illustration by John Warren, the museum's honorary architect.

Museums are in essence educational organisations, but some more than others have focused on the formal provision of educational programmes. In the early 21st century the museums and heritage sector was urged to reflect the Government's preoccupation with learning at all ages and stages, but the Weald & Downland Open Air Museum has delivered quality education since its inception.

As a teacher Roy Armstrong's deep interest in education was reflected in the museum's development. There were talks, seminars and courses for adults in the early days, leading eventually to a substantial lifelong learning programme for building conservation industry professionals and those interested in pursuing rural and building trades and crafts, making the museum a pioneer in its educational work.

Schoolchildren were welcomed from the start, not least because two of the museum's prime movers were teachers. Kim Leslie, who was on the museum's promotional committee and was its first honorary treasurer, introduced the first school to the museum site. Chris Zeuner, the museum's first full-time director and a former teacher, took a lifelong interest in encouraging young people to learn at the museum, appointing the museum's

Boys from St Andrew's School, Worthing help Roger Champion re-erect the wheelhouse frame for Catherington treadwheel, 1970.

impossible in the classroom. For many, seeing history (and other subjects) in a new light can suddenly make something click into place."

One of the most extraordinary results from the first two years of opening was the number of children welcomed in school groups. In 1972 John Lowe reported a figure of 35,000 children.

In 1998, when the museum received the Interpret Britain Award for Formal Education Provision, Chris Zeuner said:

Education has been a cornerstone of the museum's work since its foundation. This is the second award we have received for our education programmes and is evidence of the dedication and hard work of Sue Shave and her intrepid team of volunteers, and the high quality of our specialist lecturers in building conservation and related courses led by our research director Richard Harris. The museum has established itself as a leading provider of education in our fields of interest, and we intend to continue and enhance our role in learning for all ages and backgrounds.

first dedicated education officer, Heather Jackson, who was also a teacher.

A visit to the Weald & Downland Open Air Museum is inspiring for children, removing them from the formality of the classroom and enabling them to learn in a more informal environment and in a totally different way. "Children enjoy change," said Chris Zeuner, "and at the museum they can make discoveries which are

The schools service develops

Anine-year-old boy appeared one weekend, clutching a grubby paper bag. He approached a volunteer steward, proudly opening the bag to show her the contents, some pieces of charcoal. He explained that he had so enjoyed his visit to the charcoal burners' camp with his school, that he built his own kiln at home and produced his own charcoal. This was 1972: real living history.

By the following year the museum was welcoming 400 school children a day. This was the maximum as it was not possible to park more than 15 coaches. The total number of children, mostly in school groups, stood at an astonishing 49,042. Museum director John Lowe wrote:

We were fully booked with schools by 1 May and after that day we had to turn away dozens of schools. This year the museum has done everything in its power to persuade all teachers to prepare their classes for their visit…. Literally hundreds of

children returned to the museum after a school visit, bringing their parents with them.

The museum's long relationship with schools began before it opened to the public. The first school to visit the museum site was St Andrew's School, Worthing, where honorary treasurer Kim Leslie taught history in the 1960s. In 1969 and 1970 he organised two work camps after school exams with 15 senior boys in each group, camping on site, with Kim living in his caravan.

They took on all sorts of tasks, helping make wattle panels for Catherington treadwheel, rebuilding the Upper Beeding toll house, preparing the site for the Saxon weavers' hut, building the charcoal kiln with Mr and Mrs Langridge, digging a hole for the sawpit, unloading heavy timbers and tiles for the Littlehampton granary, and clearing woodland for paths and picnic sites.

It was pioneering work, filmed by the BBC and making the national papers. Kim Leslie still

Working with special needs pupils   *Diana Rowsell*

The museum has always worked with children with special educational needs, but in 2002 an opportunity arose to take it to a new level. The museum was approached by Barclays PLC Community Investment Programme which funded specific projects in which their staff could become involved as volunteers. Special days were launched covering such subjects as *Shakespeare for SATs, Working Animals, Fire & Light, Chaucer* and *Harvest Home*. A great success, they attracted nearly 700 pupils in the first year and Barclays staff supplemented museum staff and volunteers in delivering the activities. The funding made possible pupils' reduced entry fee and travel, and allowed the museum to bring in specialists, such as a professional theatre company, a falconry display and musicians. The days were evaluated and refined, with Barclays staff growing in confidence and some schools booking different classes into each of the days. Numbers grew, with almost 3,000 children attending over the three-year project.

Barclays PLC was pleased with the project and offered extra funding for a free conference for teachers and education staff from other museums and heritage organisations. With the influential Professor Eileen Hooper-Greenhill speaking to 100 delegates, the museum was able to celebrate the project, promote the role of museums in supporting special needs education, and disseminate good practice within the sector. One teacher said: "This reminds us that it's not all about target setting, league tables and performance management. Our collective jobs are to light the candles of knowledge and enthusiasm and allow them to burn."

Above *Jon Roberts and Paul Pinnington teaching children with special educational needs the basics of hurdle making and willow weaving in 2002, and* **right** *sensory experiences for another group included a music workshop in 2004. The days were sponsored by Barclays PLC Community Investment Programme.*

The museum wanted to ensure that the project continued once the funding ended, and during 2005 and each year since more than 1,100 schoolchildren with special needs have been welcomed from special and mainstream schools. Alongside the focused workshops for those with special needs, bookings are accepted for mainstream pupils on teacher-led visits or for workshop sessions, an inclusive approach which encourages beneficial interaction for all the children. Most of the elements continue to be delivered by volunteers, while South Downs College students from Havant replaced the professional theatre for some workshops, enabling them to fulfil course requirements for working with younger students. Another positive spin-off is that many of the special needs' teachers now bring their pupils to visit the museum on regular days throughout the year.

occasionally hears from old boys, including one who recently e-mailed from Chicago to say his experiences had given him a lifelong enthusiasm for history. Nowadays, this type of activity would be almost impossible to organise; in those days there was no training and there were no safety helmets or steel-capped boots.

The first steps towards a museum education service came through a coincidence – just a few days before the museum opened to the public

Kim took up an appointment as education officer of West Sussex Record Office with a very wide brief: to promote the study of local history throughout the county. This gave the opportunity to link its resources with museums and other places of historical interest, and thus be in a position to take the first tentative steps towards the provision of a museum education service.

Reaching teachers and pupils through publications was Kim's major priority. The earliest of

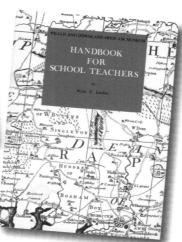

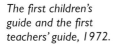

The first children's guide and the first teachers' guide, 1972.

these were three editions of the first children's guide, in 1972, 1973 and 1976, illustrated with line drawings by Marie Hett (mother of Julia, John Lowe's secretary and the museum's first secretary). Mrs Hett went on to produce cut-out models of museum buildings for children to make. There were also two editions of the *Handbook for School Teachers*, in 1972 and 1975, a pack of 12 colour slides, with notes, published in 1971 in conjunction with the Slide Centre, London, and *An Audio-Visual Kit for Schools*, published by Gateway Productions of Bristol in 1974. Courses were run at what were then known as Teachers' Centres, designed to encourage teachers to bring school parties. After a visit the pupils of Pound Hill Middle School built a full-size replica of the Saxon weavers' hut on their school field in 1972, the first of a number of reconstructions at schools.

Pound Hill Middle School's replica of the museum's Saxon weavers' hut, 1972 (on the right).

Teachers' feedback was important for the embryonic museum, and they make interesting reading now: "Not enough to see yet"; "I would remove the cows" (they were actually grazing outside the museum but obviously disturbed this writer), and "Distances between buildings too great". But most comments were more encouraging: "Personally I can't bear shut-in museums so I love Singleton"; "The children appreciated the non-starchy atmosphere of this non-museum and felt they were part of history," and "I want to come back."

The museum's first dedicated education officer was Heather Jackson (later Champion) who was to play a formative role in the museum's development, including in the curatorial department. She began a museum loans service in 1975 which included roofing and walling materials, hinges, examples of destruction by dry and wet rot and beetle infestation, carpenters' tools, and photographs of museum exhibits. From 1976 she produced a series of teachers' leaflets and trails, including a new *Children's Guide to the Museum*, published by Dinosaur Publications. School children were now visiting to work with specific exhibits, rather than as a general 'school trip' and were getting involved themselves, including applying limewash to Winkhurst and Bayleaf.

With the move to a larger portacabin office, the Goodwood granary became available to convert into a classroom and in 1977 the schools department introduced the first children's activity days on Wednesdays in August.

The British Museum recently announced a sleepover for children, but it was happening at the Weald & Downland Open Air Museum years ago. In 1983, Elizabeth Newbery, a former education officer with the Museum of London who was living in Chichester, started a monthly Junior Friends group for children aged seven and upwards. The following year a summer school was introduced, based on similar lines, with the assistance of a team of volunteers, and open to non-Junior Friends as well. The idea was to introduce children to real countryside skills, problem-solving and fresh experiences but with a heavy dose of adventure as befits the summer school holidays. Elizabeth had *Swallows and Amazons* in the back of her mind.

Children had the chance of building their own house using materials from the museum site. They examined different sorts of homes from across the world and through history, helped by watching demonstrations such as thatching, tree-felling and timber-hauling by horse. Solving problems of design and construction, they worked with the knowledge that their 'house' would have to be weatherproof for their night's sleep.

Experts were regularly asked to help out. In 1985, the children built a charcoal burners' camp and were shown how to build an oven using an oil drum in which they cooked biscuits, and how to make charcoal in an old tin. They learned how to skin rabbits, later cooked and eaten with relish. Richard Mabey, the renowned ecologist and broadcaster, took everyone on a woodland walk foraging for food. "No one was ever hurt, but almost everything we did would now be banned under health and safety regulations," says Elizabeth. "Their experience generated greater interest in the exhibits at the museum," she adds. The project was repeated for a number of years.

In 1984 Elizabeth joined the staff as education officer, a post shared with the West Sussex Countryside Studies Trust at Goodwood, an unusual partnership in those days. She developed educational materials, schools sessions and links with teachers for both. For the museum she wrote a new publication for children designed to encourage them to look and draw during their visit. *Look Here* was designed by Susan England, and the pair went on to produce a number of children's educational publications. In 1988 this included a family discovery pack, *Track Back*, linking the museum and the Goodwood Estate, Both publications received Carnegie Interpret Britain Awards.

Elizabeth left the museum in 1990 to concentrate on freelance activities, developing a successful business in educational publications. Geoff King, who took over the post, recruited an enlarged voluntary team to help deliver the expanding schools service. Themed visits for schools included *Materials for building construction, Farming through the ages, Tudor times, The technology of machines*, and *Design and decoration*.

The museum's education service took another step forward with the appointment of Sue Shave to the new post of interpretation officer in 1995, responsible for interpretation and education, a much-expanded task. She came to the museum from The ARC (Archaeological Resource Centre), York, a hands-on education centre which had been a pioneer in its field. Immersing herself in the very different world of an open air museum, Sue set about harnessing the energy of volunteers and staff.

The relocation of the shop to Longport farmhouse provided an opportunity to create an education centre in the Lavant building at the heart of the museum site. Volunteers proved

Junior Friends' monthly session in progress at the museum in the 1980s. Elizabeth Newbery is kneeling on the left.

Two publications written by museum education officer Elizabeth Newbery, Track Back *and* Side-by-Side.

Sue Shave, tasked with educational and interpretation roles, with museum gardener Bob Holman in 1996.

invaluable in preparing artefacts for education sessions and displays, and contributing to new workshops. Clore Duffield Foundation funding was secured to develop a *Getting to Grips* building materials and techniques workshop for younger

> " *When I first started [as interpretation officer], my office was on the ground floor of Crawley hall overlooking the market square. I remember Chris Zeuner appearing outside my office window one day while I was on the phone to Wimbledon Lawn Tennis Museum. He was holding two dead pheasants and waving them at me indicating that I could have them! It was impossible to have a serious conversation after that! Inhabitants of the Lavant building, where we set up the education service, included several newts, bats, and jackdaws nesting on the chimney. The mice also used regularly to eat my crayons and on several occasions I had manually to remove a mouse from my desk drawer whilst answering the phone.* "
>
> **Sue Shave, interpretation officer**

pupils; West Sussex County Council's early years' advisor was involved in the preparation.

The museum contributed to the county council's pupil enrichment scheme for gifted and talented children, creating programmes around building materials and construction methods, the study of historical and archaeological sources, woodland crafts, Tudors and Victorians, and the deserted medieval village excavations on the Downs undertaken by the Sussex Archaeological Society. Adult courses at the museum were utilised to assist the development of these programmes and others for older children. Sue Shave and volunteer Jon Roberts attended the 'identification of hard woods module' of the MSc in Building Conservation, using their new knowledge to create a workshop exploring the science behind the use of different materials in traditional construction. And Jon Roberts' attendance on timber conversion courses was crucial to the development of a carpentry workshop, enabling pupils to study timber-framed buildings and try skills such as cross-cut sawing.

Ex-farmer and volunteer Brian Weekes contributed to the development of the farming heritage element of the education programme. He and Roy Money were already guides for the *Side-by-Side* farming tours for the museum and Goodwood Estate, and Brian was also instrumental in helping launch the *Farming through the Ages* event involving local farmers and agricultural colleges. To encourage more interaction between visitors and the museum's livestock, animal experience days were held for older children and animal feeding tours were offered for general visitors.

The education volunteers developed into a creative team producing ideas for new programmes and helping to resource and deliver them. Traditional cooking sessions were held in the house from Walderton, and Ian Pearce's arrival with his knowledge of historic cooking made an important contribution to their development. The Tudor programme included bread-making, and pottage-making using onions, skirrits and edible weeds from Bayleaf farmhouse. Later, Victorian cooking sessions took place in Whittaker's Cottages, and volunteer Valerie Singer created a sample experience of a Victorian school day.

Bayleaf farmhouse was under enormous pressure from schools during the season, so the museum turned to the winter months to offer an in-depth service that was impossible during normal opening hours. The first winter workshop was based on Tudor rural life for 30 children including a tour of Bayleaf, candle-dipping by the fire, spinning using

the great wheel and threshing wheat with a flail in Cowfold barn. The response from schools was enormous with every available day booked. Victorian workshops were added and new volunteers drafted in to deliver workshops simultaneously.

> 'How would it be', I asked, 'if we were to offer a structured session of role-play in the school?' I thought back to some of the teachers of my own 1930s schooldays who were undoubtedly Victorians. I taped the memories of my older friends and relations and was greatly helped by one of our visitors, Mr Donald Hodge, who started school in the 1890s. I read up documentary and literary sources, delved into the history books and devised a programme for a Victorian School Day. This proved to be popular and helped us win a Sandford Award. ... When I am teaching in the little one-room West Wittering school I borrow the name of Annie Belam, one of my family, the gardener's daughter, who taught in the little one-room school which still stands in the village of West Stoke, a few miles from Singleton. You don't get much nearer to a real Victorian than that!
>
> **Valerie Singer, former teacher and museum volunteer**

The Junior Friends was restarted and in August there would be a four-day camp with a sleepover, with shelters built in the woodland. Sue would stay - but not sleep - in the charcoal burners' hut overnight. The Junior Friends also played a central part in the Tree Dressing event in December with the Rabble Folk Theatre, and joined in with the Christmas Carol Service in North Cray hall house.

The education service took on volunteers and work-placement students from schools, teacher training colleges, museum education courses and heritage management courses as well as students studying travel tourism. Several students joined for a few weeks, providing invaluable support with workshop delivery and helping with holiday activities and special events.

Other highlights included a medieval realms workshop, which explored contrasts between North Cray hall house and Hangleton cottage. Literacy and numeracy trails were provided, with specialist advice, based on the museum buildings. A science investigation workshop included experiments in North Cray hall house, provoking discussion about the properties of materials and their selection for use in traditional and modern building.

The expanding education service was recognised by two heritage education awards, the Sandford Award for Excellence in Heritage Education in 1997 and the Interpret Britain Award for Formal Education Provision in 1998. Educational work at the West Sussex Countryside

Above left *Children learn about a Victorian school day in 1992.*
Above right *Volunteer Jean Piggott, then also secretary of the Friends, teaching pastry-making to pupils in the house from Walderton.*

Education officer Diane Walker (second from right) with a school group at Hangleton cottage in 2002.

Left *Pupils learn what Tudor women might carry in their pocket, 2008.*
Right *Encouraging local schools to use the museum; here Singleton and West Dean primary school pupils celebrate Shrove Tuesday with pancakes made with flour from Lurgashall watermill on a visit to the museum in February 2005. The after-hours visit, enabling parents to join in, was followed up by increased use by the schools of the museum's school workshop programme.*

Studies Trust at Goodwood Estate also won a Sandford Award, with the national awards ceremony held at Goodwood House. Sue says that open air museums and traditional buildings are now in her blood. Today she is the director of Chiltern Open Air Museum, which Chris Zeuner helped with advice in the early days.

When Sue left the museum in 2000 to pursue her career at The Discovery Centre, Birmingham, her place was taken by Diane Walker, from Fort Nelson, one of the Royal Armouries' museums. She continued to develop the interpretation sessions, bringing to life the daily tasks of farmers' households from medieval, Tudor and Victorian periods, including *Fleece to Fabric*, following wool from the sheep's back to finished clothing. She developed a new version of *Getting to Grips* for

4 to 7-year-olds, and new programmes for 11 to 16-year-olds as well as vocational courses in leisure and tourism. Training for teachers continued, along with collaborative projects with the Mary Rose Trust to provide for able pupils in West Sussex. Further workshops were introduced, notably the new medieval programme, and increased training was put in place for the education volunteers. In 2001 the museum won another Sandford Award from the Heritage Education Trust.

The re-siting of Winkhurst Tudor kitchen enabled the introduction of Tudor cookery sessions, designed to appeal to teachers ever more hidebound by the demands of the National Curriculum but keen to teach history in a meaningful way. Virtually all the sessions were delivered by volunteers trained by Diane, and on one day in 2002 there were 500 schoolchildren on site.

With Diane's departure in 2003, Diana Rowsell, the museum's training co-ordinator, took over responsibility for schools in addition to her role in organising adult education at the museum, becoming head of learning. The museum withdrew from the partnership with the West Sussex Countryside Studies Trust, and made a new full-time appointment of schools services manager in Jennie Peel, who had just retired from her post as headmistress at Conifers School at Easebourne, near Midhurst.

Funding was received from The Foyle Trust to update the paper-based teacher's pack but the opportunity was taken to move with the rapidly advancing technology and launch a new website purely for schools. The new site – www.openair classroom.org.uk – took the museum's work right into schools. It includes downloadable activity

sheets which can be used directly or modified, is regularly updated, and helps teachers plan the use of museum resources and visits imaginatively, including taking advantage of a wealth of cross-curricular opportunities.

The workshops continued to expand, and responding to teachers' requests, Jennie Peel and her team of volunteers devised one-off study days for all age groups from early years to A level students. Rachel Neville (now Mercer) had joined the team as Jennie's assistant and when Jennie was lured back to Conifers School, Rachel was appointed in her place.

Education never stands still, and again the museum found itself dealing with a time of great change. Conferences were organised for teachers at the museum, covering topics such as *Cultural Entitlement, Global Citizenship, Creativity in the Classroom, Primary Citizenship* and *Transformational Learning*. All these attracted teachers who had not previously visited the museum.

A special project was run in 2007-08 for DEFRA's (Department for the Environment, Farming and Rural Affairs) *Year of Food and Farming*, working with three West Sussex schools and aiming to reconnect young people with the seasonality of food and help them appreciate the

importance of farming and the countryside. Children saw wheat growing in the field, watched it being harvested and ground into flour in Lurgashall water-mill, and finally baked bread with it in Winkhurst Tudor kitchen.

In 2008 the museum was one of the first to be awarded the new Learning Outside the Classroom Quality Badge as part of a new initiative to promote practical education outside the classroom. The badge provides a national accreditation to help teachers plan high quality school visits.

In 2010 some 20,000 children were welcomed on school

Leaflet produced in 2006 to encourage schools to use the museum for cross-curricular learning.

visits. Each child receives a certificate as a memento and is offered a free visit with their family. "It is wonderful to see a child arrive with his or her family, excitedly showing them all the things they have already seen at the museum," says Diana Rowsell.

Children involved in an early music workshop at Poplar Cottage in 2009.

Children discover how wheat for bread was harvested in Tudor times, with a chance to use a flail.

Left *MSc in Building Conservation students working with special paints and historic paint finishes, and* **right** *examining period details on panelled doors and staircases during a visit to the Brooking Collection.*

Pioneering a lifelong learning service

In 1984 the museum planned to run a summer workshop to provide experience and training in the repair of traditional buildings, open to people from the building industry, associated professions and students, but it was cancelled because of lack of support. However, by the end of the decade the museum had decided to make use of its accumulated resources of skills and experience in building conservation, together with a growing range of examples on site for teaching, and so in 1991 the first professional training was offered.

The catalyst was a proposal by the newly-formed Bournemouth University to become a founding partner in the proposed *Joint Centre for Heritage Conservation and Management*. That year Richard Harris organised the first three-day training workshop in the repair of timber-framed buildings and a programme of professional seminars and conferences - formal adult learning at the Weald & Downland Open Air Museum was born.

Initial growth was in response to requests from the burgeoning building conservation industry, and Bournemouth University suggested the development of a part-time Masters programme

in Building Conservation, aimed at professionals and craftspeople wanting to work in the industry. In 1994 the museum became a partner college with the university and designed an MSc programme in Timber Building Conservation, which was validated as a stand-alone programme in 1998. This is run entirely by the museum, and taught on the museum site. In all, more than 55 students have achieved the Post Graduate Diploma, with 18 graduating with their MSc by 2010. In 2008 a second MSc programme, Building Conservation, was validated, aimed at those who wish to pursue a broader spectrum of study than the specialist timber course.

The Masters degrees draw on the knowledge and expertise of many specialists, and a programme of day schools in historic building conservation developed from them, with subjects ranging from timber decay, to wattle and daub and gauged brickwork. In the 1990s, alongside the building conservation courses, a handful of courses in traditional rural trades and crafts were developed in response to demand from museum visitors including subjects such as heavy horse experience days and pole lathe turning.

In 1997 Richard Harris set up a training workshop teaching tool skills for the first time. Over a period of 15 days a group of five students created, from scratch, a woodshed for the museum, using traditional timber-framing techniques, led by specialist framer Henry Russell. This format gradually developed into a range of practical courses centred on the unique five-day *Timber-framing from scratch*, which has been taught by the museum's resident carpenter, Joe Thompson since 2000. The completion of the Downland Gridshell

Dr Gerard Lynch – a leader in his field – has taught historic brickwork conservation since the start of the museum's adult education course programme.

Timber-framing from scratch   *Diana Zeuner*

This innovative course was introduced to the museum's lifelong learning programme in 1997, and has become the institution's signature training course.

Students on the museum's flagship course, Timber-framing from scratch *and top right Joe, Thompson, course leader.*

It offers students a rare chance to frame up a traditional building, starting with the felled tree. A timber-framed building in miniature is the result – the first was used to provide a woodshed for Bayleaf farmhouse.

The course was originally designed by Richard Harris and led by carpenter Henry Russell over 15 days. Now refined to five, today's students are under the guidance of the museum's carpenter-in-residence, Joe Thompson.

> ❝ *The insight gained into the evolution of methods and tools was fascinating as was the converting of timber. Hewing, plumb and level marks, two-foot marks, double-cutting of tenon shoulders and draw-boring are all very familiar now. I have retired from my life as an orthorpaedic surgeon which also involved saws, hammers and chisels! Now I undertake various wood-related activities and would relish the chance to be involved in a proper timber-framing project.* ❞
>
> **Chris Chadwick**

Students are taken through all the processes involved in converting oak logs into timber which is then jointed and framed into a structure. Along the way they learn the techniques and skills involved in traditional timber framing and the use of tools and methods of 17th-century carpenters, as well as those used by timber-framing companies of today.

Joe Thompson, whose interest in working with green oak was inspired by the loss of oak trees felled in the storm of October 1987, brings his craftsmanship, passion for the material, engaging communication skills and analytical eye for historical detail to the courses, which are highly regarded in the timber-framing sector.

The profile of student participants has been varied from the start of the course – designer/builders, employees of timber-framing or building conservation companies, self-employed craftspeople, enthusiasts wishing to construct a 'one-off' building, and home-owners wanting to know more about the repair of their homes. From pilots to surgeons and IT escapees, as well as carpenters wanting to extend their skills, the course has included people from all walks of life.

2010 brochures for the museum's lifelong learning courses in historic building conservation and traditional rural trades and crafts.

> **❝** I joined the Timber-framing from scratch *course to learn how to repair and extend my Kent farmhouse in a historically appropriate way. What I hadn't expected was that, by the end of the week, I would feel absolutely confident in my own ability to construct a timber-framed building, having never previously sawn anything but a loaf of bread.* **❞**
>
> **Polly Kerss**

in 2002 led to greatly enhanced facilities for practical training.

In 1998 it was felt there was potential for significant growth in formal adult learning, but further staff resources were needed. Two charitable trusts contributed to the salary for a new post, to which Diana Rowsell was appointed with responsibility for formal and informal adult learning, the daily craft demonstration programme and the provision of demonstrators and trade stands for the museum's special event days. A wide range of new courses was developed and in response to the programmes' success two assistants were employed, Rebecca Osborne in 2002 and Lucy Hockley in 2007. The establishment of both posts was initially supported by benefactors Nick and Wendy Sargent.

Two fundamental principles underpin the programmes: courses are based on the museum collections and site resources, and all tutors are current practitioners with a flair for passing on their skills and knowledge. In addition to experts of national standing, the museum draws on local people skilled in regional traditional rural trades and crafts, and courses have been developed in such subjects as willow weaving, corn dolly making, coppice work, blacksmithing, textile

> **❝** *A good balance between theory, history and practical. Relaxed and friendly; I was delighted with the focus on practical work.*
>
> **(Repair of traditionally constructed brickwork course)**
>
> *Exceeded expectations. Everything was a whole new learning experience; many misconceptions were corrected today. First class.*
>
> **(Lime mortars for brickwork course)**
>
> *Very enlightening, in-depth information. Well planned and arranged; good tutors.*
>
> **(Joinery by hand – sash windows course)**
>
> *A wonderful balance between the academic content and the informal ambience.* **❞**
>
> **(Millennium of herbs course)**
>
> **Students' comments on the museum's adult courses**

Students taking part in the museum's lifelong learning programme. Building courses – **clockwise from top left** lime mortars, practical stone wall repairs, cob walling, flint walling, hewing and sawing, traditional plastering and traditional painting and decorating.

*Rural crafts courses – **clockwise from top left** living willow workshop, bee-keeping, pole lathe workshop, prehistoric tool-making, Tudor baking, making a bentwood chair, ploughing with working horses and natural dyeing.*

crafts, watercolour painting, experiential archaeology, uses of herbs and Tudor cooking.

The adult learning programme contributes to the museum in many different ways. Financially it

> It was precisely what the professional required … a lot of knowledge was absorbed. A very informative lecturer with an honest and instructive approach.
> **(Timber decay and its treatment course)**
>
> Exceeded my expectations by a wide margin, and provided fresh insight into the nature and characteristics of oak. Professional in its presentation and engaging.
> **(Strength grading of oak course)**
>
> Extremely informative and fascinating. Immensely stimulating.
> **(The painted house course)**
>
> Excellent instruction – just the right balance between being supervised and learning from our own mistakes.
> **(Continuous hurdle fencing course)**
>
> **Students' comments on the museum's adult courses**

is self-supporting and makes a contribution to overheads but its real value is far greater. It increases the museum's strength as a knowledge-based institution by developing a relationship with dozens of outstanding practitioners and researchers. On a daily basis it provides a background hum of activity, and there is synergy with all the museum's specialist departments which both gain from, and contribute to, the programme. Perhaps most importantly, the museum has the satisfaction of knowing that this aspect of its work makes a real difference to people's lives.

"Every course is a form of interpretation of the museum's themes and to maximise the benefit to each individual the ambience, refreshments and the friendly smile can be as important as the content of the course," says Diana Rowsell.

The museum is unique in its sector in delivering such an array of learning opportunities from evening talks to vernacular architecture study days, from historic cooking experiences to textile and greenwood crafts, from practical workshops in historic building conservation and the use of traditional tools, methods and materials to two Masters programmes. Success can be measured by adult learning's contribution to the museum and the interest shown in the programme by other cultural organisations. In 11 years numbers have grown from less than 200 student days of adult learning in 1998 to 3,565 in 2009.

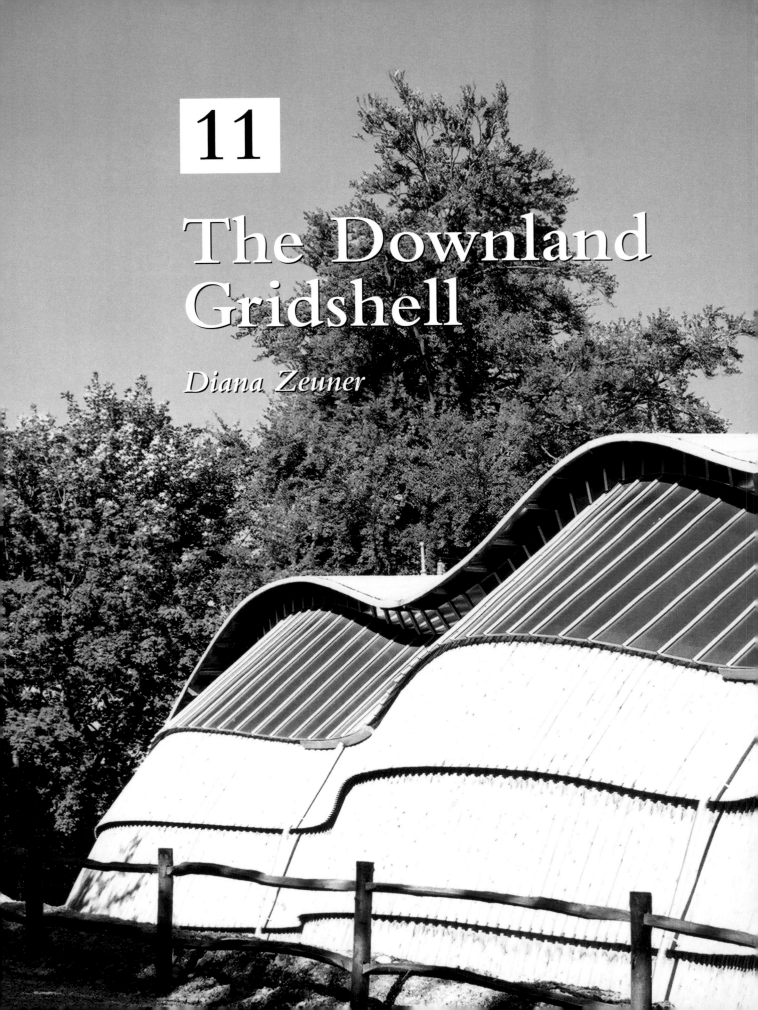

11

The Downland Gridshell

Diana Zeuner

In 1997 the museum launched a project which was by far the most ambitious in its history, and the most expensive. It successfully applied to the newly-launched Heritage Lottery Fund (HLF), for a grant towards a £1.3 million building conservation centre and collections store to be housed in an "innovative greenwood timber structure sited uphill from Longport farmhouse".

The Downland Gridshell, as it was to become, was a pioneer modern structure utilising timber and a range of new techniques, enabling the museum to move its collections and its buildings workshop onto the site, where visitors would have much improved access. They would be able to watch historic timber-frames being restored ready to join the other building exhibits on site. They would also be able to see close-up the many artefacts in the rural life and building parts collection established over 30 years. The building itself was to be an integral part of the project, through which the museum could show how sustainable natural materials can be used in modern buildings in the countryside.

Following research into a suitable architectural practice to lead the design, the museum chose one from what Richard Harris described as "the first 11" – Edward Cullinan Architects, in partnership with Buro Happold Engineers. Both had considerable track records in their respective fields and together they had worked on timber buildings at Hooke Park, Dorset, for furniture designer and manufacturer, John Makepeace. Quantity surveyors were London and Bognor Regis-based Alex Sayer Ltd. The initial development work was made possible by a grant from the Friends.

By the following year a major campaign was under way to raise the matching funding required for all Heritage Lottery Fund projects, and the Gridshell was now increasingly seen as the museum's project to mark the millennium. The venture, for which £1.05 million was expected to come from HLF, had already attracted £170,000 by the end of the first year. In the event HLF granted the museum £1.185 million.

A crucial element was the design of the building itself. "It is entirely appropriate for a museum of buildings to reflect its interest in the subject in a new and innovative structure," wrote Chris Zeuner. "The development offers a major opportunity to define public perception of the museum through a building of high quality, practical operation and ground-breaking design." The museum hoped that by exploring new techniques in greenwood timber construction it would encourage the use of traditional and

Architect Ted Cullinan (left) and Buro Happold engineer Richard Harris on site for an early design meeting.

locally available materials married to modern technology.

Edward Cullinan and Buro Happold Engineers were among the few with expertise in this specialist field of building, and at Ted Cullinan's London practice Chris Zeuner watched ideas emerge from his pen of a gridshell structure built of locally-sourced greenwood on walls of chalk and clad in timber, inspired by the shape of the South Downs surrounding the museum. The museum's own expertise in the restoration and building of historic structures and design of visitor facilities enabled it to play a central role in the evolution of the new centre. The site chosen provided a challenging opportunity, set into the hillside and framed with beech and sycamore, with westerly views across the museum site and along the downland valley.

By 1999 the purpose of the new structure was being further refined from its original objectives. Chris Zeuner spoke of its importance in providing a spacious workshop on site where visitors could watch craftsmen restore buildings; replacing the increasingly inadequate workshops and stores off-site at Charlton and removing the rent payment; giving the museum a well-serviced base for teaching and training; and enabling visitor access to collections stored in better environmental conditions.

E A Chiverton Ltd, of Bognor Regis, was chosen as the main contractors, with The Green Oak Carpentry Company responsible for the construction of the timber gridshell. Buro

Awards

- RIBA (Royal Institute of British Architects) Architecture Award (2002)
- Runner-up for the RIBA Stirling Prize (2002)
- British Construction Industries Small Projects Award (2002)
- American Institute of Architects Excellence in Design Award (2003)
- Institute of Structural Engineers David Alsop Commendation (2003)
- Full Civic Trust Award (2003)
- Short-listed for an RICS (Royal Institute of Chartered Surveyors) award (2003)
- Wood Awards: Winner (structural category) and Gold Award overall winner (Carpenters Company) (2003)
- European Wooden Façade Contest (Nordic Timber Council) (2004)
- Ted Cullinan receives RIBA Gold Medal for his contribution to architecture (2008)

> ❝ *I remember those early days of planning the Gridshell as heady times. The Heritage Lottery Fund was in its infancy and determined to support innovative structures. A visit to Ted Cullinan's offices in London assured Chris that the museum had chosen the right man to design their building; he returned full of tales of Ted's ability to draw 'flowing sketches' of a building which was to be revolutionary for an open air museum at the time and had the ability to establish for the museum far wider and broader credentials than it could have hitherto imagined.* ❞
>
> **Diana Zeuner**

Happold – whose chief timber engineer was also called Richard Harris – worked with the University of Bath on a computer model for the design of the gridshell, and Edward Cullinan's job architect, Steve Johnson, produced much of the detailed design. Work began on the museum site in 2000, with both the museum and the Heritage Lottery Fund confident that the shortfall in funding could be found well before the completion of the project. The Wolfson Foundation had awarded the project £50,000 the previous year. By now it was clear that the structure would be the largest gridshell building in the UK, and an architect's model and exhibition went on tour countrywide.

Chris Zeuner's sudden and unexpected death in January 2001 robbed this major development of its project manager, as much as it did the museum of its leading figure. The task of seeing it to completion and raising the final funds now fell to the new museum director, Richard Harris, and the trustees led by museum chairman David Tomlinson.

By the beginning of 2001 the Gridshell site was dominated by what Richard Harris called "an enormous forest of scaffolding, 150 feet long, 85 feet wide and 40 feet high [45 x 25 x 12 metres]". On top of this structure the laths of the gridshell were being assembled. The sawn oak laths, eventually sourced from France for the best material, were scarf-jointed together to make what were believed to be the longest pieces of oak ever produced. In a new method for gridshells specially developed by Buro Happold and Edward Cullinan, the grid of flexible oak members – 2 inch x 1.5 inch (50 x 35 millimetres) in section and 120 feet (36 metres) long – was first formed as a flat 'mat' on top of the scaffold with the scaffolding gradually lowered and removed to form the double curvature that gives the structure its strength.

The scaffold – provided by specialist contractor PERI – remained inside the peanut-like frame to be used in cladding the exterior. The whole sequence was an extraordinary visual experience; a platform was erected to enable visitors to watch safely, and a time-lapse video of the process was made.

Led by Steve Corbett, later to become a museum trustee, the carpenters were like 'acrobats'

scattered across the grid, lowering the scaffolding jacks by pre-determined amounts, adding further laths across the diagonals and fixing the joints in place. On 19 April, after seven weeks of bending, the edges of the grid at last touched down on the perimeter of the timber deck which forms the ceiling of the basement store. The external cladding consisted of three overlapping rows of vertical western red cedar, with polycarbonate glazing at high level, topped with a ribbon roof of 'RoofKrete' curving over the three humps of the gridshell.

Inside, the building consisted of two parts, the cavernous 5,000 square feet (1,500 square metres) basement sunk into the hill for energy efficiency, to be filled with roller-racking storage for the museum's collection of some 10,000 artefacts, and a base for the curator and his staff; and the upper floor enclosed by the gridshell which was to be the museum's building conservation workshop where timber frames and other structures would be repaired and conserved. There would also be space to accommodate the growing range of training courses and demonstrations, serviced by two enclosed workshops at one end, and the conservation of larger items from the collections, such as wagons, at the other. A key benefit would be the

building's open access, with visitors able to take guided tours of the collections and to watch the activity taking place in the workshop.

The Chris Zeuner Memorial Appeal had received a remarkable response with nearly 500 individual donations, raising just over £60,000 by autumn 2001. Nearly 20 major trust funds and other organisations contributed. Among them were the Garfield Weston Foundation (£100,000), the Jerwood Foundation (£80,000) – the upper portion of the building was to be known as the Jerwood Gridshell Space – and the Mitford Foulerton Trust (£30,000) for the east end of the basement – to be known as the Mitford Foulerton Studio.

In June the following year the Downland Gridshell was officially opened by Sir Neil Cossons, president of the Association of Independent Museums and chairman of English Heritage.

The 157 feet (48 metre) long Gridshell received a number of major awards, being finally pipped to the post by only one vote in the Stirling Prize, the major annual award for British Architecture (the first prize went to the Gateshead Millennium Bridge). The judges said: "The building is inclusive, accessible, innovative, (truly) sustainable and beautiful. Rather than construct a fake barn to

The Gridshell grows. **Clockwise from top left** *The semi-elliptical end framework is hoisted into position; Steve Corbett, leader of the Green Oak Carpentry Company team, checks the jacks used to lower the grid of oak laths into place; the gridshell is slowly lowered into position; one of the carpenters scaling the framework to adjust the intersections where the 120 feet (36 metres) long oak laths meet; the shape develops; cladding the framework with western red cedar, and the final form of the building's exterior is revealed.*

house the storage and workshop space it needed, the museum decided to commission a new work of architecture that would reflect the relevance of the vernacular tradition today. The project fostered creativity and exceptional craftsmanship. We felt it was ground-breaking and lovable."

Jonathan Glancey, architecture correspondent of *The Guardian*, called the Gridshell "one of the finest and most original of all British buildings of the past 25 years". Ted Cullinan had told Glancey: "I liked making this building as much as designing it. We had brilliant carpenters and other craftsmen and technicians who knew exactly how to bend long stretches of green wood to best effect... Making this building was like knitting with great threads of architecture", and he added "...here we

had exceptional clients who really care about architecture. Most potential clients would opt for the sort of portal-framed timber building you can see advertised in *Exchange & Mart*." When Ted Cullinan received the RIBA (Royal Institute of British Architects) Gold Medal in 2008 the Gridshell was the project he chose to feature prominently for the occasion.

"It takes a great deal of courage and commitment from everyone to make a success of an innovative project such as this," said Richard Harris, as the project was completed. "One thing is certain – entering the Gridshell for the first time will be an unforgettable experience and will help to make a visit to the museum even more memorable."

12

Influence and Recognition

Diana Zeuner

In the early days the museum was a pioneer. There were plenty of open air museums in Europe but few in this country. The study of vernacular architecture was in its infancy. Historic buildings were being razed to the ground. There was little interest in timber-framing and repair techniques. "Today you can seek people's advice," Roger Champion says. "Then there wasn't anybody to ask."

The museum grew from a small regional project to one of the big ideas in the British museum sector in the last quarter century.

In 1980 the *Shell Guide to Country Museums* commended the museum as "a museum with great style, which has known from the beginning exactly what it was trying to do and which has never departed from its original standards". Two years later *The Good Museums Guide* reported that there were "no concessions to mass entertainment, no ice-creams, no guided tours, but plenty of walking, a place where you can learn and breathe at the same time".

Sir Neil Cossons, chairman of English Heritage and director of The Science Museum,

"... a place where you can learn and breathe at the same time."

Sir Neil Cossons, chairman of English Heritage and president of the Association of Independent Museums, officially opens the Downland Gridshell in 2002.

writing Chris Zeuner's obituary for *The Independent* in January 2001, wrote:

Twenty years on those same qualities apply; uncompromising standards of excellence in research, in scholarship and in revealing the subtleties of buildings and place in what is one of the most engaging and beautiful museums in England.

The appointments of Chris Zeuner as director and later, Richard Harris, as research director, had "set the scene for the growth of the Weald & Downland museum to its current position of pre-eminence," he said.

Today it is widely recognised in Britain and Europe as a leader in the study and practice of building conservation, and especially of timber

" Traditional buildings used to be seen, patronisingly, as a junior branch of the wider study of architectural history – distinctly inferior in not being connected with a named architect or patron, but not uninteresting in a primitive sort of way. Over the last 30 years this attitude has become less common, and vernacular architecture is now valued for the insights it gives into the cultures and values of society. "

The museum's application for designation as an outstanding collection, 1998

buildings. This work extends into woodland and coppice management and the training of building-trade craftsmen, all supported by an outstanding research collection and library on vernacular architecture and craft skills.

Recognition of the museum's work came in many different forms and at the highest level. Roy Armstrong, the museum's founder, was awarded the MBE in 1972, and Chris Zeuner received the OBE in 1990. Roy received an honorary degree of Doctor of Letters from the University of Sussex in 1992, and Chris Zeuner received an honorary MA from the University of Southampton in 1998. The awards of the National Heritage Museum of the Year Award in 1975 and the Times/Shell Community Museum of the Year Award in 1989 were the most notable among a raft of awards the museum received.

When the Museums & Galleries Commission lobbied for museums to benefit from the newly-announced National Lottery in 1992, its chairman, Graham Greene, made this appeal:

Scholarship is not in any way confined to the large national museums. The display of more modest collections also needs a basis of scholarly research and interpretation. A good example – one of the many that could be cited – is the Weald & Downland Open Air Museum in West Sussex, where research into historic building methods and materials precisely complements its displays and reconstructed buildings.

In 1997 the museum celebrated 30 years since the project's establishment. Chris Zeuner wrote:

Roy Armstrong's dream developed into an award-winning museum which appealed to all ages and became one of the most popular attractions in the south-east, with some 150,000 visitors a year. Even more importantly, it developed into an institution with a sound research base and has contributed significantly to our understanding of vernacular buildings. Thirty years on our objectives remain firm, with perhaps an even greater commitment to encouraging the rural skills so important to the original occupants of our buildings and which still have a relevance today with our increasing concern for the environment in which we live.

The Weald & Downland Open Air Museum was one of a small number of projects determined to save and present to the public elements of our history which in the 1970s were largely being ignored by the museum establishment. They grouped together to become the Association of Independent Museums (AIM) in 1977, a self-help organisation which was to punch above its weight as the decades progressed. Independent museums, many of them operating as charitable trusts, were characterised by a pioneering spirit, a can-do attitude and an innovative, entrepreneurial approach.

> **"** Meeting Roy Armstrong and so many of his fellows involved in setting up the museum, I feel fortunate to have known people core to the ongoing development of the open-air museum movement in the UK. **"**
>
> **Bob Powell, curator**

This new breed of museums – such as Ironbridge Gorge Museums, Shropshire; the National Motor Museum, Beaulieu, Hampshire; the Gladstone Working Pottery Museum, Stoke-on-Trent and the Bass Museum, Burton-on-Trent – had been established by community groups focusing largely on industrial, rural and transport heritage. They were often led, not by museum professionals, but by charismatic personalities from a wide range of backgrounds – described in *Museums Journal* (June 2007) as "young guns" with a dedication to their projects and subjects.

Most of all these museums were independent – free from local authority or national government control. They raised their own revenue from admission fees and commercial activities. And they had fun. Sam Mullins, today the director of London Transport Museum and a former chairman of AIM, but then a young council officer in Shropshire, was struck by the contrast with the sedate world of museums he knew, telling *Museums Journal* (June 2007): "I was hugely impressed by the notion the independents had of capturing, rather than collecting, which seemed much more proactive. They talked as if it were big-game hunting."

AIM's first chairman, Neil Cossons, who ran Ironbridge Gorge Museum Trust before joining The Science Museum, said Museums Association meetings in the late 1970s were always dominated by worries over budget cuts. "At AIM meetings you could hardly hear yourself speak, there was so much noisy chat and enthusiasm." Despite some antagonism from the established museum sector,

Sir Arthur Drew, then chairman of the Standing Commission on Museums and Galleries (the forerunner to the present Museums, Libraries & Archives Council), was very supportive of the new independents. He famously described them as the "primordial slime" of the museum world, an epithet AIM has always rather enjoyed.

It was into this background that the Weald & Downland Open Air Museum firmly fitted, playing, through Chris Zeuner's membership of AIM Council from its foundation to his death in 2001, a significant role in the entrepreneurship which was to have such an influence on the wider museum world. Sam Mullins, again, has spoken of how having a charitable constitution gives an extraordinarily strong purpose to an organisation's activities. The independents introduced to museums the concept of being socially entrepreneurial and having a commercial attitude, which had not existed before. The charitable trust model popularised by independents is now being followed by ever more local authorities as a method of freeing their museums from local government shackles (and dependence on budgets), demonstrating how influential the independent sector has been. The Weald & Downland Open Air Museum both benefited from, and contributed to, this great cultural movement – the independent museums.

The Government's award of designated status to the museum in 1998 for the national and international importance of its entire collection, was a

The charitable trust model is favoured by independent museums. The role of a museum trustee extends beyond his or her primary legal responsibility for the efficient management of the organisation to that of ambassador in the wider world and cheerleader for staff and supporters. Here, trustee Michael Burton, right, talks to museum director Chris Zeuner, at the Rare Breeds Show in 1996.

considerable achievement. Supporting the museum's application for designation were four prominent figures from the UK and overseas.

John Fidler, head of architectural conservation at English Heritage identified four areas in which he felt the museum was "pre-eminent": interpretation of historic fabric, repair methods, use of traditional materials, and a resource for the building conservation industry.

The museum had been a pioneer in showing how important historical information could be obtained from the dismantling and analysis of buildings, including the development of new methodologies, with the re-erected buildings serving as "a model of interpretation". A laboratory for developing, testing and field-trialling remedial treatments for historic buildings, it had explored all available methods of repairing timber-framed structures for example, not simply following the well-understood methods of cutting out decayed wood and piecing-in new material. "It has developed criteria which combine visual discretion with clear expression of historical development, while ensuring maximum retention and protection of historic fabric," he said.

The museum had shown how to achieve authenticity within a re-erected building without deceiving or confusing the non-specialist visitor, through pioneering dismantling methods and an uncompromising attitude to the use of appropriate materials in reconstruction, underpinned by technical research. "In using these materials the museum has set an excellent example to others

and has also been instrumental in opening up and maintaining sources of supply for the wider museum and conservation community." The museum's collections had become a "three-dimensional text book of building and repair methods". John Fidler commended the development of professional training, especially the unique MSc in Timber-Framed Building Conservation for which the museum had "effectively written the syllabus for the subject".

Professor Gwyn Meirion-Jones of the University of Reading said it was "by far the best museum of traditional buildings in the UK", with an importance much more than regional. From his experience with European museums he felt confident in claiming that the museum's collection and its national significance placed it "in the front rank of international buildings museums".

His view was backed by Professor Dr Claus Ahrens of the Open Air Museum of Kiekeberg, Hamburg-Harburg, Germany and Professor Dr Jan Vaessen, director of the Netherlands Open Air Museum at Arnhem. Dr Ahrens said he knew few open air museums which practised "practical monument conservation" and the application of science as well, highlighting the work of Richard Harris on timber-framed buildings. Bayleaf Medieval Farmstead was singled out for particular praise: "You get the impression that the farmer and his family only went away for a short time." There was no complex comparable in European open air museums at that time.

Jan Vaessen wrote of the contribution Chris

Zeuner made whilst president of the Association of European Open Air Museums in promoting debate aimed at developing a better understanding of the special nature of open air museums:

Without exaggeration it can be said that the development of open air museums all over Europe towards a more public-oriented (environment-oriented) behaviour is at least partly a result of those discussions. Mr Zeuner's position was a very convincing one because of the results he achieved in his own museum at Singleton.

The major qualities of the museum, in the perception of European colleagues, are the very careful design of the museum as a whole (the landscaping, the sense of the buildings as historical artefacts) and furthermore the creativity in the development of educational services and the high standards to which they conform.

His own museum developed a building project for schoolchildren, "heavily inspired by the Singleton examples".

By the late 1990s there was increasing concern among British rural museums that their subject matter was of less and less interest to the ever-more sophisticated and urban population. They needed to address rural issues of the day, such as factory farming, GM (Genetically Modified) crops, major epidemics such as foot-and-mouth disease, and environmental concerns. Chris Zeuner's lecture *The Barn is Full – Which Way Now?* (1999), questioned how the rescued and accumulated rural artefacts in museums up and down the country could be made relevant as the 21st century approached. Despite curators' best efforts they had:

failed to establish our work in the public mind as something that is relevant to the issues of the present time. Where do we find issues of soil compaction and erosion challenged among the rows of tractors and combines? Where do we find the issue of the loneliness of the modern farm worker and the terrible rate of suicide among farmers?

He initiated a forum where participants were agreed that there was too much reliance on objects and not enough on people's stories. He told Felicity Haywood, writing later in *Museums Journal*, that the Weald & Downland Open Air Museum was working hard to increase interactivity and demonstrations, embracing the lifelong learning programme, charcoal production, working horses, woodland management and

timber framing. "The museum, through its exhibits and training programmes, has led a resurgence of self-employed charcoal burners. Its training in the repair of timber-framing is also much in demand and has attracted young people to the trade." The museum's unusual initiative to open a post office in its shop after the local Singleton Post Office closed was another way of bringing together the museum's work and people's lives, helping the local community in an entirely unexpected way.

The same year Chris Zeuner launched the idea of a meeting of rural and open air museums (as they are so closely related) under the umbrella of the Museums & Galleries Commission (MGC), to begin a dialogue leading to new thinking and co-operation. Out of this came the MGC-commissioned report from Rob Shorland-Ball, *Farming, Countryside & Museums*, urging those running rural life museums to find ways of making them interesting to a modern audience increasingly divorced from the countryside. Chris Zeuner did not live to see the subsequent development of strong links between rural and open air museums which was eventually to lead to the Rural Museums Network. This organisation – and its individual members – have made huge strides in making the connections between each other, through the 'distributed national collection' of rural artefacts, and the rural world and the public, and through exhibitions and activities which focus closely on today's rural and environmental issues.

The opening of the museum's sheepfold, with, from left, a representative of the Southdown Sheep Society, Brian Weekes (volunteer and former farmer), Tim Heymann (trustee and chairman of the Friends), Chris Zeuner (museum director) and Peter Albon (stockman and horseman). The reconstructed foldyard with its Southdown ewes and lambs represented a close link between the museum and the farming community.

Roy and Lyn Armstrong head for the car park at the end of a day spent working in the library.

The museum has undoubtedly had a substantial impact on the public. Countless visitors have shown how their eyes have been opened to the historical development of English houses through the clarity of the museum's examples restored to their original form. Its exhibits have formed the subject of large numbers of features and articles in books and journals and attracted wide media coverage. It is also true that a negative impact has been obvious, not envisaged by the museum's founders, where householders have been inspired to attempt unsuitable 'restorations' of their homes – a practice the museum deplores and discourages. The museum also feels some responsibility for the rash of 'Bayleaf imitation' houses erected in recent years, with more than one builder approaching the museum to be associated with it in return for sponsorship (all to no avail).

However, the minority building conservation movement has grown in parallel with the museum, to become a major industry with strong institutional support, with the museum's work having a considerable impact on its development. The south-east is not a widely recognised region in the way the Fens or the Lake District are known, yet it does have a strong identity and the museum's collections have helped establish and promote it. Richard Harris says in the designation application:

Perhaps the most significant impact of the museum in the longer term will derive from the maintenance of a reservoir of knowledge and skills in areas of low impact technologies and renewable resources.

In 1978 Roy Armstrong wrote:

The time will come when the museum has filled its site with as many buildings as it can accommodate – a fairly representative collection of traditional buildings, some of them furnished so far as is practicable, and with some appropriate crafts and a centre for research and information. By that time one hopes that the museum will be sufficiently integrated with, and accepted by, the community for it to be much more actively concerned with the practical care and preservation of buildings outside its site. This could take various forms, from the giving of technical advice or the training of craftsmen to the actual repair and custodianship of buildings.

Roy said he personally had no desire to see the museum grow beyond the scope of the master plan as a guide to development. Increase of area would be another matter, as that would lead to more opportunity for farmsteads to have adequate curtilages. "But it should not become so large that it defeats its purpose by overwhelming the visitor by its size and complexity." This was a view very much echoed by Chris Zeuner, who felt strongly that the museum had an optimum size, bearing in mind its regional remit, visitor assimilation and financial viability, beyond which it would simply be 'empire-building'. There was much that could be done in the future to further use the museum as an outward-looking resource in the fields of building conservation, agricultural and rural life, the arts and environmental education.

"Although we have many buildings in store," Roy continued, "to which we must devote all our resources at present, and in the immediate future, it would be a mistake if we neglect the desirability of playing a very much wider role of influencing the environment as time goes on." Roy's vision has been met, and continues to be fleshed out with initiatives such as the museum's lifelong learning programme and educational projects.

13

The future

Diana Zeuner

What will happen to the museum in the next decades?

Many influences, currently unforeseeable, will affect its development. But maintaining a strong commitment to its twin themes – vernacular buildings and rural life – will be essential for a continued dedication in explaining history and the project's own sustainability and pursuit of excellence.

The museum has been one of the success stories of the tourist sector over the last 40 years, but has remained steadfast in maintaining its academic purpose whilst at the same time welcoming visitors for an enjoyable day out. To lose this balance would be catastrophic and consign the museum to a second-rate leisure attraction.

There remains much to do. There are still some 15 buildings in store to re-erect, and the museum especially hopes to rescue and re-erect a 19th-century farm complex, enabling it to illustrate the vernacular development of homesteads over five centuries. Further buildings may yet be threatened with destruction and be saved for re-erection as the museum continues to tell the story of traditional architecture in its region. Although not in the vernacular tradition, perhaps the museum will add exhibits telling the story of 20th century buildings and rural structures – this has certainly been proposed in the past. And as sustainable living has become such an important concern in the early 21st century, perhaps a modern domestic timber-frame structure or a straw-bale building incorporating the latest eco-technology would be appropriate additions.

But even after its main physical development has been achieved it will no doubt continue to attract audiences. One of the great open-air museums, at Bokrijk in Belgium, has not added an exhibit building for 25 years, but visitors still remain entranced by its presentation.

Museums such as the Weald & Downland have a role in facing up to contentious issues raised by their themes. The perception of cottages, old houses and barns as picturesque and their occupants as being safe and secure is misplaced; in reality their lives were fraught with difficulty and danger. How can this be presented?

Rural life museums are increasingly concerned with making the link between today's largely urban population and their rural forebears. This is being tackled through subjects such as the changing face of today's countryside, the challenges of modern farming, food and environmental sustainability, and rural deprivation. The museum could do more and make deeper links with the regional rural community. In a paper given in 1999 on the *Interpretation of Agriculture in Open Air Museums* Chris Zeuner described open-air museums as being in a special position to serve as a "cultural bridge".

The museum's rural life collections will continue to be supplemented by new donations, and myriad different means of making this rich resource available will be found. The collections – both buildings and rural life – will certainly be used in the future in ways we could never have imagined.

Richard Harris has pointed out that there is still no well-established centre in England for vernacular studies. Perhaps the museum could follow the example of Ironbridge, which hosts the Institute for Industrial Archaeology and Den Gamle By (The Old Town) at Århus, Denmark, which has established the Danish Centre for Urban History.

Vernacular studies could cover a wide range of disciplines and the institute would be formally linked to a university.

Close partnerships with other organisations outside the museum sector will continue to develop – as they already have with bodies such as the West Sussex Countryside Studies Trust, Bournemouth University, the University of Chichester, West Sussex County Council and Chichester District Council. These links foster the sharing of skills and expertise and strengthen the museum's position in the wider community. Such a focus enables the museum to be seen as a 'social enterprise', driven by the creation of social and environmental benefits at the same time as meeting economic targets. The museum is currently involved in discussions about an education-led economic regeneration partnership for rural West Sussex, and about its role as a 'gateway' at the heart of the new South Downs National Park.

All these are objectives of which Roy Armstrong would surely approve – a mixture of history, education, social responsibility and economic sustainability. At the heart will be people – staff, volunteers, supporters – who have made the museum the strong institution it is today – the successors to the energetic and determined founders of the museum who set out to realise a dream some 40 years ago.

> **“** This is an enterprise worthy of the support of all who love the Weald and Downland. It is not a vague plan for a problematical future, but a very immediate and exciting way of dealing with the increasing threat to the magnificent heritage we are all fortunate to possess in this part of England. The museum is not intended to provide a 'home' for buildings inconveniently situated in our modern world. No building will in fact be accepted unless demolition is unavoidable, but its reconstruction as it was originally built may make us all more aware of what we still have, but so often fail to recognise or understand. **”**
>
> **Appeal message from the museum's first president, the Duke of Norfolk, in April 1970**

These lists give the names and dates of service of trustees of the museum and members of the committee of the Friends of the museum in date order

Trustees

J R Armstrong (1969–1993)
M Hallam (1969–1992)
J E Whittome (1969–1975)
P West (1969–1984)
N West (1969–1981)
Maj Gen L Hawes (1969–1985)
J Warren (1969–1991)
K Leslie (1969–1997)
C Barson (1969–1981)
Dr K M E Murray (1969–1972)
J Lowe (1969–1977)
Ald J Farmer (1969–1991)
Sir Geoffrey Thistleton-Smith (1970–1977)
G Godber (1971–1997)
W Cox (1971–1982)
D Durbin (1971–1982)
P Longley (1973–1978)
B Smeed (1973–1979)
R McDowall (1974–1987)
D Blacker (1975–1979)
The Hon S Sainsbury (1975–1980)
D Russell (1975–2007)
Lord Egremont (1976–1981)
E M Holdsworth (1976–1990)
Sir James Waddell (1978–1997)
V Sheppard (1978–1980)
B Johnson (1978–1983)
A McHaffie (1978–1979)
Col C Jefferis (1979–1984)
E Kay (1979–1984)
J Kessler (1979–1984)
P Tye (1979–1985)
J Illius (1979–1990)
D Biart (1979–1997)
J Woollings (1980–1991)
Col W Harrison (1981–1992)
N Talbot-Ponsonby (1981–1991)
Viscount Watkinson (1982–1988)
Brig W Greenway (1984–1990)
P Careless (1984–1985)
C Hawkins (1984–1993)
Lady Elizabeth Benson (1986–)
J Harding (1986–1997)
P Garland (1986–1995)
M Caroe (1986–1999)
L Armstrong (1986–1995)
Dr A Hayes (1986–1994)
T Heymann (1986–2008)
R Hunt (1986–1995)
J Veltom (1986–1993)
C Lucas (1986–1987)
V Lyon (1986–1996)

M Holt (1986–1995)
W Renwick (1986–1990)
J Oliver (1986–1995)
N Stephens (1987–2000)
M Roberts (1988–2002)
N McGregor-Wood (1988–2007)
M Beale (1988–1990)
D Bandey (1989–1997)
N Hart (1989–)
L Weller (1990–1995)
M Doran (1991–1995)
D Hopkinson (1991–1997)
J Ashurst (1992–1992)
Dr J Godfrey (1992–)
P Gray (1992–1999)
B Smith (1992–1994)
M Burton (1993–)
Dr D Streeter (1993–)
P Bryant (1993–2010)
Lord Nathan (1994–1997)
D Tomlinson (1995–)
M Sharpe (1995–2000)
N Clutton (1997–)
M Garston (1997–)
J Houlton (1998–)
A Ferrier (2000–)
M Pollock (2000–)
E Burch (2005–2010)
P Rigg (2007–)
S Corbett (2008–)
Dr J Jarvis (2008–)
D Chiverton (2008–)
R Back (2008–2010)
K Mosse (2008–)

Friends committee

D Bryant (1970–1976)
J Kessler (1970–1983)
D Robertson-Ritchie (1970–1972)
N West (1970–1997)
F Taylor (1970–1971)
C Barson (1970–1978)
J R Armstrong (1970–1983)
D Wilson (1970–1973)
K Leslie (1970–1976)
Maj Gen L Hawes (1971–1978)
J Lowe (1971–1976)
C Zeuner (1973–1974)
J Hill (1973–1974)
C Hawkins (1973–1975)
D Zeuner (1974–1979)
P Minet (1974–1976)
B Johnson (1975–1985)

E Kessler (1975–1984)
J Leslie (1976–1978)
Sir James Waddell (1976–1989)
V Lyon (1976–1996)
L Armstrong (1979–1984)
C Hawkins (1979–1993)
P Lewison (1979–1986)
Brig W Greenway (1983–1985)
B Rush (1983–1995)
J Brooks (1983–1987)
Dr B Pailthorpe (1983–1992)
M Hum (1983–1992)
E Buvyer (1983–1998)
E Newbery (1984–1986)
P Vincent (1985–1994)
M Doran (1985–1995)
N Hutson (1986–1989)
K Gunns (1987–1993)
J Hutson (1987–2009)
G Bevis (1987–1988)
S Snow (1988–1991)
T Toseland (1989–1990)
J Eyre (1989–1993)
A Allen (1990–2002)
C Sharman (1990–1991)
R Stock (1991–1992)
J Herniman (1992–2004)
M Ashdown (1992–)
D Wigmore (1992–1994)
F Broad (1993–1995)
T Heymann (1993–2002)
J Piggott (1993–2009)
D Buxton (1994–2006)
M Pollock (1995–)
G Lewis (1995–1998)
B Bickmore (1996–2001)
G Shirt (1996–2004)
D Everett (1998–1998)
F Messenger (1998–2008)
J Symons (1998–)
J Elliott (1998–2000)
C Rivett (1998–)
G Claridge (1999–2010)
M Tomlinson (2000–)
P Wilkinson (2001–)
S Casdagli (2003–)
D Zeuner (2004–2008)
C Brinson (2005–2006)
P Spence (2005–)
F Fisher (2006–2007)
S Davis (2006–2008)
R Wilde (2007–)
A Baker (2009–)
C Weekes (2009–)

Prepared by Richard Harris, Carol Brinson and Jean Piggott

This series of charts shows figures which are standardised as far as possible over the 40 year period.

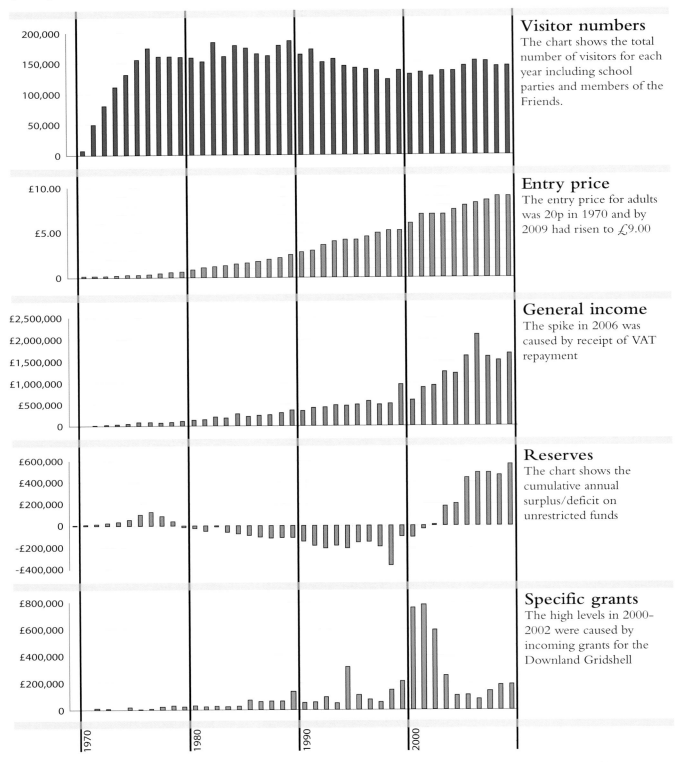

Visitor numbers
The chart shows the total number of visitors for each year including school parties and members of the Friends.

Entry price
The entry price for adults was 20p in 1970 and by 2009 had risen to £9.00

General income
The spike in 2006 was caused by receipt of VAT repayment

Reserves
The chart shows the cumulative annual surplus/deficit on unrestricted funds

Specific grants
The high levels in 2000-2002 were caused by incoming grants for the Downland Gridshell

The museum is indebted to Neville Lacey of Jones Avens, the museum's accountants since 1969, for preparing the series of financial figures used here.
Charts prepared by Richard Harris

Index to people and places

Index

The authors

Diana Zeuner

Diana Zeuner has been closely involved with the Weald & Downland Open Air Museum since 1971 after meeting Roy Armstrong and becoming a volunteer. In 1975 she married Chris Zeuner, the museum's first full-time director. Her volunteering duties have covered all areas of the museum, from making paths and planting trees, stewarding and car parking to interpretation and livestock care. As chief reporter working for Portsmouth & Sunderland Newspapers on the *Bognor Regis Observer* and *West Sussex Gazette*, her skills were in demand by the museum for news releases, exhibition texts, guidebooks (*The Bayleaf Medieval Farmstead: The Research – A Road of Discovery*), photography and in the production of the museum's twice-yearly magazine, which she continues to edit. Diana has edited the *AIM Bulletin*, the Association of Independent Museums' bi-monthly magazine since 1980, as well as papers in its Guidelines and Focus series. Since 1987 she has published and edited *Heavy Horse World*, the only specialist magazine covering draught horses in the UK, and is the author of *Working Horse Manual* (1998) and *Heavy Horses* (2004). After Chris's death in 2001 she undertook the part-time management of the museum's heavy horse stables for two years. In 1995, with Richard Pailthorpe, she revised and edited Roy Armstrong's *A History of Sussex*.

Richard Harris

The museum's current director, Richard Harris was research director from 1979 until Chris Zeuner's death in 2001, responsible for the research, interpretation and reconstruction of many of the building exhibits at the museum. In addition Richard has followed a career in teaching building conservation, specialising in timber buildings, and has played a crucial role in developing the extensive adult learning programme at the museum. After reading economics at Cambridge, Richard studied for an AADip at the Architectural Association, gaining experience as assistant to Freddie Charles, architect at the Avoncroft Museum of Buildings, Worcestershire. He founded the Hereford & Worcester Architecture Record Group. After meeting Roy Armstrong at the Institute for Advanced Architectural Studies in York, he became his assistant at the Weald & Downland Open Air Museum, becoming research officer (later director) in 1977. His freelance work has included the dismantling and recording of a farmstead for the Museum of American Frontier Culture and advising on the reconstruction of the Globe Theatre, London. He is the author of *Discovering Timber-Framed Buildings* (1978).

Kim Leslie

Kim Leslie has spent much of his career promoting the study of local history throughout West Sussex. Now retired, he was formerly education officer with West Sussex Record Office. He was actively involved in establishing the Weald & Downland Open Air Museum as a founder subscriber and trustee from 1967, when he first met Roy Armstrong, to 1997. He was honorary treasurer of the promotion committee from 1967 to 1969 and of the museum company from 1969 to 1979, as well as honorary treasurer of the Friends from 1970 to 1972. In 1990 he wrote *Weald & Downland Open Air Museum: The Founding Years 1965-1970*. Kim founded the Sussex Industrial Archaeology Society, has served the Sussex Historic Churches Trust as its secretary and treasurer, and has been a council member of the Sussex Archaeological Society. He directed several West Sussex County Council heritage initiatives, including the West Sussex Blue Plaque Scheme and the West Sussex Parish Maps Project, involving some 2,000 volunteers and resulting in a pioneer book on community map-making, *A Sense of Place: West Sussex Parish Maps* (2006). In 2008 he wrote *Sussex: Tales of the Unexpected*. He lectures and writes on Sussex local history and is co-editor of a major work of reference, *An Historical Atlas of Sussex* (1999).

Carol Brinson

Carol Brinson (Hawkins until her marriage in 1997) has undertaken a plethora of tasks involved with the operation of the museum since its earliest days. Arriving as a volunteer in 1972 she helped in the ticket office, the shop, with car parking, stewarding Winkhurst, and thatching and spar-making in the woodcraft area. Assistant to John Eves, director of the adjacent West Dean College, she achieved a Diploma in Arts & Leisure Administration from the Polytechnic of Central London in 1977 and was appointed administrator at The Farnham Maltings Arts & Community Centre until 1993. She became minutes secretary of the newly-formed Friends of the museum, eventually becoming a committee member and then, from 1983 to 1993, honorary secretary. She organised the Friends' spring tours from 1987 to 1993. Whilst continuing with voluntary work, she also took on a part-time fund-raising administration role at the museum in 1984, when the Development Fund Appeal was launched. In 1988 she became one of the part-time wardens, later becoming organiser of the Dovetail arts programme, adult education courses and then events co-ordinator until the end of 2005. She continues to volunteer in a variety of capacities.